D1426497

1001 QUESTIONS & ANSWERS

WORLD OF KNOWLEDGE

Edited by

Victoria Egan and **Neil Champion**

Vineyard
BOOKS

Photographic credits

4tl Royal Observatory, Edinburgh; 8cr Kitt Peak National Observatory; 82tl Derek Hall;
83tr Matthew Kneale; 84-5b E. Lawrie/Hutchison Library; 112l Matthew Kneale; 113r Matthew
Kneale; 119r Matthew Kneale; 122b Bruno Barbey/Magnum Photos; 145b McLaren Cars Limited.

Authors
SPACE: Chris Oxlade
EARTH: Dougal Dixon
NATURE: Adam Johnstone and Dr. Paul Sterry
HISTORY: Struan Reid
HUMAN WORLD: Neil Morris
SCIENCE AND TECHNOLOGY: John Clark

Special thanks go to Dr. John Haywood

Planned and produced by
Andromeda Oxford Limited
11-15 The Vineyard
Abingdon, Oxon OX14 3PX
England

Published in 1997 by
Vineyard Books, an imprint of
Andromeda Oxford Limited
11-15 The Vineyard
Abingdon
Oxon OX14 3PX

Copyright © Andromeda Oxford Limited 1997

ISBN 1-86199-025-1

Printed in Italy

CONTENTS

WHAT IS THE UNIVERSE ?

THE Universe contains everything that exists. It includes the Earth, the Sun and Moon, the other planets in our solar system, all the billions of stars, and all the space between them. With powerful telescopes and other scientific instruments, astronomers have found out a great deal of information about the Universe and how it works. But there are still many unexplained mysteries.

Stars and shining clouds of gas and dust fill the night sky. Those shown here are within the constellation of Orion.

HOW OLD IS THE UNIVERSE ?

MOST astronomers believe that the Universe began about 15,000 million years ago with a gigantic explosion, which they call the Big Bang. The Earth was formed 4,500 million years ago.

IS THERE OTHER LIFE IN THE UNIVERSE ?

ASTRONOMERS think that the chances of other life existing are very high. There is no reason to think that our solar system is particularly special, so there are probably other Earth-like planets orbiting some of the billions of other stars like our own Sun.

WILL THE UNIVERSE END ?

THERE are different theories about what will happen to the Universe. One theory, called the Steady State Theory, says that the Universe will keep expanding. Another, the Oscillating Universe Theory, says that it will gradually shrink, and then there will be another Big Bang. This will happen about every 80,000 million years.

WHAT WAS THE BIG BANG ?

THE Big Bang is the name given to the explosion which astronomers think started the Universe. It was an unimaginably enormous explosion. All the material in the Universe was in the form of energy, condensed into a tiny space. The temperature was probably about 10,000 million °C. When the Big Bang happened, the energy began to spread out. The temperature fell and atoms started forming. Gradually the atoms clumped together and the first galaxies were made. The outer galaxies of the Universe are rushing away into space at great speed, showing that the Universe is still expanding after the Big Bang.

Matter formed in the Big Bang collected in clouds. The clouds collapsed inwards and formed galaxies.

HOW FAR AWAY ARE THE STARS ?

IT IS tens of millions of millions of kilometres just to the Sun's neighbours, and most stars are thousands of times further away than that. Stars at different distances from Earth seem to change position slightly as the Earth moves in its orbit. This effect is called parallax. By measuring the amount a star seems to move, astronomers can work out how far away it is.

A nearby star will seem to change its position (P1 to P2) when seen from different viewpoints of the Earth's orbit (E1 and E2).

WHO FIRST UNDERSTOOD THE SOLAR SYSTEM ?

IN 1543 Nicolaus Copernicus put forward a theory that the Sun was at the centre of the Universe, and that the planets moved round it. But the Catholic Church refused to accept this, believing that the Earth was at the centre of the Universe, and Copernicus' theory was banned.

WHAT IS A "LIGHT YEAR" ?

DISTANCES in space are so huge that measuring in kilometres is impractical, so astronomers measure in "light years": the distance light travels in a year. Light travels at nearly 300,000 km/s, so a light year is about 9.5 million million km.

WHICH IS OUR NEAREST STAR ?

APART from our own Sun, the nearest star to Earth is Proxima Centauri. It is 4.2 light years away, or 40 million million km. The Sun is a mere 8 light minutes away from Earth.

IS THERE ANYTHING BEYOND THE UNIVERSE ?

WE CANNOT see the edges of the Universe, so it is impossible to tell if there is anything beyond it. Scientists cannot even tell whether the Universe has edges as we think of them.

WHO WERE THE FIRST ASTRONOMERS ?

MORE than 4,000 years ago, Chinese astronomers were making accurate observations of the stars and planets. About the same time the Babylonians were recording the night sky. They believed that the stars revealed the ways of their gods. Many of the constellations are named after the gods of ancient times.

WHEN WERE TELESCOPES FIRST USED ?

THE first time a telescope was used for astronomy was in 1609, by the Italian scientist Galileo Galilei. He discovered the four large moons of Jupiter, and supported Copernicus' theory that the planets move round the Sun.

In Roman times the god Jupiter was lord of the skies.

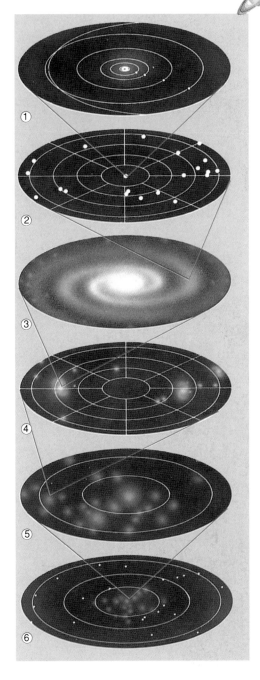

Our solar system (1) forms part of a group of nearby stars (2), which is part of a galaxy (3). Many galaxies form our Local Group of galaxies (4), which is one of many groups that form the Local Supercluster (5). This in turn forms just a small part of the observable Universe (6).

HOW BIG IS THE UNIVERSE ?

THE Universe is so vast that it is difficult to imagine. The most distant objects astronomers can see are quasars, which are up to 15,000 million light years away. The light from these quasars left them soon after the Big Bang. There may be objects further away than that, but we will never be able to see them because their light will never reach us.

The black hole Cygnus X-1 (1) is orbiting a blue supergiant star (2), which it is slowly pulling apart. As the star spirals down onto the black hole it forms an incredibly hot disc around it.

HOW CAN BLACK HOLES BE DETECTED ?

AS A black hole and its companion star rotate around each other, the gas from the star is funnelled by the force of gravity into a disc around the black hole. The gas molecules in the disc swirl around the black hole so fast that they heat up and emit X-rays. These X-rays can be detected from Earth.

WHAT IS A BLACK HOLE ?

WHEN a giant star comes to the end of its life, it grows into a huge ball and blows itself apart in an explosion called a supernova. The material left collapses in on itself until it becomes a tiny point in space. The gravity in the area around the point is so strong that not even light can escape, which is why it is called a "black hole".

WHERE DO COMETS COME FROM ?

COMETS are bits of dust, ice and gas that are zooming through space. Astronomers think that there is a huge cloud of icy lumps beyond Pluto's orbit. When a lump is pulled from the cloud, it orbits around the Sun as a comet. We see comets when their orbits bring them close to the Sun. Some come close every few years, but others take thousands of years to return.

WHY DO COMETS HAVE TAILS ?

WHEN a comet approaches the Sun, its ice begins to melt. This releases dust and gas, which make a cloud around the comet. The cloud is pushed into a tail by streams of particles from the Sun called the solar wind. The tail always points away from the Sun.

WHAT ARE THE NORTHERN LIGHTS ?

THE Northern Lights, or Aurora Borealis, is a greenish-blue glow of light that makes slowly changing patterns in the sky near the North Pole. It happens when electrically charged particles from the Sun (the solar wind) are drawn to the Earth's magnetic poles. When they reach the Earth's upper atmosphere they become trapped, bombarding the atoms there and emitting radiation.

Light path bent around galaxy

Quasar

Galaxy

Direct view of quasar

WHAT IS A QUASAR ?

IN THE 1960s, astronomers detected radio waves coming from immense distances in space. The waves were coming from objects which, through a telescope, looked like faint stars in our own galaxy. Studying the radio waves revealed that the objects were zooming away from us at almost the speed of light. These objects, known as quasars, are the most distant objects we can see, and are hundreds of times smaller and brighter than galaxies.

If a quasar lies behind a galaxy, we see a double image of it from Earth because gravity makes light from the quasar bend around the galaxy to reach us.

Earth

The impact of a meteorite (1) causes a shock wave (2) in a planet's crust, which forces rock upwards in the centre of the crater (3).

WHAT ARE SHOOTING STARS ?

AS FRAGMENTS of rock from space, called meteors, hurtle into the Earth's atmosphere, they burn up. This is visible as a streak of light, making them appear like stars shooting across the sky.

WHAT MADE THE CRATERS ON THE MOON ?

A CRATER is made when a meteorite crashes into the surface of a planet or moon. Most of the craters on the Moon were made soon after it was formed, as it was hit by thousands of meteorites. The craters are still there because the Moon has no atmosphere to erode them.

WHAT DID ASTRONAUTS FIND ON THE MOON ?

FOR thousands of years, people had no idea what the Moon was made from. This mystery was only solved when astronauts brought back many samples of lunar rock and dusty soil. The samples showed that the Moon's surface contains a volcanic rock similar to basalt.

DO ALL PLANETS HAVE AN ATMOSPHERE ?

EACH of the planets is surrounded by a blanket of gases called an atmosphere. Earth's atmosphere is made up mostly of oxygen and nitrogen, and protects us from the Sun's harmful rays. The other planets' atmospheres consist of different gases.

The Martian atmosphere is pinkish because it contains dust. The temperature (red line) changes, the higher you go above the surface.

WHAT IS A PULSAR ?

WHEN a large star comes to the end of its life, it can collapse in on itself to form an extremely dense, spinning star called a neutron star. Because it sends out a beam of radio waves as it spins, a neutron star is also called a pulsating star, or pulsar.

WHY DO STARS SEEM TO MOVE ACROSS THE SKY ?

IF YOU take a quick glance at the sky, the stars seem to be fixed in place. But look again a few minutes later and they will appear to have moved slightly. The movement is caused by the Earth spinning in space.

Altitude in km

Stratosphere

2 km thick cloud layer

Troposphere

Clouds

Dust

WHY DO SOME PLANETS HAVE RINGS ?

THE planets Jupiter, Saturn, Uranus and Neptune have rings around their equators, made from chunks of ice, dust or boulders. These particles were either left over when the planets were formed, or they may be the remains of broken-up moons.

Saturn's rings are visible from Earth with a telescope.

100

90

80

70

60

50

40

30

20

10

0

200   400   Temperature (K)

WHAT IS A GALAXY ?

A GALAXY is a huge cluster of stars held together by gravity. There are millions of galaxies in the Universe, and even the smallest contain millions of stars. Between the galaxies are vast, starless spaces. Light from the galaxies takes millions of years to reach us.

CAN OTHER GALAXIES BE SEEN IN THE SKY ?

IF YOU have very good eyesight, you can see three other galaxies. They look like tiny, fuzzy patches of light. You cannot see individual stars in these galaxies — even with a powerful telescope — because they are so far away.

WHAT IS A NEBULA ?

A NEBULA is a gigantic cloud of dust and gas, which can be hundreds of light years across. Some nebulae look dark because they block out light from stars behind them. Other nebulae are bright because they reflect light from stars or because their gas gives off light. Some nebulae gradually clump together and form new galaxies.

WHAT SHAPES ARE THE GALAXIES ?

A SPIRAL galaxy, like the Milky Way, has a central lump with several "arms" spinning out from the centre. Elliptical galaxies are shaped like flattened spheres. Irregular galaxies have no particular shape at all.

The Milky Way galaxy is a spiral galaxy. All the stars that we see in the night sky are in the Milky Way.

The Orion Nebula is in the constellation of Orion. It is about 1,000 light years away from us and 15 light years across.

WHERE DID THE GALAXIES COME FROM ?

ASTRONOMERS think that the galaxies in the Universe were formed after the Big Bang, when space was full of energy. The energy gradually turned into atoms. Over millions of years these atoms drifted together under gravity into clouds of gas, and formed into galaxies containing stars and planets.

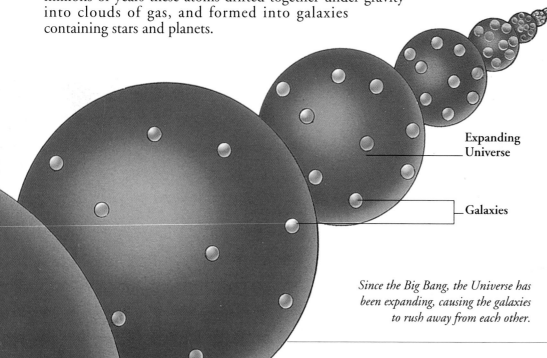

Expanding Universe

Galaxies

Since the Big Bang, the Universe has been expanding, causing the galaxies to rush away from each other.

WHAT IS THE MILKY WAY ?

THE Milky Way is the name of the galaxy to which our solar system belongs. It is also the name given to the bright band of light from millions of stars that you can see stretching across the sky on dark, clear nights.

HOW BIG IS THE MILKY WAY ?

THE distance from one end of the Milky Way to the other is about 100,000 light years, and it is about 20,000 light years deep. It contains about 100,000 million stars. Our Sun is about two-thirds of the way out from the centre on one of the spiral arms, called the Orion arm.

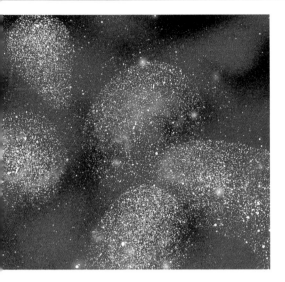

The Virgo supercluster of galaxies has a diameter of more than 100 million light years.

This is a radio map of part of the M82 galaxy.

WHY ARE RADIO MAPS USEFUL ?

A RADIO map can give a more accurate picture of a galaxy than the optical image received by a telescope. It is built up from radio waves emitted by the galaxy. These may come from a wider area than can be seen with a telescope, or their source may be a small area at the centre of the galaxy.

HOW MANY GALAXIES ARE THERE ?

ASTRONOMERS estimate that there are about 100,000 million galaxies in the Universe, gathered together in clusters. Some clusters contain thousands of galaxies. Others contain less than a hundred. Our own cluster, called the Local Group, may contain about 30 galaxies. Clusters of galaxies also group together in superclusters, which are hundreds of millions of light years across.

WHAT LIES IN BETWEEN THE GALAXIES ?

IN BETWEEN the billions of galaxies in the Universe are huge expanses of empty space. But space is not completely empty. Every cubic metre contains about half a million atoms (a hundred million million million times fewer than a cubic metre of air).

WHICH IS THE NEAREST GALAXY ?

THE nearest galaxy to our own is an irregular galaxy called the Large Megallanic Cloud (LMC for short).

WHO PROVED THAT THERE WERE OTHER GALAXIES IN THE UNIVERSE ?

IN THE 1920s, the astronomer Edwin Hubble proved that there were other visible galaxies in the night sky, outside our own galaxy and much further away.

WHAT DOES A RADIO TELESCOPE DO ?

OBJECTS in space give off a variety of electro-magnetic waves, such as light waves, radio waves and X-rays. A radio telescope detects radio waves coming from space. It can also detect quasars and other objects that cannot be seen with an optical telescope (one that collects light waves). A radio telescope has a large dish aerial that collects radio waves and bounces them into a receiver, which converts them into electrical signals.

The world's largest radio telescope, the Very Large Array, is in New Mexico, in the United States.

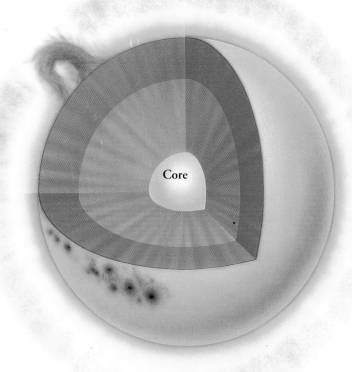

Like other stars, the Sun is a vast ball of gas with no solid surface.

Core

WHAT IS A STAR ?

A STAR is a huge ball of gas that gives off vast amounts of light and heat. The Sun is our local star. It is nearly 1.4 million km across. More than a million Earths could fit inside it. Being made of gas, it has no solid surface. Energy is made in the Sun's core, where the temperature is about 15 million °C, and travels to the surface through layers of gas to emerge as light and heat. The Sun is close enough for us to see it as a disc shape in the sky, and it provides all the energy needed to keep life going on Earth. Because they are so distant, other stars appear as points of light.

HOW MANY STARS ARE THERE ?

ASTRONOMERS estimate that our galaxy (star system) — the Milky Way — contains 100,000 million stars. There may be 100,000 million galaxies in the Universe. That is a total of 10,000 million million million stars!

WHAT ARE SUNSPOTS ?

JUST like the Earth, the Sun creates magnetic fields inside and around itself. These sometimes stop the heat from the centre of the Sun reaching the surface. In places where this happens, cooler, dark areas, called sunspots, appear. Some last just a few days. Others are as big as planets and last for months. Solar flares are another surface feature of the Sun. They are huge eruptions of flame.

WHAT MAKES THE SUN SHINE ?

THE Sun shines because it gives out light and heat, which are forms of energy. The energy is made by nuclear reactions in the Sun's core. Extreme temperatures and pressure at the core make hydrogen atoms join together to form helium atoms. This process is called nuclear fusion, and it creates huge amounts of energy. It can take a million years for the energy produced in the core to reach the surface.

At the Sun's core, the nuclei of atoms join together, releasing huge amounts of energy.

WHY ARE SOME STARS BRIGHTER THAN OTHERS ?

HOW bright a star appears to be depends not only on how bright it really is, but also on how far away it is. A dim star that is close to us can appear brighter than a more distant, brighter star.

Solar flares and sunspots are visible on the Sun's surface.

Solar flare

Sunspot

ARE ALL STARS LIKE OUR SUN ?

THE Sun is a type of star called a "yellow dwarf", because it is small compared to other types of star and gives off yellow light. Some stars are a hundred times bigger. Others are as small as the Moon.

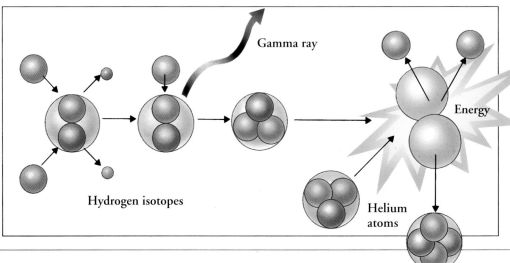

Gamma ray

Hydrogen isotopes

Energy

Helium atoms

WHAT IS A CONSTELLATION ?

A CONSTELLATION is a group of stars that forms a pattern. Some of the 88 constellations are easier to spot than others. Different constellations are visible from different parts of the Earth. Some are visible only from places in the northern hemisphere; others can be seen only from the southern hemisphere. As the Earth orbits the Sun, different constellations become visible as the Earth's dark side faces different parts of the night sky.

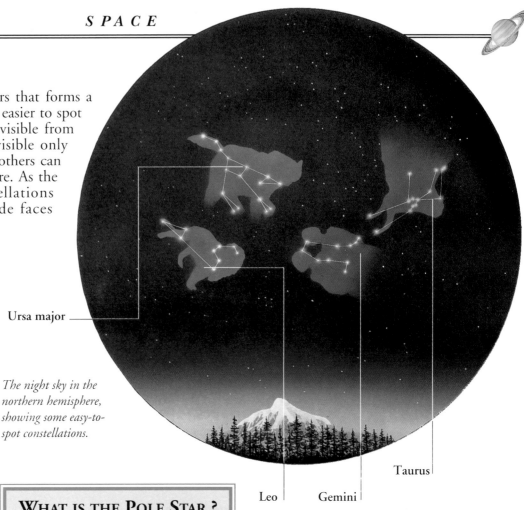

The night sky in the northern hemisphere, showing some easy-to-spot constellations.

Ursa major

Taurus

Leo   Gemini

WHO NAMED THE CONSTELLATIONS ?

OVER 2,000 years ago, ancient Greek astronomers saw the same patterns in the sky as we do today. They named the constellations after the animals, beasts and gods familiar to them.

During a total eclipse of the Sun, the Sun is completely hidden by the Moon. During a partial eclipse, only part of the Sun is hidden.

WHAT IS AN ECLIPSE ?

AN ECLIPSE happens when the Moon casts a shadow on the Earth (an eclipse of the Sun), or the Earth casts a shadow on the Moon (an eclipse of the Moon). During a total eclipse of the Sun, the Sun disappears from some places on Earth. There are about seven minutes of darkness as the Moon's shadow moves across the Earth's surface. During an eclipse of the Moon, the Moon goes dark as it moves through the shadow cast by the Earth.

WHAT IS A STAR SIGN ?

TWELVE of the constellations, called the signs of the zodiac, or star signs, lie in an imaginary belt across the night sky. The orbits of all the main planets except Pluto move through this belt. Some people believe that our lives are affected by the movement of the Sun, Moon and planets in relation to these constellations.

WHAT IS THE POLE STAR ?

THE Pole Star, or Polaris, is a star in the northern hemisphere. It is called the Pole Star because it is the nearest star to the north pole of the sky. It appears to stay still as the Earth spins and the other stars appear to move round it.

WHAT IS THE SOUTHERN CROSS ?

THE Southern Cross (also called Crux) is one of the most beautiful of the constellations visible from the southern hemisphere. Its five stars form the shape of a cross. The long bar of the cross points towards the point in space above the Earth's south pole.

DOES A STAR EVER DIE ?

A STAR does not shine forever. When the hydrogen gas in the centre is used up, the star can no longer make energy. It expands into a giant red star (1) and the core heats up (2). In some stars, the outer layers disappear into space, and the star collapses (3) leaving a small, dense star called a white dwarf. Other, larger stars end with a huge explosion, called a supernova (4).

Stars bigger than the Sun end in massive explosions called supernovae.

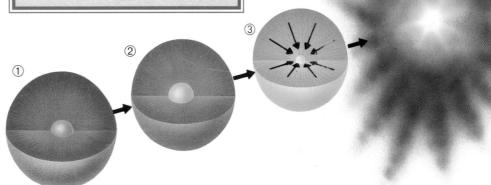

①   ②   ③   ④

WHY DOES THE MOON SEEM TO CHANGE SHAPE ?

THE half of the Moon that points towards the Sun looks bright because it is lit by sunlight. The Moon appears to change shape because we see different amounts of the lit part as the Moon orbits the Earth. When the Moon is between the Earth and the Sun, the lit side is hidden from us. As it moves around the Earth, more and more of the lit side comes into view. Then it begins to disappear again.

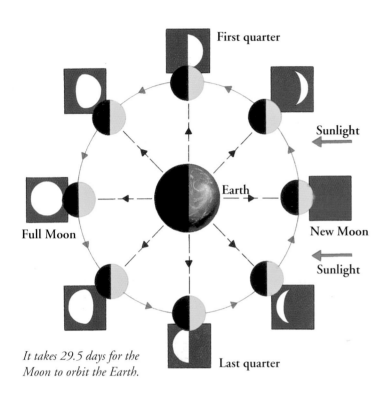

First quarter

Sunlight

Earth

New Moon

Full Moon

Sunlight

Last quarter

It takes 29.5 days for the Moon to orbit the Earth.

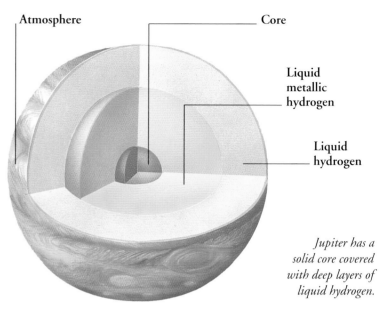

Atmosphere

Core

Liquid metallic hydrogen

Liquid hydrogen

Jupiter has a solid core covered with deep layers of liquid hydrogen.

ARE THE OTHER PLANETS LIKE THE EARTH ?

THE Earth is a rocky planet with seas and solid land masses. It is shrouded in an atmosphere of gases, which animals and plants need in order to live. The atmosphere also protects life from harmful rays from the Sun. Venus is the only other rocky planet with an atmosphere, but its atmosphere contains burning clouds of sulphuric acid. The other rocky planets are Mercury and Mars. There are five gas planets, including two giant planets, Jupiter and Saturn. They are called gas planets because they are made up of liquids, such as hydrogen, which would turn to gas on Earth.

WHICH PLANET IS NEAREST THE SUN ?

MERCURY is the planet closest to the Sun. On average, it orbits at 58 million km away. (Earth orbits 93 million km away.) Mercury is not much bigger than the Moon, and it looks quite like the Moon, too. The side of Mercury nearest to the Sun gets blisteringly hot. The surface temperature is more than 400°C. The next-closest planet to the Sun is Venus, followed by Earth, Mars, Jupiter, Saturn, Uranus, Neptune and Pluto.

WHAT MAKES THE MOON GO ROUND THE EARTH ?

THE Moon keeps moving in its circular orbit around the Earth because the force of gravity between the Earth and the Moon acts like an invisible tether. If there were no gravity, the Moon would fly off into space. If the Moon stopped moving, it would crash down to Earth.

Nine planets orbit the Sun. Mercury is the closest and Pluto the furthest away.

WHAT IS THE SOLAR SYSTEM ?

THE solar system is the Sun, the nine planets, the planets' moons — there are 62 in all — and the millions of other objects, such as asteroids and comets, that orbit the Sun.

Mercury Venus Earth Mars   Jupiter   Saturn

DO ALL THE PLANETS HAVE MOONS ?

ALL planets but two (Mercury and Venus) have moons. The Earth and Pluto have one each, Mars has two, Neptune has eight, Uranus has 15, Jupiter 16, and Saturn 19. Jupiter's largest moon is larger than the planet Mercury.

WHAT ARE ASTEROIDS ?

APART from the planets, other lumps of rock, called asteroids, orbit the Sun. Astronomers have identified several thousand asteroids, but there are probably millions in all. Most lie between the orbits of Mars and Jupiter, in areas called Asteroid Belts.

Our entire solar system was formed from a cloud of dust and gas.

WHERE DID THE PLANETS COME FROM ?

ALL the material that makes up our solar system — the Sun, planets, moons, asteroids and comets — is thought to have formed from a gigantic cloud of gas and dust in space. About 4,600 million years ago, this cloud began to swirl around and collapse inwards (1). The centre heated up, and jets of gas shot out (2). The cloud flattened into a disc (3) and the hot core became the Sun. Other material slowly clumped together to become planets, moons, asteroids and comets (4).

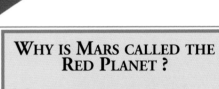

WHY IS MARS CALLED THE RED PLANET ?

MARS is called the Red Planet because it is covered in reddish-brown rocks and soil. Most of the surface is flat, but there are several enormous, extinct volcanoes. Like Earth, Mars has an icy cap at each of its poles.

WHICH IS THE BIGGEST PLANET ?

JUPITER is by far the largest planet. It is big enough to contain all the other planets put together. Huge storms rage in its hydrogen atmosphere, including one that has lasted for many centuries, called the Great Red Spot.

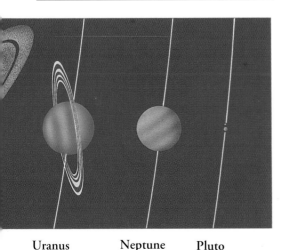

Uranus   Neptune   Pluto

Pluto's orbital path sometimes crosses over Neptune's.

WHICH PLANET HAS THE LONGEST ORBIT ?

PLUTO is the furthest planet from the Sun, and has the longest orbit. On Pluto, a year lasts for 248.5 Earth years. Pluto's orbital path is unusual because it is elongated. When furthest from the Sun, it is 7,380 million km away — nearly 50 times further away than the Earth. Pluto is by far the smallest planet, and its Moon is half its size. There may be other planets outside the orbit of Pluto, but they must be very far away, otherwise they would already have been found.

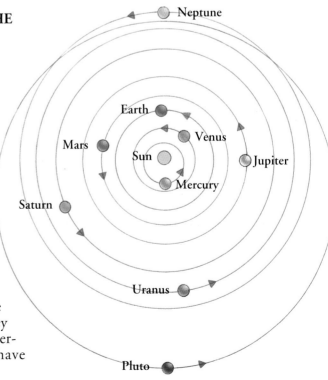

WHAT IS A SPACE PROBE?

A SPACE probe is an unmanned spacecraft that travels through space to explore planets and moons. Probes carry cameras and scientific instruments. These measure such things as magnetic fields, X-rays and other cosmic radiation. Space probes have sent back vast amounts of information about the Sun, the planets and their moons. Astronomers have found out far more than they could have by using telescopes alone.

Voyager 1 flew past Jupiter in 1979.

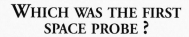

HAVE PROBES LANDED ON OTHER PLANETS?

TWO American Viking probes travelled to Mars in 1976, and each carried a landing craft that was parachuted down to the Martian surface. More than twelve Soviet Venera probes have landed on Venus, where the atmospheric pressure is 90 times that of Earth. Although all were crushed, several survived long enough to send back data and pictures.

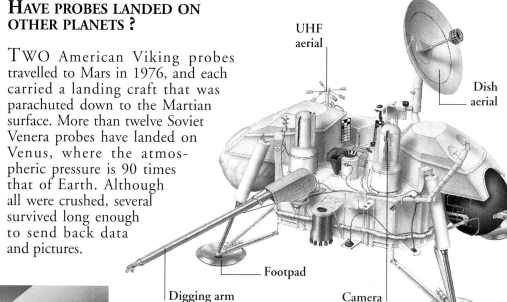

UHF aerial

Dish aerial

Footpad

Digging arm

Camera

One of two identical Viking landing craft or "landers".

WHAT DID THE SPACE PROBE GIOTTO DO?

IN 1986, the Giotto space probe was one of five probes sent to study Halley's comet. It flew through the cloud of dust and gas around the comet at 68 km/s, passing within 500 km of its icy core. Giotto photographed jets of gas spouting from the black surface of the comet's nucleus.

Camera

Solar energy cells

Aerial

The Giotto probe went to investigate Halley's comet as it flew near the Earth in 1986.

WHICH WAS THE FIRST SPACE PROBE?

THE first successful probe was the Soviet probe Luna 1, which flew within 6,000 km of the Moon in January 1959. Luna 2 landed on the Moon in September 1959.

HOW LONG DOES A PROBE TAKE TO REACH MARS?

IT TAKES about six months for a space probe to reach Mars. The probe flies in a big curve, gradually catching up with Mars' orbital path. This makes it easier for the probe to orbit the planet.

WHICH PLANETS HAVE SPACE PROBES VISITED?

SO FAR, space probes have visited every planet except Pluto, the furthest planet from the Sun. They have also flown past many of the other planets' moons. Voyager 2 took 12 years to reach Neptune. A trip to Pluto would take at least 10 more years.

WHAT DID THE VIKING LANDERS FIND OUT?

THE Viking landers photographed the Martian surface, analysed the soil, measured "Marsquakes" and reported on the weather. The temperature was between -43 and -123°C. They tested for signs of life in the soil, but found none.

WHAT IS THE HUBBLE TELESCOPE ?

THE Hubble Space Telescope is a reflecting telescope that orbits the Earth as a satellite. It was launched by a space shuttle in 1990. Unfortunately, the main mirror, which is 2.4 m across, had a fault in its shape, and was not able to create clear images. It had to be repaired in space by a space shuttle astronaut. It now sends back amazing pictures of the stars, galaxies and planets.

The Hubble Space Telescope's on-board computers control its cameras and send pictures back to Earth.

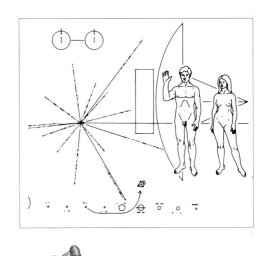

Camera

Solar panel

Light enters here

WHY DOES HUBBLE NEED TO BE IN SPACE ?

TELESCOPES on Earth look at space through the atmosphere, which contains dust, moisture and air currents. It is like looking through an uneven, dirty window. From outside the atmosphere, Hubble can see 50 times further than telescopes on Earth.

WHICH PROBE IS FURTHEST FROM EARTH ?

IN 1997, Pioneer 10 was nearly 10 billion km from Earth. It left the solar system in 1986. Eventually it will be overtaken by Voyager 1, which is travelling faster. Both probes will take tens of thousands of years to reach other stars.

DO SPACE PROBES HAVE ENGINES ?

SPACE probes can travel for years at tens of thousands of kilometres per hour, but they do not need engines because there is no air in space to slow them down. They are launched into orbit around the Earth and then fired on paths that will enable them to intercept the planets they are to visit. They have small thrusters that send out streams of gas. These can slow a probe down, speed it up or make it spin.

DO SPACE PROBES RETURN TO EARTH ?

SPACE probes are not designed to return to Earth. Some orbit other planets, taking photographs. They will carry on orbiting their planets for ever. Others make "fly-bys" of planets without going into orbit. Some, such as Voyager 2, are heading out of the solar system and into deep space. Both Pioneer 10 and Voyager 2 are carrying messages from Earth in case they are ever found by other intelligent beings.

Earth   Moon
Sun   Jupiter
Uranus   Saturn

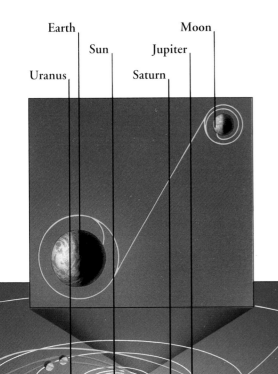

Probes to the outer planets can have complex orbits. Voyager 2 reached Neptune via Jupiter, Saturn and Uranus.

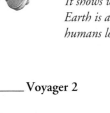

This is a plaque on board Pioneer 10. It shows where the Earth is and what humans look like.

Voyager 2

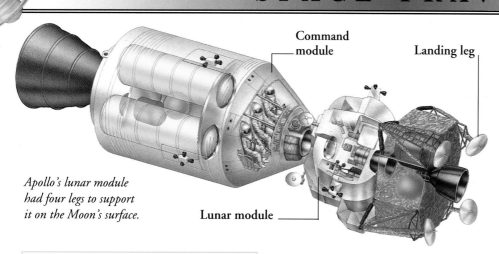

Command module

Landing leg

Apollo's lunar module had four legs to support it on the Moon's surface.

Lunar module

HOW DID ASTRONAUTS GET TO THE MOON ?

A COMPLETELY new type of spacecraft, called Apollo, was developed to send astronauts to the Moon and get them back safely. To launch Apollo into space a new rocket, the Saturn V, was built. The Apollo spacecraft was made up of two parts: the command and service module, in which the astronauts travelled on their journey to and from the Moon, and the lunar module, which actually took them to the surface of the Moon.

HOW LONG DID THE FIRST JOURNEY TO THE MOON TAKE ?

APOLLO 11 made the first Moon landing on July 20, 1969. The mission lasted 195 hours and the astronauts travelled more than 1.5 million km. Neil Armstrong and Edwin "Buzz" Aldrin spent 22 hours on the Moon.

HOW DID *APOLLO 11* LAND ON THE MOON ?

WHILE the command and service module stayed in orbit, the lunar module descended to the Moon with two astronauts on board. Only the lunar module's top half blasted back into orbit to rejoin the rest of the spacecraft.

HOW LONG DOES IT TAKE THE SHUTTLE TO GET INTO SPACE ?

THE space shuttle normally orbits the Earth at a distance of about 250 km. The journey into orbit takes about 10 minutes. The two rocket boosters fall away after the first 45 km, which takes just two minutes. The fuel tank is jettisoned after eight minutes.

Backpack

Backpack control

The space suit's backpack contains an oxygen supply so that the astronaut can breathe in space.

WHAT IS A SPACE WALK ?

WHEN astronauts leave their spacecraft on a space walk, they do not really walk at all; they simply float in space. They have to do space walks to make repairs to satellites, space telescopes, or even their own spacecraft. Sometimes they use a special backpack called a manned manoeuvring unit (MMU for short).

An astronaut fires tiny gas jets from the manned manoeuvring unit in order to move about.

Apart from its rocket boosters and fuel tank, the space shuttle is a reusable spacecraft.

WHY DO ASTRONAUTS WEAR SPACE SUITS ?

SPACE is an inhospitable place. In the shadow of Earth it is extremely cold. In full sunlight, without the protection of the Earth's atmosphere, it is very hot. As there is no air pressure, an astronaut's blood could boil. A space suit keeps an astronaut's body at a comfortable temperature and protects him or her from the Sun's rays.

WHAT HAPPENED TO SKYLAB ?

THE US space station Skylab was launched in 1973. Although badly damaged during lift-off, it allowed many scientific experiments to be carried out successfully. It fell out of orbit in 1979 after circling the Earth 34,981 times, and was destroyed as it re-entered the Earth's atmosphere.

HOW DO ASTRONAUTS GET INTO SPACE ?

SPACE starts only 150 km above the Earth's surface, but getting there is a huge struggle against gravity. Spacecraft stay in orbit by travelling extremely fast. They must reach 28,000 km/h in order not to fall back to Earth. To reach this speed, they need powerful rocket motors.

HOW DO ASTRONAUTS GET BACK TO EARTH ?

THE main problem in returning to Earth is the heat produced by friction (over 1,000°C) as the spacecraft re-enters the atmosphere. The craft starts its descent by slowing down, which makes it fall back towards Earth. A heat shield protects the craft from intense heat as it hurtles into the atmosphere. In the past, most American craft parachuted into the sea. The space shuttle lands on a runway.

Re-entry module

The Russian Soyuz spacecraft's re-entry module is designed to touch down on land.

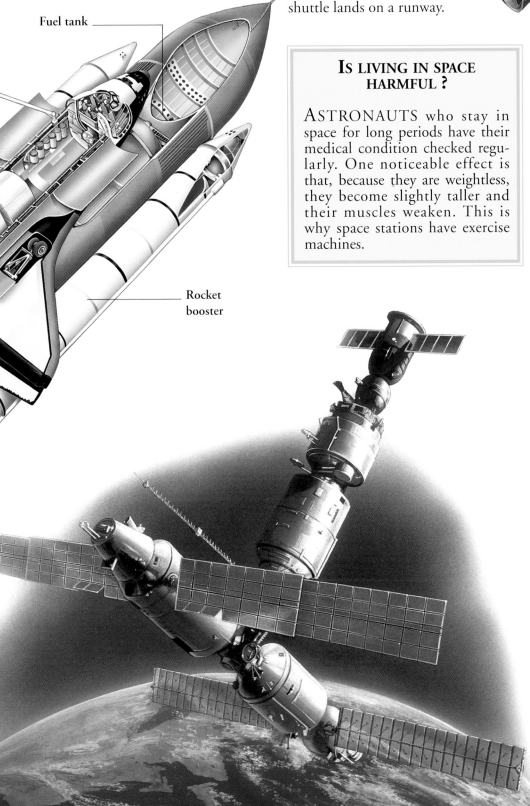

Fuel tank

Rocket booster

IS LIVING IN SPACE HARMFUL ?

ASTRONAUTS who stay in space for long periods have their medical condition checked regularly. One noticeable effect is that, because they are weightless, they become slightly taller and their muscles weaken. This is why space stations have exercise machines.

WHAT IS DOCKING ?

WHEN astronauts move from one spacecraft to another in space, the two craft have to join together. This is called docking. The craft are manoeuvred slowly until they lock together with an airtight join.

HOW LONG WOULD IT TAKE TO REACH THE STARS ?

A MODERN spacecraft, travelling at about 40,000 km/h, would take years to reach the edge of our solar system. Even if it could travel at the speed of light (300,000 km/s), it would still take more than four years to reach the next star.

WHAT IS A SPACE STATION ?

A SPACE station is a spacecraft that permanently orbits the Earth. On board, astronauts and scientists carry out scientific experiments and see how people react to living in the weightlessness of space. Space stations have living areas and working areas. People sleep in bags on the walls, and there are washrooms adapted for weightless conditions. Solar panels turn sunlight into electricity, which the station needs in order to work.

The Russian Mir space station has been in orbit around the Earth since 1986.

WHAT IS INSIDE THE EARTH ?

THE Earth is like a giant ball with different layers building out from its centre. The centre is the core, made from iron and nickel. The inner core is under such pressure that it is a solid mass, while the outer core is liquid. Next is the mantle, made up of rocky material. This is hot, and in some places it moves very slowly. On the surface of the Earth is the crust, which can be up to 50 km thick.

The core, mantle and crust are the Earth's three components.

618 km

2,220 km

1,738 km

1,545 km

Lower mantle

Outer core

Inner core

Crust

Upper mantle

WHAT IS THE EARTH'S CRUST MADE FROM ?

THE Earth's crust is its outer layer. Oceanic crust, which lies beneath the oceans, is made largely of heavy basalt rock. Continental crust is less dense, and is made mostly of granite.

WERE THE CONTINENTS ONCE JOINED TOGETHER ?

THE continents are continually moving, centimetre by centimetre. About 200 million years ago they were all joined together, forming a huge supercontinent. We know this because the rock types at the edges of the continents match up with each other. We also know, from studying fossils, that when the continents were joined the same animals lived all over the world.

HOW HEAVY IS THE EARTH ?

THE total mass of the Earth is 5.98×10^{24} kg. Its volume is 1.08×10^{21} m^3. The solid inner core, made mostly of iron, makes up a third of the Earth's mass.

HOW OLD IS THE EARTH ?

IT IS difficult to tell, as the Earth's surface is constantly changing and reforming. The Earth formed at the same time as the rest of the planets in the solar system. As far as we can tell, the oldest rocks on the Earth's surface formed about 4,500 million years ago.

WHY DOES A COMPASS NEEDLE POINT NORTH ?

THE Earth's solid iron core is spinning at a different speed from the rest of the Earth. It can do this because the outer core is liquid. The movement sets up magnetic fields in the Earth that make it act like a giant magnet. It has north and south magnetic poles, which attract a compass needle.

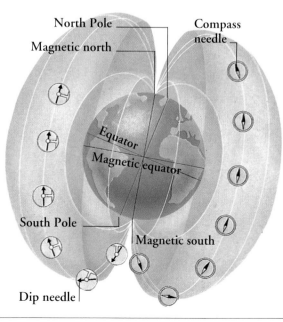

North Pole

Compass needle

Magnetic north

Equator

Magnetic equator

South Pole

Magnetic south

Dip needle

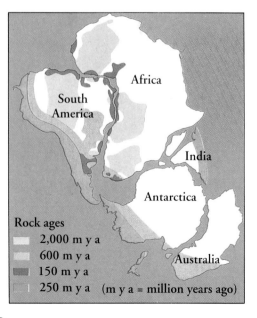

Africa

South America

India

Antarctica

Australia

Rock ages

2,000 m y a

600 m y a

150 m y a

250 m y a   (m y a = million years ago)

The continents can be fitted together like the pieces of a jigsaw puzzle, so that their coastlines interlock.

A compass needle lines up with the magnetic field, so it always points north. A dip needle can swing up or down.

HOW ARE MOUNTAIN RANGES MADE?

WHEN continents are pushed together, they crumple up at the edges. The rocks are thrust up into mountain ranges, which eventually begin to wear away by the forces of erosion.

WHAT ARE BLOCK MOUNTAINS?

WHEN a continent is pulled in different directions, the rock fractures along a fault. Whole blocks of land can rise or sink between two faults, forming flat, steep-sided mountains and valleys.

WHERE DOES VOLCANIC LAVA COME FROM?

A VOLCANO is an opening in the Earth's crust through which molten rock (lava) erupts. The molten rock may come from the mantle, or it may be formed when parts of the continental crust melts.

The layers of the atmosphere absorb and reflect different parts of the Sun's radiation.

WHAT IS AIR?

SURROUNDING the more solid part of our planet are the layers of the Earth's atmosphere. Most of the air we breathe is compressed into the lowest layer, the troposphere. Air is a mixture of gases made up mainly of oxygen and nitrogen, and it supports all life on Earth. Clouds and weather systems are also confined to the troposphere. Higher up the air becomes thinner. In the stratosphere, a layer of ozone helps to filter out the radiation from the Sun which is harmful to life.

WHY IS THE EARTH HOT INSIDE?

SOME heat remains from when the Earth was first formed; some is caused by the pressure the rocks are under; and some is released by radioactive chemicals.

HOW CAN WE FIND OUT ABOUT OTHER PLANETS?

UNMANNED space probes can measure a planet's gravity and density, and whether it has a magnetic field.

HOW DO THE CONTINENTS MOVE?

THE Earth's outer shell is made up of rigid individual plates, made from the Earth's crust and the topmost part of the mantle. As the mantle material slowly moves, the plates move, too. When two plates move apart, molten rock from inside the Earth wells up, filling the gap. The continents are embedded in the plates, like logs in the ice of a frozen river. As the plates move, the continents move with them.

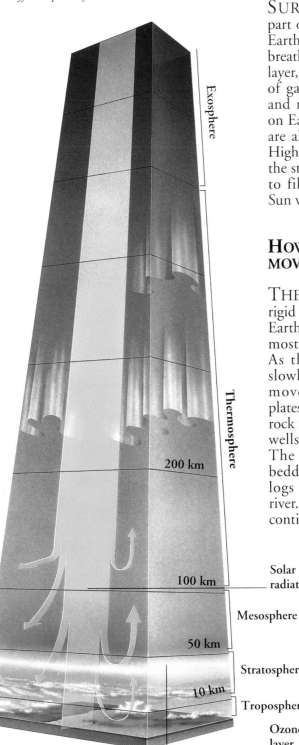

Exosphere

Thermosphere

200 km

100 km — Solar radiation

Mesosphere

50 km

Stratosphere

10 km

Troposphere

Ozone layer

When two continental plates meet, one is dragged down beneath the other.

Folds develop when sedimentary rocks are subjected to pressure. When the pressure is too great for the rocks to withstand, they shear and faults are formed.

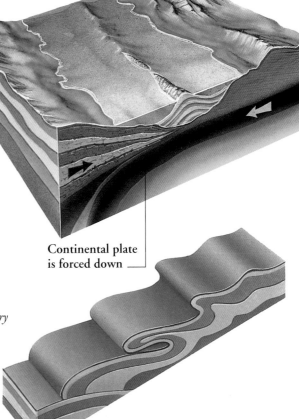

Continental plate is forced down

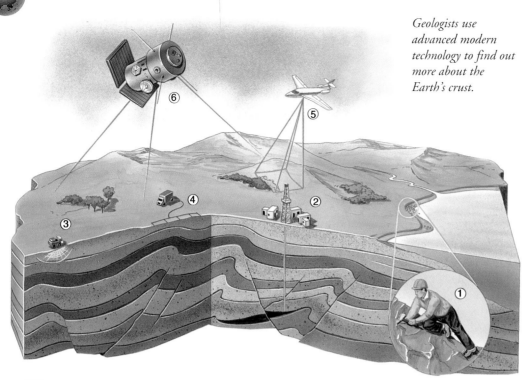

Geologists use advanced modern technology to find out more about the Earth's crust.

ARE ALL MINERALS VALUABLE?

APART from some gemstones, the only valuable minerals are the so-called "ore minerals", from which a metal can be extracted. Most other minerals that make up the Earth's rocks are not valuable.

WHAT ARE GEMS?

GEMS are stones found in the Earth's crust, used in jewellery. Most are mineral crystals. Diamond is made from carbon. Sapphire is made from corundum. Opal is a gem made from silica, which does not form a crystal.

HOW DO GEOLOGISTS FIND OUT ABOUT THE EARTH'S CRUST?

UNTIL early in the 20th century, the only way geologists could find out about the Earth's crust was to examine rock samples. This involved breaking them off with a hammer (1) and analysing their chemical composition. Today, they can also drill deep into the crust (2) to collect samples; make artificial earthquakes (3) and record the shock waves (4), in order to map the layers of rock; and use aerial photography (5) and satellites (6) to give us new information about the Earth's surface.

WHAT IS A MINERAL?

MINERALS are the building blocks of rocks. If you examine a rock through a magnifying lens, you will see that it is made up of many small particles. Each particle has a specific chemical composition. When a rock forms, the chemicals that comprise it form themselves into mineral particles. There are usually no more than six different kinds of mineral in a particular rock type.

Sometimes a mineral, such as diamond, forms a well-defined crystal.

HOW DO GEOLOGISTS STUDY MINERALS?

GEOLOGISTS are able to study the minerals of a rock by slicing the rock thinly and looking at a slice through a microscope. A thin rock slice is transparent. If polarized light is shone through it, the different minerals show up as various shapes and bright colours. The effect is like looking at a stained glass window. Geologists and mineralogists can use these false colours to identify the particular mineral types in the rock.

Minerals are studied in a laboratory as well as in the field.

HOW HARD ARE MINERALS?

DIFFERENT minerals have different degrees of hardness. Talc is the softest mineral; it crumbles in the fingers. Diamond, the hardest mineral, can cut glass. The hardness of a mineral is often used to help identify it.

WHY DO SOME ROCKS FORM IN LAYERS?

SOME rocks are formed from great masses of sand or mud, which build up on the sea floor in layers. Over millions of years, the mass is compressed by the weight of more sand, and solidifies into "sedimentary rock".

WHY DO MINERALS FORM SHAPES ?

A MINERAL is made up of atoms and molecules. As the atoms and molecules combine, they form a particular pattern. This pattern continues to grow as the mineral develops. The final shape of the mineral reflects the original atomic shape. In the same way, the square shape of a house reflects the square shape of the individual bricks. The mineral shape that is formed is called a crystal.

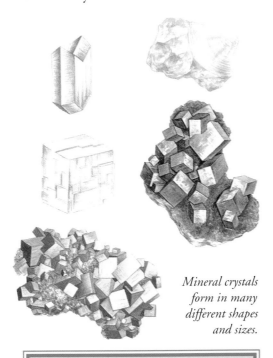

Mineral crystals form in many different shapes and sizes.

WHAT IS HARD ROCK GEOLOGY ?

HARD rock geology is the study of igneous and metamorphic rocks. Igneous rocks, like granite, are formed from the magma in the Earth's mantle. Metamorphic or "changed" rocks, like marble, are formed when other rocks have been subjected to heat or pressure.

WHAT IS SOFT ROCK GEOLOGY ?

SOFT rock geology is the study of sedimentary rocks and the way they were laid down. It examines the sediments from which the rock formed, the fossils in the rock, and the history of how the Earth's surface has changed.

HOW ARE IGNEOUS ROCKS MADE ?

IGNEOUS rocks form when hot, molten masses from the Earth's interior come close to the surface, or burst out from volcanoes, and cool. The minerals crystallize out of the molten mass, bind together and form an "igneous rock".

WHAT ARE FOSSILS ?

FOSSILS are the preserved remains of animals and plants that lived long ago. Usually a dead animal or plant decays, but sometimes it may be buried before it has decayed. Over a long period, the minerals in the ground can replace the once-living substance and preserve the dead body or plant as a lump of mineral. Other fossils may be preserved as a thin film of the animal or plant's original carbon. Sometimes fossils are just animal traces, such as footprints.

Some fossils show clearly what the ancient animal life of the Earth looked like.

HOW DO GEOLOGISTS DATE ROCKS ?

SEDIMENTARY rocks form in layers or beds. If the beds remain undisturbed, the oldest rocks lie at the bottom and the youngest at the top. A geologist can usually tell the age of a bed of rock by examining the fossils that it contains, because many fossils are of types of animals that only lived for a short time before becoming extinct.

Fossil trilobite

Trilobites lived 500 million years ago, so the shale bed that the trilobite fossil was found in must also be this old.

HOW ARE METAMORPHIC ROCKS MADE ?

METAMORPHIC rocks form when a rock that already exists is compressed in the depths of a mountain chain, or is heated until the mineral composition changes. The result is a new rock called a "metamorphic rock".

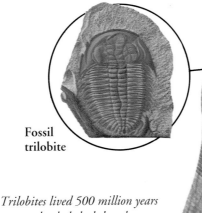

HOW DO SAND DUNES MOVE ?

SAND dunes are masses of loose sand that move across the ground in wind. The grains are blown up the windward side of a dune until they reach the top; then they drop down into the shelter of the lee (the side away from the wind). Other grains are blown up and over, burying the first. This continued action moves the dune across the landscape.

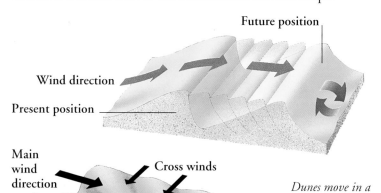

Future position

Wind direction

Present position

Main wind direction

Cross winds

Dunes move in a wave-like motion downwind.

When wind comes from different directions, irregularly shaped dunes, called seif dunes, form.

WHY DO DESERT ROCKS HAVE FANTASTIC SHAPES ?

DESERT erosion is different from any other type of erosion because there is hardly any water involved. Wind is the main force. It picks up sand grains and hurls them against exposed rocks, wearing them away into fantastic shapes and polishing them to shiny surfaces. The rock fragments that are blasted off become more sand.

HOW DO RIVERS FORM ?

RAIN falls in the hills and sinks into the ground. When the rocks and soil cannot hold any more water, the water bubbles to the surface in a spring and runs off downhill, eroding a gorge as it goes. In lower-lying land it runs more slowly, and although it is still eroding the sides of the valleys, it is also depositing the material that it has eroded upstream. Eventually the river becomes so slow that it cannot carry any more debris, and it deposits the sediment in a flood plain, before reaching the sea.

WHAT IS THE ROCK CYCLE ?

ALL rocks, whether they are sedimentary, igneous or metamorphic, are constantly being created and destroyed. Whenever a rock is exposed at the surface the forces of weather and erosion slowly break it down. The broken particles are carried along by winds or rivers and eventually accumulate, forming sedimentary rocks. These may melt and solidify as igneous rocks, or may be compressed to form metamorphic rocks. If they reappear at the surface, the process, called the rock cycle, starts all over again.

The minerals that form rocks take part in an endless round of construction and destruction.

WHAT IS WEATHERING ?

RAIN, wind, frost and all kinds of other weather effects can, over time, break down the rocks of the Earth's surface. Even sunlight, heating up rocks by day and allowing them to cool at night, has an effect. All of this erosive action is known as weathering.

Over time, the constant flow of freshwater in a river changes the landscape.

WHAT SHAPES THE CLIFFS ALONG THE SEASHORE ?

COASTAL cliffs are continually battered by the sea, and the waves compress the air in their cracks. A headland is worn away from each side, becoming narrower, until caves and arches are punched through. These eventually collapse, leaving the offshore parts standing as sea stacks.

DO ROCKS DISSOLVE?

IN A rock such as granite, one of the mineral components, feldspar, is dissolved by acid rainwater to form clay. This makes the other minerals in granite — quartz and mica — fall loose to form sand.

CAN LIVING THINGS BREAK DOWN ROCKS?

TREE roots reach down through the soil and force their way into cracks in the rock beneath. As they grow, they can force these cracks open and, over the years, help to erode the landscape.

WHAT MAKES WATERFALLS?

A FAST-FLOWING river erodes its bed downwards. This erosion is not constant, but depends on the hardness of the rock over which the water is passing. When there is a particularly hard bed of rock in the river, it erodes so slowly that the river falls over it as a waterfall. The downstream rocks are eroded into a "plunge pool". Eventually the hard rock at the top of the waterfall is undermined and the river can cut back into it as a gorge.

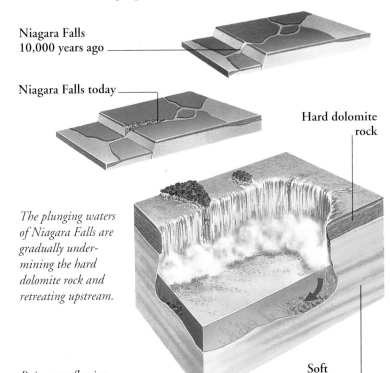

Niagara Falls
10,000 years ago

Niagara Falls today

Hard dolomite rock

The plunging waters of Niagara Falls are gradually undermining the hard dolomite rock and retreating upstream.

Soft sandstone

HOW ARE CAVES MADE?

RAINWATER absorbs carbon dioxide gas from the air, which makes it acidic. The acid attacks some kinds of rocks, particularly limestone. A limestone bed can be hollowed out by the acidic water passing through it. Weak areas, such as cracks or the gaps between beds are eroded first, forming horizontal caves along the water table. The water table is the level at which the rocks are saturated with water. When the water table changes, different levels of caves are hollowed out.

Rainwater flowing underground can hollow out rocks such as limestone and form caves.

WHAT IS AN OXBOW LAKE?

ON A flood plain, a river erodes the outside of each bend, while beaches of mud build up on the inner curves. Eventually the neck of a bend wears through, and the river takes up a straighter course, leaving behind an oxbow lake.

IS ALL EROSION SLOW?

MOST of the erosive processes on Earth take thousands and thousands of years to wear away rocks. However, some erosive events, such as landslides, avalanches and floods, can be sudden and disastrous.

WHAT IS SCREE?

THE sides of some mountains are covered in pieces of broken rock, called "scree". Scree forms as a result of frost. When water that has gathered in cracks in the rocks freezes, it expands. The force of expansion is so great that it can split rocks apart into smaller and smaller pieces.

HOW LONG HAS THERE BEEN LIFE IN THE SEA ?

THE sea is where the Earth's first living creatures evolved. The earliest clear fossils date from 570 million years ago. Before then, animals had no hard parts and so did not fossilize. Some 175 million years later, fish were well-established in the sea and were spreading to rivers and lakes. Some 195 million years ago, squid-like creatures with shells were common. Giant squid up to 20 m long survive today in the ocean depths.

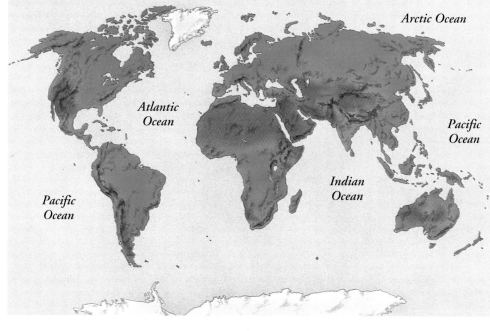

A world map shows at a glance just how much of the Earth's surface is covered by water.

Two giants of the ocean depth are the giant squid and the sperm whale, which can be more than 18 m long.

HOW MUCH OF THE EARTH IS COVERED BY SEA ?

SOME scientists have said we should call our planet Water instead of Earth, since water covers about 71 percent of the planet's surface. The area of the ocean surface is 3.62×10^8 km^2. The area of the land surface is 1.49×10^8 km^2. There is over 2.4 times as much water area than land area.

WHY DOES SEAWATER TASTE SALTY ?

WHEN rivers flow down to the sea they carry with them minute traces of soluble minerals that have been washed out of the rocks. Over thousands of millions of years, these have built up in the oceans. Sodium chloride, or common salt, is the most abundant.

IS THE OCEAN FLOOR FLAT ?

THE floor of the ocean has a very varied topography. A series of volcanic ridges cuts through all the oceans. These ridges mark the sites where the Earth's surface plates are being created. Deep ocean troughs occur in places where one of the Earth's plates is being pulled down beneath another and destroyed. Volcanoes that rise up from the ocean floor produce chains and arcs of islands.

WHAT CAUSES WAVES ?

WIND over the sea pushes surface water particles along with it. This sets up a rolling motion in the water, moving the water particles in a vertical, circular path. The water itself does not travel far, but the movement, transferred from one particle to another, makes waves that cross the oceans.

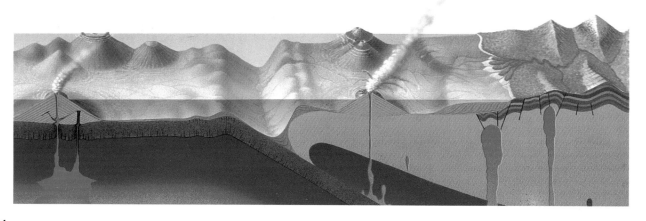

Landscape features on the ocean floor include mountains taller than Mount Everest, 10-km deep trenches, valleys, ridges and volcanoes.

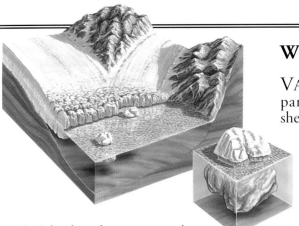

Ice is less dense than seawater, so huge masses of ice can float in the ocean.

WHAT IS AN ICEBERG ?

VAST sheets of ice cover the coldest parts of the Earth. When these ice sheets meet the sea, parts break off and float away, forming icebergs. In the Arctic, lumpy and angular icebergs form when the ice in a glacier meets the sea. In the Southern Hemisphere, icebergs break off the ice cap that covers Antarctica. These broad, flat icebergs can be as large as a country.

ARE TIDAL WAVES CAUSED BY THE TIDES ?

NO! TIDAL waves happen as a result of a great disturbance in the sea. Underwater volcanic eruptions, underwater earthquakes, or landslides into the sea can set up a devastating wave that can travel half way round the world. Such waves are called "tsunamis", but are also known as "tidal waves".

WHY DOES THE TIDE COME IN AND GO OUT ?

AS THE Moon and the Earth swing round one another, ocean water is thrown to the side of the Earth away from the Moon. At the same time, the Moon's gravity attracts water to the side facing the Moon, resulting in two periods of high tide every 24 hours.

WHAT ARE OCEAN CURRENTS ?

OCEAN currents are movements of warm or cold seawater through water of a different temperature. Vertical currents happen because cold water sinks through warmer water. It then travels along the ocean beds as undersea currents. Surface currents are made by the wind blowing water ahead of it.

Great Barrier Reef

Australia

Australia's Great Barrier Reef is the largest coral reef in the world.

HOW HAS THE OCEAN BED BEEN MEASURED ?

THE Seasat satellite was able to measure variations in the height of the sea bed using radar. It built up a picture of the average surface level of the sea by measuring the reflection time of radar waves off the sea's surface. A surface level above average indicated a steep slope on the sea bed.

HOW DOES THE SEA AFFECT THE CLIMATE ?

WATER takes longer to warm up and cool down than land does. This has an effect on the air above it. As a result, lands close to the sea have winters that are warmer than those inland, and summers that are cooler.

HOW DO CORAL REEFS FORM ?

A CORAL is a small animal that lives all its life in one place. It thrives in warm, shallow seawater. The coral builds a shell, which it cements on to the dead shells of other corals, and so a great mass of rocky shell material is built up. If the sea bed sinks, the corals continue to grow upwards, forming a reef. Many sinking islands in the Pacific Ocean have disappeared, leaving only a coral reef behind.

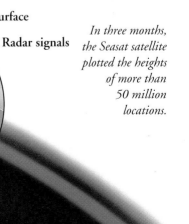

Sea bed
Sea surface
Radar signals

In three months, the Seasat satellite plotted the heights of more than 50 million locations.

ARE THERE CURRENTS AT GREAT DEPTHS ?

AT THE bottom of the ocean the water is constantly in motion. The deep ocean current pattern is quite different from the pattern of the currents on the surface.

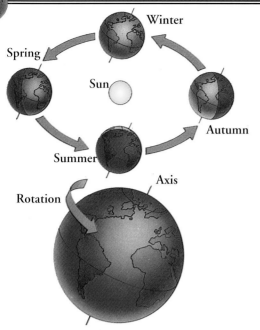

The tilt of the Earth causes different amounts of sunlight to fall on different parts of the globe.

WHY DO WE HAVE SEASONS ?

THE Earth is tilted at an angle of 23.5° from the vertical. During the Earth's yearly orbit of the Sun, for part of the time the North Pole is tilted towards the Sun, giving a northern summer. Six months later it is tilted away, giving a northern winter. Summer in the north coincides with winter in the south, and vice versa.

WHERE DOES RAIN COME FROM ?

THE Sun makes water evaporate from the surface of the sea, turning it into water vapour in the air. The vapour is blown inland by the wind. Over hills, this moist air rises and the water condenses, falling as rain or snow. The rainwater eventually finds its way back to the sea via rivers.

Evaporation

Ground-water

Snow and rain

Water vapour blown inland

Evaporation from sea

Rainfall over sea

The constant circulation of water that produces rain is called the water cycle.

WHAT IS AIR PRESSURE ?

AIR has weight, and so the air at ground level is compressed by the weight of the air above pressing down. This gives us air pressure. Low-pressure areas at ground level are caused by warm air rising and cooler, denser air moving in. Wind always blows into a low pressure area.

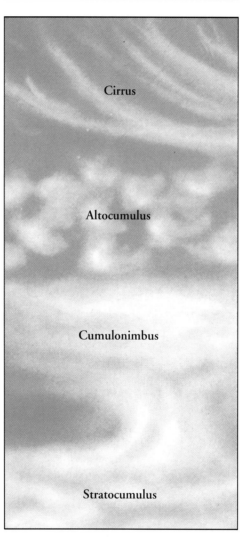

Cirrus

Altocumulus

Cumulonimbus

Stratocumulus

WHAT IS THE TROPOSPHERE ?

THE troposphere is the lowermost layer of the atmosphere. This is the layer in which all life exists, and where all the weather processes occur. Its upper limit varies from place to place, but it usually extends to about 10 km above the Earth's surface.

WHAT ARE CLOUDS ?

WHEN water in the air condenses, it forms tiny droplets. These are so light that they do not fall as rain; instead millions of them gather together as clouds. Fluffy-looking clouds have the word "cumulus" in their name. Clouds formed in layers are called stratus. Wispy ice clouds are called "cirrus".

Different layers of the atmosphere produce different types of cloud.

WHAT IS HAPPENING TO THE OZONE LAYER ?

IN THE stratosphere, the second-lowest layer of the atmosphere, there is a thin layer rich in a kind of oxygen, called ozone. This absorbs much of the harmful radiation of the Sun, but it is being broken down by gases produced by industry and by volcanoes.

WHAT IS CONVECTION ?

THIS is the name given to the movement produced when warm, light air rises and cool, dense air descends to take its place. Most of the Earth's wind patterns are determined by convection.

WHERE DO HOT AND COLD WINDS BLOW ?

AS A rule, hot winds blow from the equator towards the higher latitudes. Cold winds usually blow in the opposite direction.

At a cold front, hot air is forced up over cold air, resulting in unstable weather.

WHAT IS A WEATHER FRONT ?

WHEN two air masses of different temperatures meet, the boundary between them is called a front. When a warm air mass meets a cold air mass, the warm air mass tends to rise up over the cold one. The moisture carried by the warm air then condenses and falls as rain. We can often see a front approaching, bringing bad weather, by the layers of light and dark cloud which appear to meet.

The winds that blow outwards from the poles are diverted to east and west by the Earth's rotation.

WHAT ARE THE PREVAILING WINDS ?

THE winds are described as prevailing because they always blow in the same pattern. This happens because of two effects: convection, in which hot air rises and cool air flows in to take its place, combined with the Earth's rotation. There are always winds blowing towards the equator, and others that blow away from the tropics.

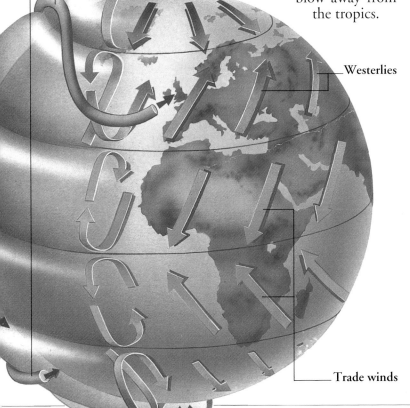

Earth's rotation

Jet streams

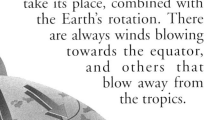

Westerlies

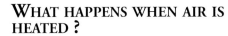
Trade winds

WHAT IS THE "GREENHOUSE" EFFECT ?

THE "greenhouse" effect is the name given to the increase in temperature that results from an increase of some gases in the atmosphere. Sunlight passes through the atmosphere and heats up the ground. Warmth is radiated from the ground as infrared rays, which usually pass straight back up through the atmosphere. The greenhouse gases, like carbon dioxide (CO_2), produced by industry, trap the infrared rays and act like a blanket, raising the temperature.

Radiation in balance

Unnatural greenhouse effect

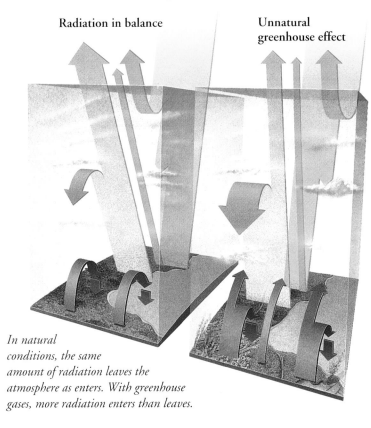

In natural conditions, the same amount of radiation leaves the atmosphere as enters. With greenhouse gases, more radiation enters than leaves.

WHAT HAPPENS WHEN AIR IS HEATED ?

WARM air is lighter than cold air, and so when air is heated it rises. Colder air then rushes in at ground level to take its place. On a small scale, this effect can be seen when the Sun heats up a field and the air above it rises in a thermal; you can often see birds like eagles soaring on these air currents.

Birds can soar upwards on columns of warm, rising air, called thermals.

Bird's flight path

Thermal

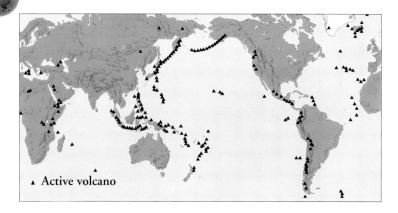

▲ Active volcano

WHERE ARE EXTINCT VOLCANOES FOUND ?

NEARLY every part of the world has been volcanic at one time or another. Many old hills in "non-active areas" are actually extinct volcanoes that have eroded away. Some erupted hundreds of millions of years ago.

Sinking cold air speeds up winds

WHERE DO VOLCANOES HAPPEN MOST ?

A GREAT deal of energy is produced where the Earth's surface plates are being created and destroyed. In these areas, molten material may erupt from the Earth's interior in volcanoes. There are so many around the Pacific Ocean that it is called the "ring of fire".

Most of the world's active volcanoes are found along the edges of the Earth's plates.

A section through a volcano shows how the cone is built up from solidified lava, ash and rock debris deposited by successive eruptions.

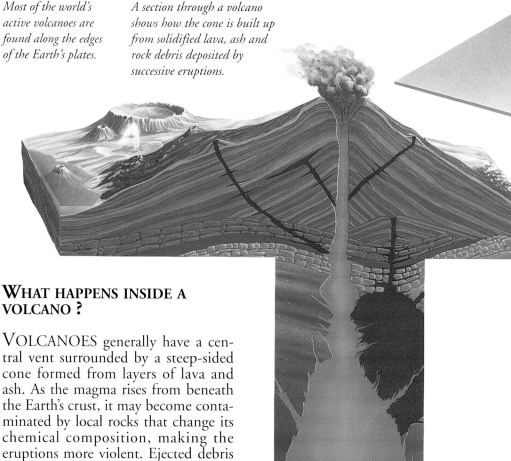

WHAT MAKES AN AVALANCHE SO DEADLY ?

IF YOU press snow in your hands to make a snowball, the snowflakes compress to form ice. Snow tumbling down a mountain turns to hard ice as it hits rocks, making it highly destructive.

WHAT CAUSES LANDSLIDES ?

STEEP slopes can be undercut by rivers, the sea or road building. This can cause the rock structure of the slope to split along lines of weakness, creating a landslide.

WHAT HAPPENS INSIDE A VOLCANO ?

VOLCANOES generally have a central vent surrounded by a steep-sided cone formed from layers of lava and ash. As the magma rises from beneath the Earth's crust, it may become contaminated by local rocks that change its chemical composition, making the eruptions more violent. Ejected debris may range from ash to huge volcanic bombs that weigh several tonnes.

WHAT CAUSES AN EARTHQUAKE ?

WHEN two of the Earth's plates move against one another, pressure builds up along the boundary. Often the plates are locked together, unable to move as the pressure increases. Eventually the stress is so great that the crust ruptures, the rock masses jump past one another, and shock waves spread out in a destructive burst of energy. The result is an earthquake.

An earthquake is most violent at its epicentre, the point on the surface directly above the source.

Epicentre — Source

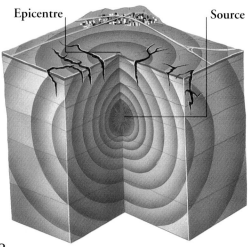

ARE SOME VOLCANOES MORE DANGEROUS THAN OTHERS ?

LAVA produced from magma coming straight up from the mantle is very runny and erupts in slow lava flows, which form broad, low volcanoes like those in Iceland. If the lava is made of old plate material it is very sticky and erupts explosively and without warning, like Mount Saint Helens in the United States.

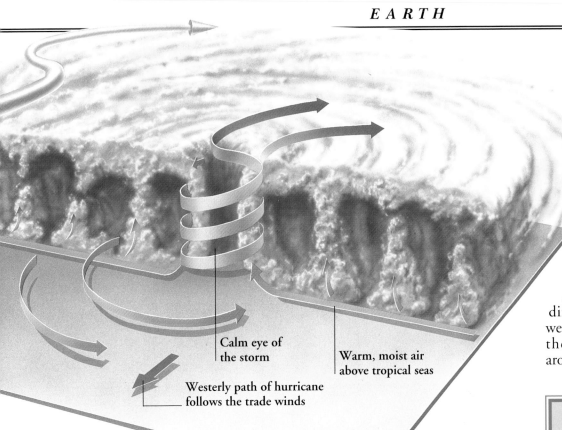

Calm eye of
the storm

Warm, moist air
above tropical seas

Westerly path of hurricane
follows the trade winds

IS A TYPHOON THE SAME THING AS A HURRICANE ?

HURRICANES form over tropical seas. As an intense area of low pressure develops, the surrounding air spirals inwards and upwards, creating winds of up to 300 km/h in the spiral. The whole system is blown by the prevailing winds, only dispersing when it reaches land. A hurricane has different names in different parts of the world. In the west Pacific it is called a typhoon, in the Indian Ocean a cyclone, and around Australia a willy-willy.

At the very centre of the hurricane's turbulent, spiralling winds there is a calm area called the "eye of the storm". This is surrounded by the eye-wall, with the hurricane's highest-velocity winds.

IS A TWISTER LIKE A HURRICANE ?

A TWISTER, or tornado, is like a small hurricane in that strong winds are sucked into a tube of intense low pressure. It may be just a few metres in diameter and usually occurs on land.

WHAT IS A CALDERA ?

A CALDERA is formed when some or all of the magma drains away from the chamber below the cone of a dormant volcano, causing the cone to collapse. On the island of Thira, Greece, a huge caldera is all that remains of the volcano that erupted in 1500 BC, wiping out all life on the island.

WHAT IS A WATERSPOUT ?

WHEN a tornado passes across the sea it sucks up droplets from the surface into an intense, waving white tube called a waterspout. The seawater is dispersed some hours later as salty rain.

CAN DISASTERS BE PREDICTED ?

ALTHOUGH we know how volcanoes and earthquakes occur, it is still not possible to predict precisely when or where they will take place.

HOW DOES WILDFIRE SPREAD ?

SOME habitats thrive because of fire. Grasslands, for example, develop in dry areas where fires are frequent. The grass regenerates quickly and the animal life has adapted to such conditions. But fires can burn out of control. In a forest, it can spread through leaf litter and undergrowth, or through the crowns of trees. Sometimes fire storms develop, in which vicious winds are whipped up by the convection currents produced by the heat, pulling animals and firefighters into the heart of the blaze.

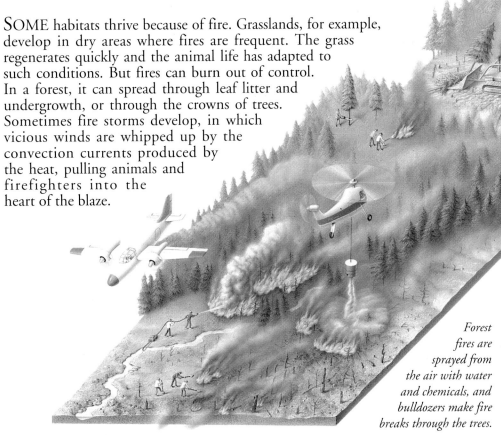

Forest fires are sprayed from the air with water and chemicals, and bulldozers make fire breaks through the trees.

WHERE DO MOST OF THE WORLD'S TREES GROW?

TIMBER has been exploited as a resource for thousands of years, first for heat, light and as a building material, and later as the raw material for paper. Gradually the area of natural forest has decreased; it once covered two thirds of the land and now covers only about one third. The main areas are the coniferous forests of Canada and northern Asia, and the tropical rainforests of South America, Africa and southeast Asia. Today, planted forests supply most of the world's timber products.

Natural forest is being lost most quickly in South America.

☐ Deforested areas

☐ Original forest

WHAT RESOURCES ARE USED TO BUILD A HOUSE?

A TYPICAL house can contain almost every type of natural resource: brick formed from clay, cement derived from limestone, metals extracted from ores, wood cut from forests and glass made from sand, limestone and soda ash.

WHY IS THERE LOTS OF HEAVY INDUSTRY IN CERTAIN AREAS?

MANUFACTURING industries often develop where raw materials occur naturally. These include deposits of coal to supply energy, and deposits of iron or other ores to supply the raw materials.

HOW DO ORE DEPOSITS FORM?

HEAVY mineral-ore particles, from which metals can be easily extracted, can be washed together by rivers or deposited in rock cracks by the Earth's hot magma. Only easily workable deposits are useful to industry.

HOW DO WE GET POWER FROM FLOWING WATER?

SINCE ancient Egyptian times, water wheels that turn in a river's current have been used to drive mills. The same principle is used to make electricity. Water is released from a dam, and as it falls, its energy is used to turn a set of turbines, each of which drives an electrical generator.

Electricity is generated in hydroelectric power plants.

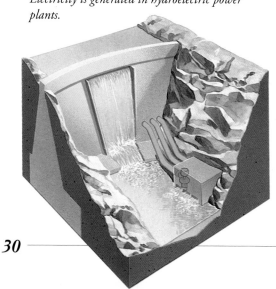

HOW IS IRON OBTAINED FROM ITS ORE?

IRON ore consists of the element iron combined with other elements, mostly oxygen. During smelting, the iron ore is heated with carbon. The carbon combines with the oxygen and carries it away, leaving iron. Carbon was originally obtained from charcoal derived from wood, but in the early 1700s furnaces began to use coke derived from coal. Blast furnaces are so hot that they melt the iron, which is drained off and poured into moulds to form bars, called ingots.

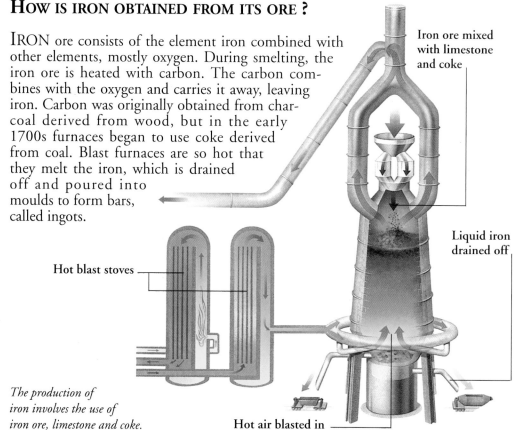

Iron ore mixed with limestone and coke

Liquid iron drained off

Hot blast stoves

Hot air blasted in

The production of iron involves the use of iron ore, limestone and coke.

Rubber, steel, diamond, coal and ink are examples of carbon-based products.

HOW DOES COAL FORM ?

IF THE wood of an ancient forest is buried and compressed for millions of years, its carbon increases. This produces coal, an impure form of carbon, which can be used as fuel.

WHAT IS CARBON USED FOR ?

CARBON is the most important element. It is a major component of our bodies, but it also makes up many of the things we use. Fossil fuels such as coal, oil and gas are carbon based. Diamond, the most valuable gemstone, is pure carbon. Rubber, which has numerous uses in industry, is a carbon compound. Even the paper used in this book and the ink used to print it are formed from carbon.

WHAT IS A RENEWABLE RESOURCE ?

MOST of the Earth's resources cannot be replaced once they have been used up. But some are renewable, relying on natural processes to replace them, for example wind used for power and wood grown as a raw material.

WHAT IS RECYCLING ?

RECYCLING means using a particular resource over and over again. For example, old aluminium cans may be melted down and turned into new cans, and waste paper can be pulped to make more paper.

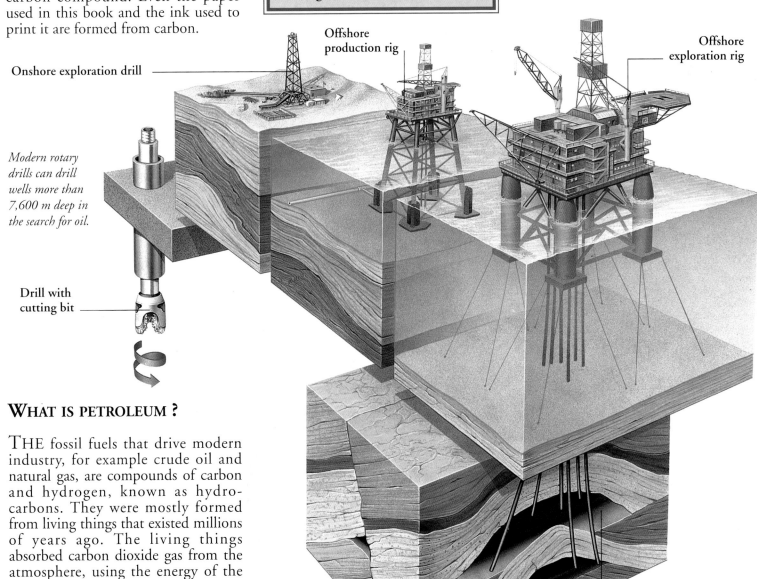

Onshore exploration drill

Offshore production rig

Offshore exploration rig

Modern rotary drills can drill wells more than 7,600 m deep in the search for oil.

Drill with cutting bit

Oil and gas deposit

WHAT IS PETROLEUM ?

THE fossil fuels that drive modern industry, for example crude oil and natural gas, are compounds of carbon and hydrogen, known as hydrocarbons. They were mostly formed from living things that existed millions of years ago. The living things absorbed carbon dioxide gas from the atmosphere, using the energy of the Sun, and were then trapped and preserved. When fossil fuels are burned today, the carbon dioxide returns to the atmosphere and energy is released.

WHAT IS EVOLUTION ?

IF YOU could travel back into the distant past, you would find that the animals and plants looked different from how they do today. This is because living things change gradually, over millions of years, to survive in the changing world around them. We call this evolution. For example, the original horse was a small creature with toes on its feet. As marshlands turned into plains it evolved longer legs and hardened hooves.

Over millions of years the horse has evolved from a small animal with toes into a big animal with hooves.

HAS MANKIND CHANGED THE COURSE OF EVOLUTION ?

HUMANS often affect the way that animals evolve. We have hunted many species to extinction. We have bred many species, like dogs, into shapes that we prefer. We have changed the environment by cutting down forests and building cities, thus favouring animals that can survive in a world full of buildings. For example, rats and other scavengers such as gulls and raccoons have become urban-dwelling creatures.

CAN AN ANIMAL EVOLVE AN EXTRA LIMB ?

EVOLUTION cannot make an animal suddenly produce an extra limb. It can only modify what already exists to make it do a different job. When birds evolved from dinosaurs they did not acquire a pair of wings in addition to their original four legs. Their front legs had gradually to evolve into wings. The tails of some monkeys have evolved to become prehensile; they can be used to grip branches like their hands can.

Some monkeys can use their muscular tail as an extra limb.

WHY ARE CAVE FISH BLIND ?

EVOLUTION does not always lead to animals becoming more complex. They may get simpler if this suits them for their way of life. Humans lost their tails over the course of evolution. The cave fish, which lives in the dark, has lost the ability to see.

Many clever animals have adjusted to life in cities and towns, feeding off our rubbish.

Raccoon

Herring gull

House mouse

Brown rat

DOES EVOLUTION ALWAYS WORK ?

EVOLUTION allows animals to adjust to the environment around them. But sometimes the environment changes too fast for evolution to keep up. If this happens, some animals may be in danger of becoming extinct, as happened with the dinosaurs.

DO PLANTS EVOLVE ?

PLANTS evolve, just as animals do. Their history has been one of continuous change, from the original primitive organisms of the pre-Cambrian period to the evolution of the pollen-producing flowers of today.

WHEN DID EVOLUTION START ?

EVOLUTION began, over 4 billion years ago, with the origin of molecules that could make copies of themselves. These gave rise to the first simple cells, which gave rise to the first animals.

WHEN DID FLOWERS EVOLVE ?

PLANTS evolved flowers about 120 million years ago, during the Age of Dinosaurs. Flowers evolved as the insects were evolving, because most flowers need insects for pollination.

WHY DO BIRDS HAVE BEAKS ?

THE very first birds had teeth. We think that later birds evolved a beak to help reduce their weight. It is important for a flying creature to be light, and a beak weighs less than a mouth full of teeth. Each bird has a type of beak that has been modified by evolution to suit the way it eats. For example, some have strong beaks for cracking nuts. Some have beaks like tweezers, which can be used to probe for insects.

Different birds have evolved different beaks to deal with different types of food.

WHO DISCOVERED EVOLUTION ?

CHARLES Darwin was the first person to realize that animals evolved and to explain how it happened. He wrote his ideas in a book called *The Origin Of Species*. This caused a lot of argument at first, but today most scientists agree with Darwin.

WHEN DOES EXTINCTION OCCUR ?

EXTINCTION occurs when the last individual of a plant or animal species dies out. This may happen naturally, perhaps due to a change in the climate or other conditions, or it may occur due to human activity, such as over-hunting or through habitat destruction.

IS EVOLUTION DANGEROUS ?

THE evolution of bacteria and viruses that cause disease is dangerous for humans. Creatures as small as these reproduce and evolve very quickly. Because of this, they can often evolve into new types, or strains, which are resistant to the medicines we invent to kill them.

CAN THE SAME CREATURE EVOLVE TWICE ?

THE same type of creature cannot evolve more than once, but different types of creatures often evolve similar methods for adapting themselves to their environment. This may result in similar behaviour or feeding habits, or may cause quite different animals to look alike. Many animals that live in open grassland, from wallabies to kangaroo rats, have developed the ability to run or hop on a pair of long back legs, and they may even look similar.

Many different animals have evolved the technique of bounding along on two legs.

Bridled nailtail wallaby

Common wallaroo

Quokka

HOW ARE FOSSILS FORMED ?

WHEN an animal dies its body is usually eaten or it decays. In some rare cases, when the animal dies in very dry conditions or under water, this does not happen. Instead, the body of the animal is swiftly covered by sand or mud. Over the years this piles up and is compressed to rock. Deep beneath the rock the bones of the animal absorb minerals and harden to become a fossil.

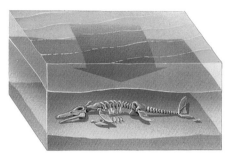

Many prehistoric organisms have been preserved by a process known as fossilization.

WHY DID ANCIENT ELEPHANTS HAVE FUR ?

THE ancient elephant, or woolly mammoth, was a huge creature that could stand up to 4.5 m high at the shoulder. The mammoth was an animal of the Ice Age, over 30,000 years ago, when the world was much colder than it is today. Its thick coat of fur helped to keep it warm. Mammoths have been found deep-frozen in the ice fields of Siberia, in Russia, with their fur, and even the food in their stomachs, still preserved.

The largest mammoths had tusks over 5 m long.

WHAT WERE THE FIRST LAND ANIMALS ?

THREE hundred million years ago there were no animals living on land. Insects and their relatives were probably the first to occupy the new world beyond the sea. The first four-legged creatures to explore beyond the shoreline were ancient amphibians. We think that these evolved from creatures such as lungfish, which could survive out of the water for a while.

WHAT WERE THE FIRST ANIMALS LIKE ?

THE first animals were probably single-celled creatures. The first animals we know from the fossil record occurred about 570 million years ago. Some were worm-like; others had shells. They probably lived in water.

HOW OLD ARE THE OLDEST-KNOWN FOSSILS ?

THE oldest-known fossils are of tiny bacteria-like creatures that lived over 3 billion years ago. They are so small that to see them you have to look at the rock they are in through a microscope.

HOW MANY FOSSILS ARE THERE ?

THERE are billions of fossils. Many types of rock have fossils embedded in them. Chalk is a white rock constructed entirely from the tiny fossil shells of ancient sea creatures.

Diatryma, *a giant meat-eating bird from ancient America.*

WHAT WERE THE FIRST FORESTS LIKE ?

TWO hundred and fifty million years ago the Earth was covered by the first forests. The trees were not like the trees of today. There were giant ferns and palm-like plants, but no flowers. No squirrels climbed the trees. No birds perched in their branches. These forests were ruled by giant scorpions and huge centipedes. Dragonflies with 0.5-m wingspans buzzed through the warm, wet air.

Prehistoric dragonflies had wings more than 0.5 m across.

WHICH ANIMALS REPLACED THE DINOSAURS ?

AFTER the last of the dinosaurs died out, 60 million years ago, and before humans evolved a million years ago, the Earth was ruled by mammals and birds. Some of these reached extraordinary sizes. There were giant, hornless rhinoceroses with long, giraffe-like necks; and 2-m high flightless, meat-eating birds, such as *Diatryma*, with its ripping beak.

WHAT IS AN AMMONITE ?

AMMONITES are coiled shells that are commonly found as fossils. We think that creatures resembling squid lived inside these shells, with their tentacles sticking out. Ammonites ruled the ancient seas before the first fish evolved.

WHAT IS A PETRIFIED FOREST ?

A PETRIFIED forest is the name given to a large group of logs and stems that have been preserved as fossils. The original wood has been replaced by minerals, turning the original forest into rock.

Many different types of organism have been preserved as fossils.

Insect in amber

Cast

Fern

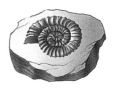

Ammonite

Petrified wood

WHY WOULD YOU BURN A FOSSIL ?

COAL is formed from the fossilized trunks of ancient trees. You can sometimes see leaf imprints in a piece of coal. Each time that you burn a piece of coal, you are burning a fossil.

ARE FOSSILS STILL BEING MADE TODAY ?

YES, the process of fossilization is a continuous one. If the conditions are right, a dead plant or animal will be preserved in the rocks of the future, just as they were in the past.

A pair of ancient amphibians resting at the water's edge.

WHAT TYPES OF FOSSIL ARE THERE ?

SEA animals are the most likely to be fossilized and, since it is the hard parts of an organism that are usually preserved, the most common fossils are those of sea shells. Many other types of fossil can be found, however, including fossil wood, fossil dinosaur droppings and the faint fossil imprints of leaves or soft-bodied creatures such as jellyfish. Insects are often found preserved in amber: the hardened sap of prehistoric trees.

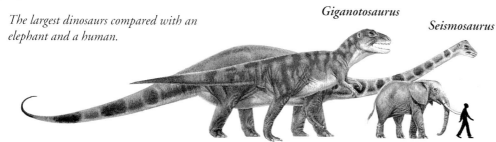

The largest dinosaurs compared with an elephant and a human.

Giganotosaurus

Seismosaurus

HOW BIG WAS THE BIGGEST DINOSAUR ?

THE biggest dinosaurs were the huge plant-eating sauropods. They had long necks allowing them to reach up to feed from the tops of trees, and long tails which helped them to balance. The longest was *Seismosaurus;* it measured 40 m in length. The biggest meat-eater was the fearsome 15-m long *Giganotosaurus.*

WHAT SOUNDS DID DINOSAURS MAKE ?

MANY of the duck-billed dinosaurs had crests on their heads. Scientists think that the chambers of air inside these crests could resonate and help them to make a trumpeting noise.

HOW WERE BABY DINOSAURS BORN ?

WE KNOW that baby dinosaurs hatched out of eggs, because we have found the fossil remains of dinosaur nesting sites. We think that some dinosaurs looked after their new-born young.

WHY DID THE DINOSAURS DIE OUT ?

THERE are many theories about the extinction of the dinosaurs. One theory is that a huge meteorite struck the Earth and sent up clouds of dust that blocked out the Sun. Without any sunlight, many plants would have died and the dinosaurs would have starved.

WHAT COLOURS WERE DINOSAURS ?

DINOSAUR skin has been discovered but, because it is fossilized, we cannot tell what colour it was. Dinosaurs may have had colours like today's reptiles.

Tyrannosaurus was a fierce, meat-eating dinosaur over 12 m in length.

The sharp teeth of a tyrannosaur could grow up to 15 cm long.

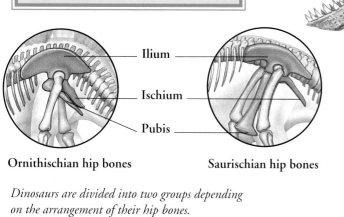

Ilium

Ischium

Pubis

Ornithischian hip bones

Saurischian hip bones

Dinosaurs are divided into two groups depending on the arrangement of their hip bones.

WHY SHOULD YOU LOOK AT A DINOSAUR'S HIPS ?

THERE are two main types of dinosaur. Dinosaurs like the long-necked *Diplodocus* and the fierce *Tyrannosaurus* are called saurischians. Dinosaurs like the three-horned *Triceratops* are called ornithischians. The difference between the two groups is in the arrangement of their hip bones. Saurischians have one hip bone pointing backwards and one pointing forwards. Ornithischians have both bones pointing backwards.

DID DINOSAURS EAT PEOPLE ?

THE fierce *Tyrannosaurus* must have been a terrifying predator. With its huge jaws full of 15-cm long teeth, it could reach as high as a second-storey window. It would certainly have been able to swallow a person in one bite, but we know that this never happened because the last of the dinosaurs died out over 60 million years ago, long before there were any people living on the Earth, even primitive cavemen.

WHY DID DINOSAURS HAVE TAILS ?

SCIENTISTS used to think that dinosaurs were sluggish and slow moving. In old-fashioned pictures dinosaurs are often shown leaning back on their tails or dragging them along the ground. Nowadays we think that dinosaurs were active and fast-moving creatures. We think that they held their tails up off the ground, stretched out behind them, to help them balance as they walked or ran along. Some museums have changed the way their dinosaur skeletons are mounted to show this.

A running dinosaur uses its tail to balance as it chases a giant insect.

WERE DINOSAURS INTELLIGENT ?

MANY dinosaurs had very small brains, especially given their huge body size, and they are unlikely to have been as clever as modern mammals. There are dinosaurs, however, that had lifestyles that suggest a certain amount of intelligence. For instance, some of the smaller, predatory dinosaurs, like *Deinonychus*, hunted in packs. This would have required good coordination and communication.

An armoured, plant-eating dinosaur with a club on the end of its tail.

Deinonychus was a fast, meat-eating dinosaur that hunted in packs.

WHAT WEAPONS DID DINOSAURS HAVE ?

THE meat-eating dinosaurs had sharp teeth and clawed feet with which to kill their prey. Many of the plant-eating dinosaurs also had weapons, which were needed to fight off the meat-eaters. Some had clubs or spikes on the ends of their tails. Some, like *Triceratops*, had horns on their heads. They may have used these to fight each other as well, in the way that stags clash antlers today.

ARE THERE ANY DINOSAURS LEFT ?

ALL the dinosaurs are dead and gone, but they did leave behind some very successful descendants. It is thought that all modern-day birds evolved, originally, from the dinosaurs.

WHAT DOES THE WORD "DINOSAUR" MEAN ?

THE word "dinosaur" means "terrible lizard", and comes from the Greek words *dino* (meaning "terrible") and *saur* (meaning "lizard"). When scientists first discovered dinosaur fossils, they imagined them to be the remains of huge lizards from the past.

HOW LONG DID DINOSAURS RULE THE EARTH ?

DINOSAURS first appeared on Earth about 200 million years ago. They became the dominant life forms, until their sudden extinction at the end of the Cretaceous Period about 65 million years ago.

COULD DINOSAURS FLY ?

NO-ONE has ever found any fossils of flying dinosaurs. There were, however, many kinds of flying reptiles living at the same time as the dinosaurs. These included the pterodactyl, as well as creatures such as *Pteranodon* and the giant *Quetzalcoatlus*, the largest flying reptile known. It had a huge 12-m wingspan.

WHAT USE IS A SKELETON?

AN ANIMAL that lives on land needs a skeleton to support it and to help it move. Some animals, including humans, have a skeleton on the inside. Some animals, like insects and spiders, have a hard skeleton on the outside. Many simple animals that float in the sea, like the jellyfish, do not have a skeleton at all. They do not need one because the water they float in gives them all the support they need.

The umbrella-shaped jellyfish swims by rhythmically contracting its body.

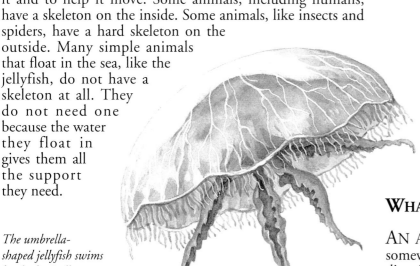

The body of an amoeba is made from a single cell.

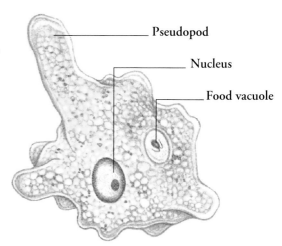

Pseudopod

Nucleus

Food vacuole

WHAT SHAPE IS AN AMOEBA?

AN AMOEBA has no definite shape. If it wants to move somewhere it can extend part of its body in the appropriate direction to form a temporary foot, or pseudopod. The rest of the body then flows up to it. If it encounters food it can make part of its body stretch out to surround and engulf the food.

WHAT IS INSIDE AN EARTHWORM'S BODY?

AN EARTHWORM'S body is made up of compartments called segments. The segments are filled with a fluid which the earthworm's muscles push against to enable it to move. The intestine and nervous system run the length of the body. Its brain, five hearts and reproductive organs are found near the front of the body.

An earthworm burrows through the soil by extending the front part of its body and pulling the rest up behind it.

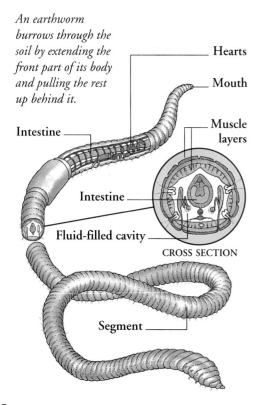

Hearts

Mouth

Muscle layers

Intestine

Intestine

Fluid-filled cavity

CROSS SECTION

Segment

WHAT IS CORAL MADE FROM?

A LIVING piece of coral is full of tiny holes. Inside each of these holes lives a microscopic coral animal. These animals build the chalky coral to provide a safe and protective home for themselves.

HOW MANY LEGS HAS A CENTIPEDE?

IT IS often thought that centipedes have one hundred legs but, depending on the species, centipedes may have between 15 and 70 pairs of legs. One pair of legs is carried on each body segment.

WHAT COLOUR IS A WORM'S BLOOD?

BLOOD is used to carry oxygen round the body. In humans, the molecule that carries the oxygen is red in colour, giving us red blood. Other organisms may use different-coloured molecules to carry their oxygen round. Many worms have red blood; some have green.

WHY DO SCORPIONS DANCE?

WHEN a male scorpion courts a female scorpion, he first takes hold of her pincers with his own pincers and then they begin to shuffle back and forth, like a man and woman in an old-fashioned dance. The male is not doing this for fun, but to stop the female from eating him. He holds her pincers to prevent attack and dances to convince her that he is not food.

The scorpion is famous for its deadly stinging tail.

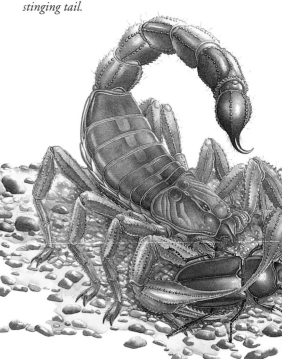

Some sea urchins have an intimidating array of spines.

Crabs and lobsters have tough shells that help to protect them.

WHY DO SQUID CHANGE COLOUR ?

SQUID can produce an amazing display of bright colours that continuously shift and change across the surface of their bodies. We think that these patterns of rapidly moving stripes and flickering shapes are used by the squid to communicate with one another or to confuse prey.

WHY DOES A CRAB HAVE A SHELL ?

WE HUMANS have skeletons on the inside of our bodies, with muscles attached to the bones. The crab has its skeleton on the outside, in the form of a shell. The crab's shell helps to protect it, like a suit of armour. As long as it is wearing its armour, the crab cannot grow. It has to get rid of its shell, and grow a new one, in order to get bigger.

WHY DOES A SEA URCHIN HAVE SPINES ?

THE sea urchin's spines help it to ward off predators. The spines are sharp and often contain a poison. The sea urchin can also point them towards the source of danger. The ability to move the spines allows some sea urchins to employ them as a battery of rigid legs. They can tiptoe along the sea bed on their spines.

ARE SEA ANEMONES ANIMALS OR PLANTS ?

ALTHOUGH they look like flowers, and even have a flower's name, sea anemones are animals. They live attached to rocks and catch other small creatures with stinging cells on their tentacles. The mouth is in the centre of the ring of tentacles.

The cone shell is capable of catching and eating fish.

HOW DO YOU GET INK FROM AN OCTOPUS ?

AN OCTOPUS has eight legs, covered in suckers, with which it can capture crabs and small fish. The octopus itself, however, may be threatened by a larger fish. To help it escape from danger it has the ability to squeeze its body into the smallest of crevices in the rock. In extreme situations it can produce a cloud of black ink to cover its escape.

Siphon

The octopus uses its tentacles to capture prey.

HOW DOES A CONE SHELL HUNT ?

MOST molluscs, like snails or the creatures that live inside sea shells, are not active carnivores. They feed by scraping tiny plants off the rock surface or by sieving microscopic organisms out of the seawater. The cone shell is an exception. It has a long, projecting spine with a sting on the end. With this it can kill and feed off fish.

WHY DO PRAYING MANTIDS PRAY?

PRAYING mantids are fierce predators. When waiting for prey they keep their forelegs folded back close to the body in a position that resembles a person praying. If a mantid spots an insect it creeps slowly towards its victim. When the insect is in range, the mantid shoots out its front legs and grabs it. Sharp spines and barbs on the inner edge of the legs help secure the struggling prey, which the mantid then eats at its leisure.

This praying mantid has just spotted its next victim.

This dragonfly has just caught a damselfly in flight.

HOW DO DRAGONFLIES CATCH THEIR PREY?

DRAGONFLIES are large insects that patrol over ponds and lakes in summer. They catch smaller insects in flight, and their large eyes allow them to spot any likely victim from a distance. Two pairs of powerful wings enable them to fly fast. The insect prey is caught by the dragonfly's legs, and spines on the legs prevent the victim from struggling free. The insect prey is usually eaten while the dragonfly continues flying.

WHAT IS AN INSECT?

INSECTS are animals without backbones but whose bodies have a hard outer casing. There are three pairs of jointed legs, and many adult insects have wings and can fly. The body is divided into a head, thorax and abdomen.

WHAT IS A SPIDER?

SPIDERS are related to insects, but they have four pairs of jointed legs. They also have bodies that are protected by a hard outer casing. All spiders are carnivores, and they produce silk for making webs. Spiders do not have wings.

An impressive atlas moth rests on forest leaves.

WHY DO MALE RHINOCEROS BEETLES HAVE HORNS?

RHINOCEROS beetles are large insects that live in the forests of southeast Asia. Males are larger than females and may reach 16 cm in length. The species takes its name from the long horns on the heads of the males. The horns are used when two rivals fight for the right to mate with a female. The horns often lock together and are sometimes used to turn an opponent on to his back. The strongest beetle with the longest horns usually wins the contest.

WHICH IS THE LARGEST MOTH?

LARGE moths can be found throughout the tropical regions of South America, Asia and Australia. The largest is Australia's hercules moth, with a wingspan of 28 cm. Almost as big is the atlas moth from southern Asia. It is bigger than many of the birds that share its rainforest habitat. Although it has colourful markings, it blends in well among fallen leaves and bark on the forest floor.

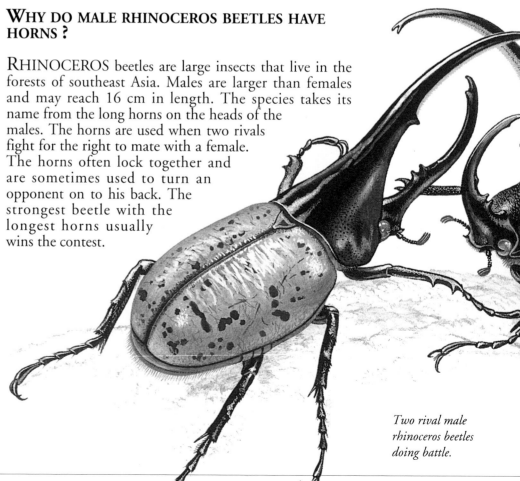

Two rival male rhinoceros beetles doing battle.

HOW DOES THE MALE SPIDER COURT HIS MATE?

MOST male spiders are considerably smaller than females of the same species. Courtship is a dangerous process for the male because he must make sure the female recognizes him as a potential mate and not a meal. He takes great care to advertise his arrival at her web by vibrating the silk at a special frequency. If he is successful, he can then approach her and mate. If not, he will probably be eaten.

A male orb web spider carefully courts the much larger female.

A deadly black widow spider spins her untidy web.

WHICH IS THE MOST DEADLY SPIDER?

BLACK widow spiders are usually thought to be the most deadly of their kind. There are several very similar species found across North America and Australia. They like dark, shady places and often find their way into houses; several people die each year after being bitten. Black widow spiders make untidy webs, and feed mainly on small insects and other spiders. Although deadly, they are not especially impressive to look at, being small, black and shiny.

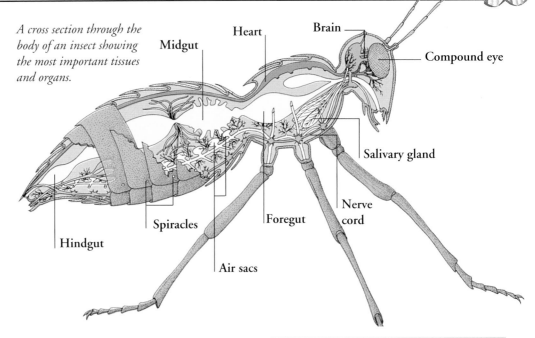

A cross section through the body of an insect showing the most important tissues and organs.

Heart
Brain
Midgut
Compound eye
Salivary gland
Nerve cord
Foregut
Spiracles
Hindgut
Air sacs

WHAT IS INSIDE AN INSECT?

THE soft tissues in an insect's body are protected by its hard outer casing. The digestive system runs along the length of the body, and the heart bathes the important organs with blood. The nervous system connects all parts of the body to the brain. Openings called spiracles allow oxygen to enter the body.

HOW DO FLYING INSECTS MOVE THEIR WINGS?

A FLYING insect moves its wings using muscles inside its body. The muscles are attached to the base of the wing at one end and to the inside of the insect's hard outer body casing at the other. By using several sets of muscles, the wings can be moved up and down to enable the insect to fly. Muscles also make the wings twist for changing direction.

HOW DO INSECTS BREATHE?

LOOK closely at an insect's body and you will see tiny openings called spiracles along the sides. These connect to a network of tubes called tracheae. Air flows along these tubes supplying oxygen to the organs.

HOW MANY DIFFERENT SPECIES OF INSECT EXIST?

IT IS impossible to be absolutely sure how many species of insects exist. Scientists have estimated, however, that there may be more than 30 million different kinds alive today. These range in size from tiny fleas to giant beetles.

WHY DO ANTS "MILK" APHIDS?

APHIDS are tiny insects commonly seen during the summer months. They feed on plant sap and produce a sugary secretion called honeydew. Ants pay frequent visits to the aphids to collect this liquid, and often encourage them to produce more by touching them with their antennae. This behaviour is called "milking". In return for a rich supply of food, the ants protect the aphids from insect predators.

Ants in the process of "milking" a group of aphids.

WHICH FISH NEED LIGHTS ?

IF YOU sank down into the black depths of the sea, thousands of metres beneath the surface, you would find yourself surrounded by glowing specks of light. On closer examination you would discover that many of these glowing specks were fish with luminous bodies. Deep-sea fish emit light so that they can locate one another. Some, like the angler fish, use light to hunt. The angler fish has a long thread dangling from its head, on the end of which is a light. Smaller fish are attracted to the light and then devoured.

HOW DO FISH BREATHE ?

FISH need oxygen just as land animals do, but they get their oxygen from water rather than from air. The oxygen is absorbed out of the water into the fish's delicate, feathery gills. Blood vessels in the gills carry the oxygen to the body organs.

Many deep-sea fish are phosphorescent, which means that they glow in the dark.

WHICH IS THE BIGGEST FISH ?

THE biggest fish is the whale shark, which can grow up to 18 m long. It lives in warm, deep waters. Luckily for us it is a harmless creature that feeds only on tiny animals and plants.

HOW FAST CAN FISH SWIM ?

FISH swim by sweeping their muscular tails from side to side. The fastest fish is the sailfish, which can drive itself through the water at more than 100 km/h.

WHAT IS UNUSUAL ABOUT THE SEAHORSE ?

IN MOST fish the young develop outside the body of their mother. The female sheds her eggs into the water and the male sheds his sperm nearby. The sperm and eggs join and a fertilized egg is produced, which will then develop into a baby fish. The seahorse is unusual, however, because the fertilized eggs are stored in a special pouch on the male parent until they are ready to hatch.

Lantern fish

Viperfish

HOW DO FISH FLOAT ?

MANY fish have a swim bladder. This is a gas-filled sac inside the body of the fish that allows it to float. When a goldfish swims up to the surface of a pond to take in air, it is doing this not because it needs the air to breathe, but in order to fill up its swim bladder. The swim bladder allows the fish to hang suspended in the water while it uses its fins to manoeuvre.

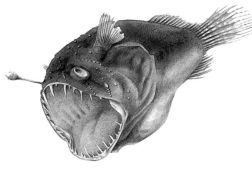

Angler fish

HOW DID THE ARCHER FISH GET ITS NAME ?

THE archer fish has a clever trick for catching insects. It can squirt an accurate jet of water up into the air. It uses this to knock down insects resting on vegetation overhanging the water.

The archer fish cruises just below the surface of the water looking for prey.

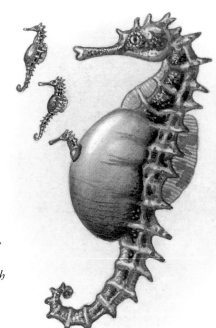

The male seahorse gives birth to live young.

Sharks will go into a feeding frenzy if they scent blood in the water.

The flying fish has fins that can be stretched out to form wings.

CAN FISH FLY ?

FISH are not capable of true flight but some, like the flying fish, can glide through the air for short distances. If a flying fish is being chased by a predatory fish, it will rapidly swim towards the surface. As it leaps from the water it spreads its wing-like fins and glides for over 30 m before splashing down.

HOW DOES A FISH BUILD A NEST ?

SOME fish build nests to protect their developing eggs. The male stickleback first excavates a hollow in the mud. It then builds a tube-shaped nest over it, using weeds glued together with mucus.

CAN FISH GENERATE ELECTRICITY ?

YES, a number of fish can generate and detect electric current. Some use this ability to sense other fish near them. Some, like the electric eel, can stun their prey with an electric shock.

WHAT ATTRACTS SHARKS TO THEIR PREY ?

DURING the Second World War many sailors were told that sharks were cowardly creatures that could be frightened away by splashing. Although the sailors were told this to make them feel less frightened, sharks are, in fact, often attracted to splashing or other disturbances in the water. They are also attracted to the scent of blood. Scientists believe sharks sometimes attack humans because they mistake them for seals or other prey.

DO ALL FISH LAY EGGS ?

NO, SOME species, such as the sailfin molly, keep their eggs inside themselves until the young hatch. Then they give birth to up to 200 live young.

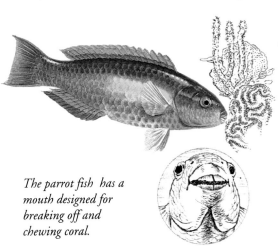

The parrot fish has a mouth designed for breaking off and chewing coral.

WHICH FISH NEEDS A BEAK ?

FISH feed on many different types of food. Sharks have rows of razor-sharp, backward-pointing teeth with which to kill their prey. Manta rays have a filter that allows them to sieve tiny creatures from the seawater as they swim along. The parrot fish has a tough, beak-like mouth that it uses to break off bits of coral. The parrot fish grinds up the coral to get at the tiny coral animals inside.

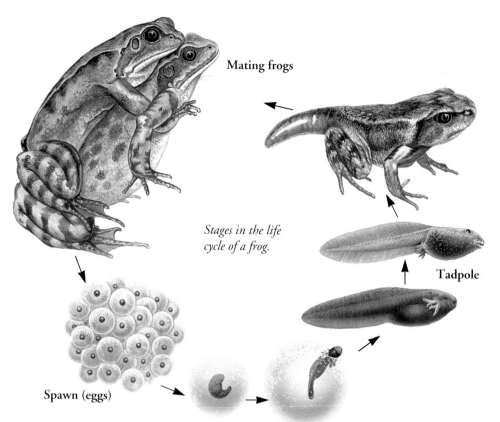

Mating frogs

Stages in the life cycle of a frog.

Tadpole

Spawn (eggs)

HOW DO FROGS BREATHE ?

TADPOLES have feathery gills sticking out of the sides of their necks that allow them to absorb oxygen from the water. Adult frogs need to breathe in air. They have lungs like us and can also absorb some oxygen through the linings of their mouths and through their moist skin.

WHY DO FROGS CROAK ?

MALE frogs croak during the mating season. Female frogs listen to the croaking and this allows them to find the males. The louder a male frog croaks the more likely he is to attract a partner. For this reason many types of male frog have special air sacs that help to make their croaking louder. A puffed-up air sac acts as a resonator, boosting the volume of each croak.

WHAT IS METAMORPHOSIS ?

IF AN animal changes shape at some stage in its life, turning from one sort of creature into another, then we call this metamorphosis. Many amphibians, such as the frog, go through metamorphosis. When a baby frog is first born it has a strong tail for swimming and gills that let it breathe under water. We call it a tadpole. As it grows older the tadpole gradually develops legs, first two, then a full set of four. Eventually it loses its tail and gills and becomes a fully formed frog.

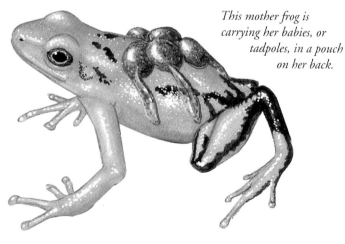

This mother frog is carrying her babies, or tadpoles, in a pouch on her back.

DO MOTHER FROGS CARE FOR THEIR YOUNG ?

MOST baby frogs grow up without any help from their parents. The mother frog deserts her eggs, or frogspawn, as soon as she has laid them. Some types of frog are more caring. A mother marsupial frog carries her young around in a pouch on her back until they have grown from tadpoles into froglets. The young of the mouth-brooding frog spend their early life in a very strange nursery, the mouth and vocal sacs of their father!

A bullfrog inflates its air sac to make its croak sound louder.

WHAT DO BLACK AND YELLOW MEAN ?

IN THE animal world black and yellow are warning colours. They show that an animal is poisonous or can sting. If a predator has an unpleasant encounter with a poisonous or stinging animal, it will try to avoid that animal in the future by watching out for the warning colours. This is why wasps and bees have black and yellow stripes. Some amphibians, like the fire salamander, are coloured black and yellow to warn predators that they can produce a dangerous poison.

A fire salamander produces poison from pores behind its eyes.

WHICH IS THE BIGGEST FROG ?

THE biggest frog is the goliath frog. It measures over 0.3 m in length from its nose to the end of its body. Its eyes are as big as a fully grown human's.

WHICH FROG LIVES IN A FLOWER ?

THE ivory-coloured arum frog lives in the flowers of the arum lily. It waits there, camouflaged, until unsuspecting insects come visiting the flower. It then quickly snaps them up.

The newt is an amphibian with a long, slender body like that of a lizard.

WHICH AMPHIBIAN NEVER GROWS UP ?

THE axolotl is an amphibian that never completes its metamorphosis. It spends its whole life as a large tadpole-like creature and can never leave the water to explore dry land.

HOW CAN A FROG SURVIVE IN A DESERT ?

THE water-holding frog of the Australian desert swells up with the water stored inside its body. In very dry spells, when even its own water store is used up, it can bury itself beneath the sand to prevent further water loss.

HOW DO AMPHIBIANS MATE ?

A FEMALE frog sheds her eggs into the water. The male sheds his sperm nearby so that they can join with the female's eggs. The result is frogspawn, which will soon develop into tadpoles. When newts mate the male newt sheds a little package of sperm that the female picks up and places inside her body, near her eggs, in order to fertilize them.

HOW DO YOU CATCH A FROG ?

THE edible frog is considered a tasty morsel by many people. When fishing for frogs the fisherman dangles a brightly coloured lure in front of the frog. As the frog tries to grab the lure in its mouth, the fisherman flicks the frog out of the water. It is important that the fisherman keeps the lure moving, because frogs are accustomed to leaping up at moving insect prey.

HOW DO FROGS JUMP ?

A FROG jumps in just the same way as it swims. When jumping, it lifts its front legs off the ground and pushes off with its powerful back legs. It lands on its front legs and chest, then gathers in its back legs ready for another jump.

CAN FROGS FLY ?

WALLACE'S flying frog of southeast Asia is so called because it can launch itself and glide to another tree, using the large webs of skin attached to its feet as a kind of parachute.

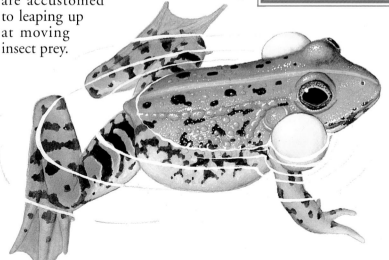

The edible frog has a pair of air sacs underneath its ears.

HOW DO ALLIGATORS LOOK AFTER THEIR YOUNG ?

MANY alligator and crocodile species show a great deal of protection towards their offspring. For example, the American alligator first lays its eggs in a mound, which it then guards against predators. Once the young have hatched, they are carried carefully by the parents to specially excavated pools where they can begin their development in safety.

WHY DO LIZARDS SHED THEIR TAILS ?

SOME lizards have tails that are designed to break off easily from their bodies. When a predator catches such a lizard by the tail, the lizard simply runs away, leaving its tail behind. Afterwards the lizard grows a new tail.

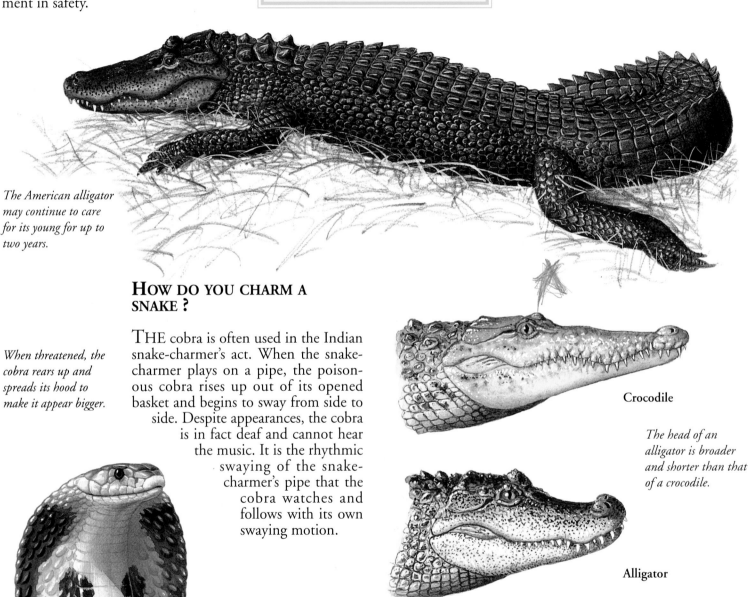

The American alligator may continue to care for its young for up to two years.

When threatened, the cobra rears up and spreads its hood to make it appear bigger.

Crocodile

The head of an alligator is broader and shorter than that of a crocodile.

Alligator

HOW DO YOU CHARM A SNAKE ?

THE cobra is often used in the Indian snake-charmer's act. When the snake-charmer plays on a pipe, the poisonous cobra rises up out of its opened basket and begins to sway from side to side. Despite appearances, the cobra is in fact deaf and cannot hear the music. It is the rhythmic swaying of the snake-charmer's pipe that the cobra watches and follows with its own swaying motion.

HOW CAN YOU TELL THE DIFFERENCE BETWEEN A CROCODILE AND AN ALLIGATOR ?

AT FIRST glance, crocodiles and alligators look very similar, but there are differences that tell them apart. When a crocodile closes its mouth, the fourth tooth of the lower jaw sticks up outside the top jaw. When an alligator does the same thing, this tooth is hidden. Also, the head of an alligator is shorter and broader than the head of a crocodile.

HOW LONG DO REPTILES LIVE FOR ?

SOME reptiles, like the tortoise, can live to a great age. A giant male marion tortoise, which lived in the British artillery barracks in Mauritius, is known to have reached the age of 152.

CAN LIZARDS FLY ?

MOST lizards move about on all fours, but some have more unusual ways of getting around. The Jesus lizard can stand up on two legs and sprint for short distances. It moves so fast and is so light that it can even run across water. The flying lizard has rigid flaps of skin on either side of its body that allow it to glide through the air after it has leapt from a branch.

A flying lizard glides swiftly through the air.

DO REPTILES CRY ?

YOU may have heard the expression "crocodile tears", which means false or pretend tears. Many reptiles do cry, including crocodiles, but they do this because the flow of tears helps to clean out and protect their eyes, not because they are unhappy. The sea turtle spends its life in the warm oceans of the world, feeding on jellyfish and sea snails. As it swims it often swallows salty seawater. The turtle cries to get rid of excess salt.

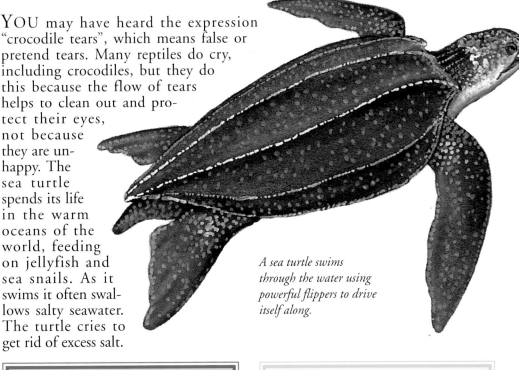

A sea turtle swims through the water using powerful flippers to drive itself along.

DO REPTILES HAVE COLD BLOOD ?

THE blood of a reptile is not always cold, but its body temperature depends on the temperature of its surroundings. A reptile cannot make heat inside its body in the way that a mammal or a bird can.

CAN A CHAMELEON REALLY CHANGE ITS COLOUR ?

YES, chameleons can change the colour of their skin, though they cannot exactly match their background. If you put a chameleon on a striped towel, it will not become striped itself. It may turn black, however, to show that it is angry, because chameleons can change colour according to how they are feeling.

WHEN DID REPTILES FIRST EVOLVE ?

REPTILES first appeared on Earth over 300 million years ago. Some reptiles, such as crocodiles, have remained almost unchanged throughout this time.

ARE ALL SNAKES POISONOUS ?

MANY snakes are harmless to humans and do not have poison fangs. Some big snakes, such as pythons, kill their prey by squeezing it until it suffocates.

HOW BIG IS THE BIGGEST LIZARD ?

THE Komodo dragon of the Indonesian islands is the biggest lizard in the world. It can grow to over 3 m long, and feeds on large animals such as monkeys, pigs and even deer.

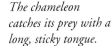

The chameleon catches its prey with a long, sticky tongue.

HOW DO BIRDS HUNT PREY ?

BIRDS of prey kill birds or other animals for food by using their sharp claws and powerful beaks. Hawks, eagles and falcons hunt by sight. Those that hunt other birds will usually "stoop", meaning they dive at high speed on to prey when in flight. The force of impact knocks the victim out of the sky. When hunting ground animals, birds of prey usually land suddenly, pinning the victim to the ground with their talons. Most owls hunt at night, using their acute hearing to locate prey. Owls' wing feathers are adapted for silent flight, allowing the owl to hear prey more easily.

A monkey-eating eagle swoops down to capture its prey with its long talons.

WHICH IS THE MOST NUMEROUS BIRD ?

SEVERAL types of birds exist in large numbers, but none is as numerous as the red-billed quelea, which lives on the open plains in Africa. There are thought to be around 2,000 million of these birds alive at the moment.

WHY DO SOME BIRDS FLY AWAY IN WINTER ?

SOME birds live all year in one place. Others spend the summer months in one part of the world and, as winter approaches, they fly off to a warmer region in search of food. Such journeys are called migration.

WHICH BIRDS LIVE THE LONGEST ?

THE longest-living birds are the larger parrot species, which may live for over 50 years. The greatest undisputed age reported for any bird is for a male sulphur-crested cockatoo, which died in 1982 at London Zoo, England, aged 80.

WHICH BIRDS ARE USED AS SYMBOLS ?

THE owl has been used to symbolize wisdom since the time of the ancient Greeks. Eagles symbolize strength and courage. The bald eagle is the symbol of the United States of America, while a two-headed eagle was used by the Hapsburg emperors to show they ruled two powerful kingdoms: Austria and Hungary. The beautiful quetzal bird is the national symbol of Guatemala, the Central American country where it lives.

The striking male quetzal bird was believed to be sacred by the Aztecs in the 16th century.

WHY DO OTHER BIRDS RAISE CUCKOO CHICKS ?

CUCKOOS do not build their own nests. A female will find another bird's nest, wait for the parents to be absent, then dart in to lay her own egg. First, though, she removes one of the original eggs. When the cuckoo chick hatches, it pushes any other eggs and chicks out of the nest. Its bright red mouth acts as a stimulus to the foster parents to feed it constantly. As soon as the cuckoo is old enough to fly it leaves its foster parents forever.

WHICH BIRD SLEEPS IN THE AIR ?

THE swift sleeps, feeds and even mates in the air. With its long, swept-back wings, it is perfectly built for flying, but its legs and feet are so weak it can barely walk.

A female cuckoo removes an egg from another bird's nest before laying her own egg in the nest.

HOW FAST CAN AN OSTRICH RUN ?

SEVERAL birds have lost the ability to fly altogether. For example, the New Zealand kiwi escapes hunters by hiding in undergrowth, and the African ostrich simply runs away very fast. The ostrich is the largest bird of all, standing at 3 m tall. Its long legs and powerful muscles enable it to run at speeds of up to 70 km/h.

Hummingbirds can hover, fly forwards and backwards and up and down in their search for nectar.

WHY DO HUMMINGBIRDS HUM ?

HUMMINGBIRDS gain their name from the noise made by their wings. They can beat their wings 100 times each second — and a few can beat their wings even faster than that. This rapid beating, which produces the characteristic hum, is essential for the birds as they need to hover above a flower in order to suck the nectar on which they feed.

The long legs of the ostrich allow it to run at high speed, but they are also powerful weapons when used for kicking.

The ostrich lays the largest egg of any bird. Each egg may be up to 20 cm long.

A male royal flycatcher with crest raised in display.

WHY DO SOME BIRDS HAVE BRIGHT, SHOWY FEATHERS ?

MANY birds have large or brightly coloured feathers that are used to signal to other birds. Perhaps the most attractive feathers are those of the bird of paradise from New Guinea. The colourful display feathers are used to attract females at nesting time, or to frighten away rival males.

WHEN DID THE FIRST BIRD LIVE ?

THE oldest-known fossil bird is about 150 million years old. Scientists have named it *Archaeopteryx*, which means "ancient wing". It lived in forests and probably could not fly very well.

HOW MANY TYPES OF BIRD ARE THERE ?

IT IS thought that there are about 8,700 different species of bird alive today. They are grouped together in orders such as the penguins, herons and parrots. There are 27 of these orders.

HOW DEEP CAN A BIRD DIVE ?

SEVERAL types of bird dive beneath the water in search of fish, weeds or other food. The deepest diving bird of all is the emperor penguin of Antarctica, which can reach 270 m beneath the sea surface.

DOES THE KILLER WHALE DESERVE ITS NAME?

YES, the killer whale is a fierce and ruthless hunter. Included in its diet are penguins, seals, dolphins and even other whales. It is not just the sharp teeth and streamlined speed of the killer whale that make it such a deadly predator, but the way that it uses its intelligence. When killer whales attack another, larger whale, a number of them will grab on to its tail to tire it out and slow it down, while the rest bite at its vulnerable lips and tongue.

The polar bear is an excellent diver and can be found swimming over 160 km from land.

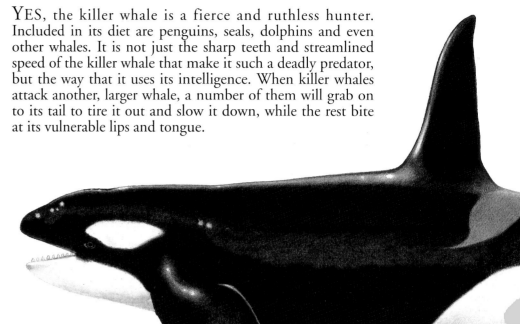

The sharp teeth and streamlined shape of the killer whale make it a deadly hunter.

WHAT IS A SEA MAMMAL?

A SEA mammal is a mammal that spends some, or all, of its life in the sea. Whales and dolphins spend their whole lives at sea. Seals and walruses spend most of their time in the water, but must return to land to mate and give birth. Polar bears often hunt at sea.

WHY DO WHALES SING?

WHALES communicate by singing. We know very little about the content of their songs, but we do know that each whale has an individual signature tune that it sings at the start of each message.

WHICH IS THE BIGGEST WHALE?

THE biggest whale, and indeed the biggest mammal, that has ever existed on Earth is the blue whale. It can grow up to 30 m long and can weigh as much as 30 African bull elephants.

WHY DO WHALES SPOUT?

WHEN a whale dives, the pressure forces water into its nostrils and air tubes. Just as a diver has to blow water out of his snorkel when he surfaces, so the whale has to spout.

ARE MERMAIDS REAL?

MUSEUMS used to display the preserved bodies of creatures that people believed were mermaids. Today we know that these mermaids were in fact fakes. They were made from the body parts of dead monkeys and dead fish stuck together. Some people think that when sailors first saw a sea-cow, they mistook it for a woman with a fish's tail, and that this is how the legend of the mermaid began.

HOW DOES A WHALE LEAVE A FOOTPRINT?

WHEN a whale dives, the up-thrust of its tail drives water towards the surface. On the surface this can be seen as a round, calm area of flat water, known as a whale's footprint.

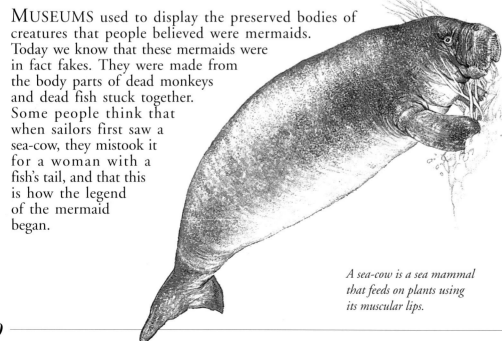

A sea-cow is a sea mammal that feeds on plants using its muscular lips.

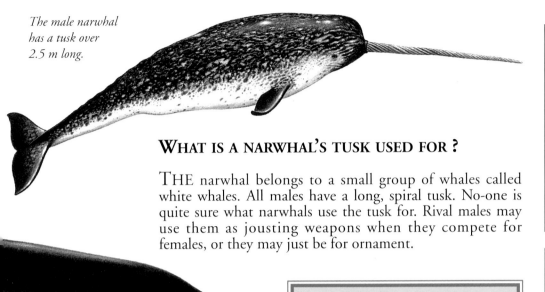

The male narwhal has a tusk over 2.5 m long.

WHAT IS A NARWHAL'S TUSK USED FOR ?

THE narwhal belongs to a small group of whales called white whales. All males have a long, spiral tusk. No-one is quite sure what narwhals use the tusk for. Rival males may use them as jousting weapons when they compete for females, or they may just be for ornament.

WHY DO DOLPHINS BEACH THEMSELVES ?

SOMETIMES whole schools of dolphins will strand themselves on a beach. Though this may look like mass suicide, it is more likely to be due to an infectious disease that has disabled the dolphins' sonar. Dolphins use sonar to help them find their way about.

HOW DID THE RIGHT WHALE GET ITS NAME ?

SAD though it may seem, early whalers gave the right whale its name. They considered it to be the "right" whale to catch because it was a slow swimmer and floated after it had been killed, making it easy to tow back to their ship.

WHY DOES THE ELEPHANT SEAL HAVE AN INFLATABLE NOSE ?

THE huge elephant seal weighs up to 4 tonnes and has a trunk-like nose over 0.3 m long. When excited, it can pump air into its nose to double its size. This probably acts as a display to frighten away enemies.

HOW DOES A SEAL KEEP WARM ?

MANY seals, such as the leopard seal shown below, live in very cold conditions. Fur is good at keeping land mammals warm, but it stops doing this when it gets very wet. However, fat will keep an animal warm in or out of the water. This is why seals have a thick layer of fat, called blubber, which lies beneath their skin.

WHAT IS THE DIFFERENCE BETWEEN A SEAL AND A SEALION ?

MOST seals belong to a family called true seals, and sealions to one called eared seals. Eared seals have small ear flaps, but true seals have none. Eared seals swim using mainly their foreflippers, whereas true seals use their hindflippers.

WHY DOES A WALRUS HAVE TUSKS ?

THE great tusks of the male walrus are used in battle against other males. The winner of the fight gets to mate with all the females on the beach. The loser must haul himself off. A walrus can also use its tusks to dig clams out of the mud or to smash breathing holes in the ice. Tusks are also useful when a huge male, which can weigh over 1,600 kg, is trying to haul itself along the ice.

Two huge walrus bulls engaged in battle.

A leopard seal chases penguins through the cold waters of the Antarctic.

WHAT IS A MARSUPIAL ?

A MARSUPIAL is a type of mammal that gives birth to its young when they are still small and unformed. These tiny babies continue growing inside their mother's pouch, feeding on her milk, until they are big enough to live on their own. Kangaroos, koala bears and wombats are all examples of marsupials.

The hare's large ears help it to keep cool.

A kangaroo is a marsupial mammal. The young develop inside a pouch on the mother's body.

Leopards feed on animals of all sizes, from rats to antelopes.

HOW DOES A HARE KEEP COOL ?

THE large ears of the hare help it to listen out for any sign of danger. They also help it to keep cool. As the hare's hot blood flows beneath the thin skin of its ears, heat is rapidly lost to the surrounding air. This is why hares that live in hot climates have particularly large ears, while hares that live in cold places, for example the Arctic hare, have relatively small ears.

WHY DOES A LEOPARD HAVE CLOSE-SET EYES ?

IF YOU look at a leopard face on, you can see that its eyes are set close together on the front of its head. The hare, on the other hand, has eyes that are spaced far apart on either side of its head. A hunter, like the leopard, needs both eyes at the front so that it can judge the distance of its prey. An animal that is hunted by others, like the hare, needs eyes on the sides of its head so that it can spot danger approaching from any direction.

WHY IS IT AN ADVANTAGE TO BE WARM BLOODED ?

MAMMALS, along with birds, are animals which are warm blooded. This means they can make heat inside their bodies, and can stay active even when it is cold. As a result they can hunt even in the chill of the night and live in places as cold as the polar wastes.

WHAT DID THE FIRST MAMMALS LOOK LIKE ?

THE first mammals evolved over 100 million years ago, long before the dinosaurs became extinct. These early mammals were insect eaters, rather like modern shrews or voles. They hid from the dinosaurs by burrowing or feeding at night. All modern-day mammals are descended from these tiny creatures.

HOW DOES AN ARMADILLO HIDE ?

THE scaly armadillo is a slow-moving mammal that feeds on insects and other small animals. It has powerful forelegs and is an expert digger. It uses this ability to construct a large burrow for itself. If it is threatened it will try to hide in its burrow. If it cannot get to its burrow in time, it curls up into an armoured ball.

A heavily armoured armadillo searching for insects to eat.

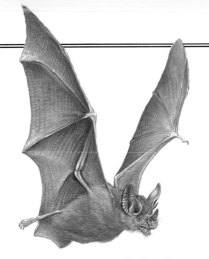

A bat's wings are made from leathery flaps of skin.

HOW DOES A BAT FIND ITS WAY IN THE DARK ?

MOST bats live in dark caves and only fly out to feed at night. They manage to navigate in the dark, and to find night-flying insects to feed on, by using a sonar system. As a bat flies along it sends out a series of high-pitched sound pulses. It uses its large ears to detect the echoes from these pulses as they bounce back off surrounding objects in its path.

A gibbon calls out to other gibbons as it leaps from branch to branch.

WHICH MAMMAL HAS THE LONGEST HAIR ?

HUMANS have the longest hair of all mammals. In the past, when women did not cut their hair, it was common to see hair that reached the floor. After humans, the mammal with the longest hair is the musk ox.

CAN MAMMALS LAY EGGS ?

MOST mammals give birth to live young, but there are some mammals — the monotremes — that lay eggs like birds and reptiles do. The platypus and the echidna are both examples of monotremes.

HOW DO MONKEYS AND APES COMMUNICATE ?

MONKEYS and apes communicate in lots of different ways. They gesture, make noises and have facial expressions. These facial expressions may be similar to those of humans, but they do not always mean the same thing. When a monkey "smiles", it is threatening you by revealing its teeth.

The African elephant can weigh up to 6 tonnes.

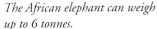

WHICH MAMMAL CAN JUMP THE HIGHEST ?

THE puma, a member of the cat family, holds the record for the highest-jumping mammal. It can leap up to 6 m in the air from standing, and is a very agile climber.

HOW DO YOU MAKE A NEW MAMMAL ?

FOR thousands of years people have controlled the mating of mammals like the dog and the horse. For example, all the different varieties of dog, from great danes to spaniels, have been produced, by human interference, from a wolf-like ancestor.

WHICH IS THE LARGEST LAND MAMMAL ?

THE African elephant is the largest land mammal alive today. A bull elephant can grow up to 3.5 m high at the shoulder. Even a baby elephant is nearly 1 m high when it is born. The mother elephant is pregnant for almost two years while the baby is growing inside her. In the prehistoric past there lived even larger land mammals that may have weighed up to two or three times as much as an elephant. All of these are now extinct.

Pine cone

Fir cone

Cones are the reproductive structures of conifer trees.

WHAT ARE CEREALS ?

CEREALS are members of the grass family. They are grown for their grain, or seed, which is used to feed people all over the world. Wheat is the most common cereal plant; its grain is used to make bread and pasta. Rice and millet are important in developing countries, where they are eaten by millions of people. Maize or corn is also popular, and is fed to animals as well as being eaten by people.

Cereal plants include wheat, rye, oats, barley, maize and rice.

WHAT ARE CONES FOR ?

CONES are the reproductive structures found on conifer trees. Male cones produce pollen, which is carried by the wind to fertilize the female cones. After the female cones have been fertilized, they become bigger and produce seeds. Each seed is protected by one of the scales that make up the cone. There may be a hundred or more seeds in a single cone.

WHICH ARE THE TALLEST TREES ?

GIANT redwoods are the tallest trees. They grow in the Sierra Nevada mountains of California. The largest-recorded tree was 83 m tall, but is now dead. There are several others, however, which are more than 73 m tall.

HOW ARE FUNGI DIFFERENT FROM PLANTS ?

ALMOST all plants are able to make their own food from sunlight energy, water and a gas found in air called carbon dioxide. Fungi are different. They get their food from decaying or sometimes living plants or animals. The food is digested outside the body of the fungus and then absorbed through a network of tiny, root-like threads.

WHAT ARE LICHENS ?

LICHENS are curious plants. They are made up of algal cells, surrounded by a fungus. The algal cells can live alone, because algae can make their own food by photosynthesis. The fungus needs the algae for survival, however. Lichens live on stones and trees and grow slowly.

WHAT IS THE OLDEST PLANT ?

BRISTLECONE pines from California's White Mountains are probably the oldest plants. Some individuals are more than 4,000 years old. Because they live in a cold environment at high altitudes, they grow very slowly and look rather stunted.

WHAT IS A TOADSTOOL ?

A TOADSTOOL is the spore-producing body of a fungus. It produces millions of spores that are carried by the wind. If they land in a suitable area, the spores will grow to form a new fungus. There are many different sorts of toadstools. Some look like edible mushrooms and have gills or pores under the cap, from which the spores drop. In puffballs, the spores are found inside the toadstool. They are puffed out when the puffball is knocked or hit by raindrops.

A selection of common and colourful toadstools.

Bracket fungus

Conifer tree

WHY ARE PLANT LEAVES GREEN ?

PLANT leaves are green because they contain a pigment called chlorophyll, which traps sunlight energy and allows the plant to make its own food from water and carbon dioxide gas. This process is called photosynthesis.

WHY DO PLANTS PRODUCE SEEDS ?

PLANTS produce many seeds to ensure the continuation of the species. The seed contains the embryo that will later grow into a new plant.

ARE ALL TOADSTOOLS POISONOUS ?

ONLY a few toadstools are poisonous. Many more simply taste unpleasant. A few are edible and tasty. Some poisonous ones are easy to recognize, but others need an expert to identify them.

Many North African trees survive by having spiny or needle-like leaves, which reduce water loss and deter grazing animals.

WHAT IS AN EVERGREEN TREE ?

AN EVERGREEN tree is one that keeps its leaves all year round. Most conifer trees are evergreen. They can be found in most parts of the world, except the hotter parts of the tropics. Broadleaf trees from cool climates usually lose their leaves in the autumn, but those that grow in hot, dry parts of the world are often evergreen. Their leaves usually have a waxy coating to stop them losing too much water in the heat of the Sun.

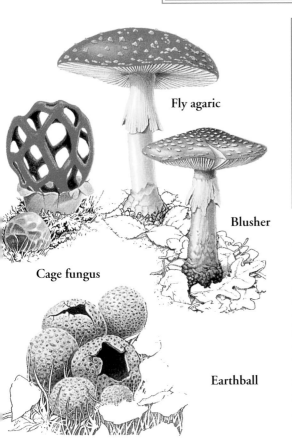

Fly agaric

Blusher

Cage fungus

Earthball

HOW MANY SPECIES OF PLANTS ARE THERE ?

THE plant kingdom consists of about 350,000 species, ranging in size from tiny algae to huge trees. Of all the plant groups, by far the biggest is the angiosperms, or flowering plants. It has about 250,000 species.

A selection of flowers showing their varied sizes, shapes and colours.

WHAT IS A FLOWER ?

A FLOWER is the reproductive part of a plant. The male part of the flower produces pollen and this fertilizes the eggs in the female part of a flower, which is usually on a different plant. Usually, the pollen is transferred from flower to flower by insects, which are attracted to the flowers' nectar. This is known as pollination. After fertilization, the flower produces seeds.

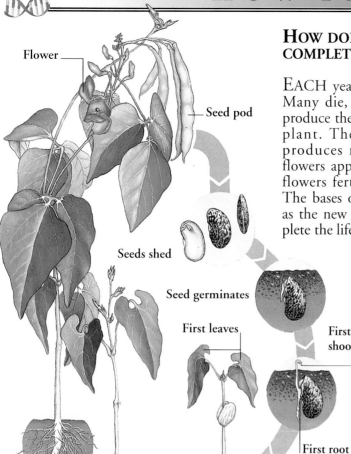

Flower

Seed pod

Seeds shed

Seed germinates

First leaves

First shoot

First root

The life cycle of a plant, from seed to maturity.

HOW DOES A PLANT COMPLETE ITS LIFE CYCLE ?

EACH year, a plant produces seeds. Many die, but some germinate and produce the roots and shoots of a new plant. The plant grows and soon produces more leaves. Eventually flowers appear. Pollen from the male flowers fertilizes the female flowers. The bases of the female flowers swell as the new seeds form, ready to complete the life cycle.

WHY DO TREES SHED THEIR LEAVES ?

TREES lose a lot of water, by evaporation, from their leaves. In cold weather it is difficult for a tree to suck up any new water, because most of the water in the soil is frozen. So the tree must shed its leaves before winter arrives to prevent water loss.

HOW DO PLANTS SPREAD THEIR SEEDS ?

SOME seeds grow inside fruits. These are eaten by animals and emerge in their dung, often some distance away. Other plants have seed cases that split open, scattering seeds in all directions. Some seeds, such as nuts and grains, are gathered by animals and stored in larders, while others have tiny hooks that cling to animals' coats. Finally, some are wind blown or carried by water.

Maple

Dandelion

Wind-blown seeds.

Fig

Blackberry

Plum

Seeds eaten by animals.

Hazelnut

Wheat

Carrot

Seeds carried by animals.

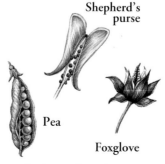

Shepherd's purse

Pea

Foxglove

Seed cases that split open.

WHY DOES A FRUIT TASTE SWEET ?

FRUITS taste sweet because they are full of sugar. The plant fills them with sugar so that animals will eat them. Inside the fruit are the plant's seeds. When an animal eats the fruit, the seeds are not digested along with the rest of the fruit but, instead, pass out of the animal's body unharmed. This may happen some distance from where the parent plant was growing. The distribution of seeds is called dispersal.

There are many different fruits and berries, but they are all sweet tasting and brightly coloured.

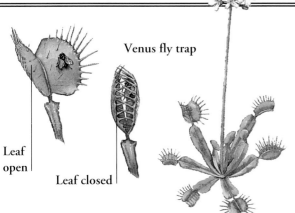

Venus fly trap

Leaf open

Leaf closed

Pitcher plant

The Venus fly trap and the pitcher plant are insect eaters.

Each ring in a stump's cross section represents a year's growth.

WHICH PLANTS CAN EAT INSECTS ?

SOME plants grow in places where they cannot get all the nutrients they need from the soil. To increase their supply, they trap and digest insects. The Venus fly trap has leaves shaped like jaws that close around a fly when it alights. The leaves of the pitcher plant make a slippery-sided trap with digestive juices at the bottom. Insects fall in and are digested.

HOW DOES A STINGING NETTLE STING ?

THE tiny hairs on the leaves and stems of stinging nettles are really tubes filled with poison. When touched, the brittle tips of the tubes break off. The rough edges scratch the skin and inject poison.

WHY ARE TREES TALL ?

TO GROW, trees must have sunlight falling on their leaves. The tallest trees in a forest are the ones that get the most light. They are not shaded by the leaves of other trees.

WHAT HAPPENS INSIDE A LEAF ?

A LEAF has tiny holes on its under-side. Through these holes it takes up carbon dioxide, which is present in the air. Water, sucked up by the plant's roots, is also sent to the leaf. In the leaf the carbon dioxide and the water are combined together to make sugar. The energy to drive this process is provided by sunlight.

HOW DO DAFFODILS SURVIVE THE WINTER ?

AFTER flowering, the stems and flowers of a daffodil wither away. During the winter the plant survives underground in the form of an onion-shaped bulb. This contains a food store.

CAN PLANTS FEEL ?

PLANTS can sense many things; the direction of the light, which way is up, and where the wettest soil is. Climbing plants can feel when they touch something. This allows them to curl around things as they climb.

HOW CAN YOU TELL A TREE'S AGE ?

EVERY year a tree grows a new layer of wood beneath the bark. If it is cut down, the layers can be seen as rings on the surface of the stump. By counting the rings you can tell the tree's age.

ARE ALL PLANTS GREEN ?

THE green colour of a plant is caused by the green pigment chlorophyll, which allows it to absorb light. Some plants, like dodder, suck food from the stems of other plants. They do not need to absorb light themselves. Their leaves are colourless instead of being green.

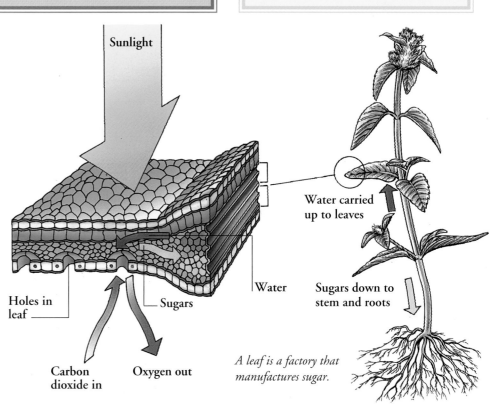

Sunlight

Holes in leaf

Sugars

Carbon dioxide in

Oxygen out

Water carried up to leaves

Water

Sugars down to stem and roots

A leaf is a factory that manufactures sugar.

WHICH IS THE MOST DEADLY TOADSTOOL ?

THE most deadly toadstool is the death cap. It is found in beech woods in Europe and appears in September and October. It certainly lives up to its name for, if eaten, less than 50 g can kill a human in six hours. The death cap can be recognized by the olive-yellow colour of the cap and its whitish gills. The base of the stalk grows from a white, bag-like structure.

The deadly death cap can easily be confused with edible types of fungi.

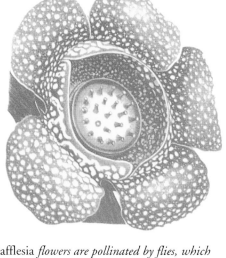

Rafflesia flowers are pollinated by flies, which are attracted by the flowers' smell of rotting flesh.

WHAT IS THE LARGEST SEED ?

THE world's largest seed comes from a plant called the giant fan palm, which grows only in the Seychelles. The seeds are shaped like rounded coconuts and a single one can weigh 20 kg.

HOW DO MANGROVE TREES BREATHE ?

MANGROVE trees live on tropical coasts around the world. Although they are land plants, they grow in saltwater and their roots are buried in thick mud that contains little oxygen. In order to breathe, the roots send up spikes that rise into the air above the level of the mud. When the tide is out, these spikes can exchange oxygen and expel carbon dioxide into the air.

WHICH IS THE LARGEST FLOWER ?

THE world's largest flower belongs to a plant called *Rafflesia arnoldii*, which grows in the rainforests of Sumatra. One flower can measure up to 80 cm across and weigh as much as 7 kg. *Rafflesia* is a parasite of tropical vines; the body of the plant consists of long threads living inside the host vine.

WHICH PLANT IS MOST SENSITIVE TO TOUCH ?

THIS plant is the mimosa. Normally the narrow, delicate leaflets that make up the leaf are spread wide. If touched, however, they quickly fold together. This protects them from damage.

WHY DO CUCKOO PINTS ATTRACT INSECTS ?

LURED by a foul smell, flies are attracted into a swollen chamber at the base of the cuckoo pint flower. This contains the reproductive parts of the flower. The insects are trapped by backward-pointing hairs. Some flies carry pollen from other cuckoo pints and fertilize the flower while trapped.

HOW DO DESERT PLANTS SURVIVE ?

DESERT plants live in hot, dry places and have to avoid losing too much water. Cacti, which are found mainly in Central America, do not have leaves. The plants' green stems have tough skins that help retain water. The strange welwitschia plant from southern Africa has a different way of avoiding water loss. It closes the pores on its leaves during the day and only opens them at night.

Cacti

The flowers of the cuckoo pint eventually produce a spike of red berries. These are eaten by birds but are poisonous to humans.

Cuckoo pint

All desert plants have evolved ways to reduce water loss through their leaves and stems.

Welwitschia

Seaweeds come in a wide range of colours, shapes and sizes.

WHAT IS AN AIR PLANT ?

AIR plants are also known as bromeliads. There are many different kinds and they are found in tropical forests in Central and South America. Air plants grow attached to the branches of certain trees. Instead of taking up water through their roots, they absorb moisture from the air through their large leaves.

HOW FAST CAN PLANTS GROW ?

GIANT kelp seaweed can grow as much as 45 cm in a single day, while some kinds of bamboo can grow nearly 1 m in a similar time. The Russian vine is sometimes called "the mile-a-minute plant". Although it is a fast grower, it can only manage 1 m or so in a week.

Despite its chemical weapons, a mature oak tree may have 300 or so kinds of insects living on it.

DO PLANTS HAVE CHEMICAL WEAPONS ?

ALMOST all plants are attacked by plant-eating animals of one kind or another. Many defend themselves by producing chemicals that either make their leaves and stems unpleasant to taste or sometimes even poisonous when eaten. Despite these chemical weapons, there are still plenty of creatures that are unaffected and happily continue to eat the plant's tissues.

WHAT ARE SEAWEEDS ?

SEAWEEDS are found growing on seashores in most parts of the world. Although many seaweeds are large, they are all in fact simple plants called algae. Unlike flowering plants, they do not have true leaves, stems or roots. Seaweeds are attached to rocks by branching holdfasts that are tough enough to withstand pounding waves.

The vast array of supporting roots help prevent the banyan tree from falling over.

WHAT IS A WATER VINE ?

A WATER vine is a long, creeping plant that climbs up the trunks of trees in the Amazon rainforest. Local people know that if you cut the vine, water gushes out and provides a refreshing drink.

WHICH IS THE SMALLEST TREE ?

THE tiny dwarf willow is the world's smallest tree. A full-grown specimen may reach a height of only 5 cm. It is found on frozen tundra in the Arctic, and grows very slowly.

WHAT IS A BANYAN TREE ?

THE banyan tree is a type of fig that is found in India and southeast Asia. It produces numerous long, trailing shoots from its spreading branches. When these reach the ground, they take root and form new trunks. These help stabilize the tree and enable it to spread. The largest-known specimen has some 1,775 supporting roots and a canopy area larger than a tennis court.

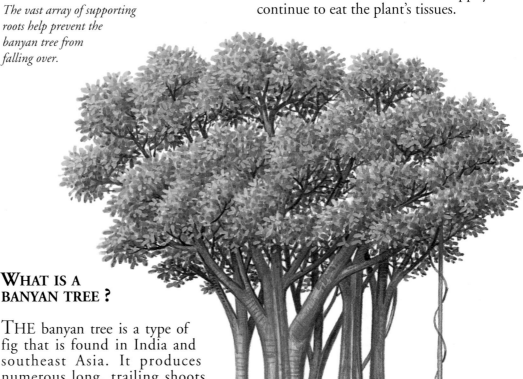

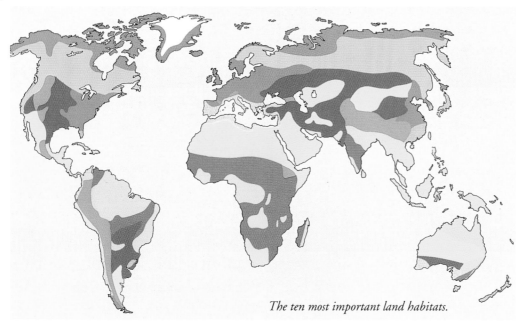

☐	Tropical rainforest
☐	Temperate rainforest
☐	Temperate forest
☐	Boreal forest
☐	Scrub
☐	Desert
☐	Savannah
☐	Temperate grassland
☐	Tundra
☐	Mountains

The ten most important land habitats.

WHAT IS A HABITAT ?

A HABITAT is the name given to the particular type of environment in which a species lives. So, for example, the habitat of a limpet is the seashore, while the habitat of a woodpecker is woodland. There is a wide range of habitats found throughout the world. The appearance of each one is affected by physical factors such as climate, soil type and rainfall, as well as by the plants and animals that live there.

WHAT IS ECOLOGY ?

ECOLOGY is the study of how plants and animals interact. For example, an ecologist (someone who studies ecology) looking at woodland birds would be interested not only in the birds themselves, but also in their food, nesting trees and predators.

WHAT IS AN OMNIVORE ?

AN OMNIVORE is an animal that eats both plants and animals. A badger is an example of an omnivore. It eats earthworms, slugs and insect grubs as the main part of its diet, but will also eat leaves in the spring and nuts, fruits and seeds in autumn.

WHAT IS A SPECIES ?

BOTH plants and animals are classified, or grouped, into species. Members of a species usually look very similar to one another. An animal or plant of any particular species can only reproduce successfully with other members of the same species.

WHAT IS A CARNIVORE ?

A CARNIVORE is an animal that eats the flesh of other animals. Lions and wolves are examples of animals with this type of diet. There are also a few examples of carnivorous plants.

The threats faced by baby turtles include being eaten by gulls, crabs and fish.

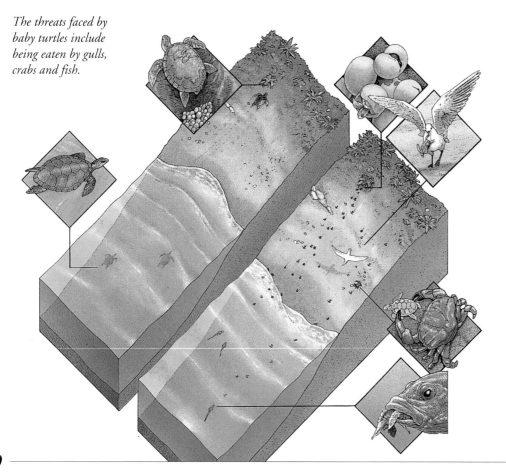

WHY DO TURTLES LAY SO MANY EGGS ?

FEMALE turtles lay their eggs on sandy beaches, burying them in deep pits. Each turtle lays 100 or so eggs. Many of the eggs are dug out of the nests by scavengers, and young turtles that do hatch are often eaten by predators. By laying so many eggs, the female turtle makes sure that a few will always survive to become adults.

WHAT IS A FOOD CHAIN?

A FOOD chain is the series of steps by which energy passes through the environment when animals feed on plants or other animals. Plants make their own food and start the chain. They are eaten by herbivores such as snails. Carnivores, including birds, eat the snails and are themselves eaten by predators such as foxes.

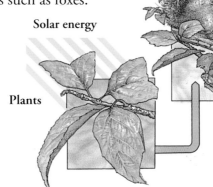

Carnivores

Herbivores

Solar energy

Plants

Predators

A typical woodland food chain.

WHAT IS THE WATER CYCLE?

WATER is recycled naturally in the environment. It evaporates from the sea and is lost through plant leaves into the air. Clouds form and rain falls both on the sea and on land, and the process, called the water cycle, is repeated.

WHAT IS A HERBIVORE?

A HERBIVORE is an animal that eats plants. Cows and sheep are herbivores; they eat grassland plants. Squirrels and mice, which eat seeds and nuts as well as leaves and shoots, are also herbivores.

WHAT IS A PARASITE?

A PARASITE is the name given to a plant or animal that lives in or on another plant or animal and uses it as its only source of food. Tapeworms are parasites that live inside the guts of mammals such as dogs and pigs.

WHY ARE SOME INSECTS CALLED PESTS?

SOME insects harm people, their livestock or their crops. The Colorado beetle damages food crops. Tse-tse flies transmit diseases to cattle. The death-watch beetle damages timber. Mosquitoes carry diseases such as malaria.

Cross sections through the soil showing the tunnels and burrows made by soil-aerating animals.

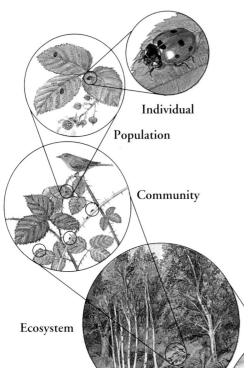

Individual

Population

Community

Ecosystem

WHAT IS AN ECOSYSTEM?

AN ECOSYSTEM is a name used in ecology to describe a collection of plant and animal communities. A woodland is an example of an ecosystem; different plant and animal communities are found on the woodland floor, among bramble patches and among the leaves of the trees. Within each community are populations of individual animals. There are lots of different ecosystems across the world, and together these make up the ecosphere.

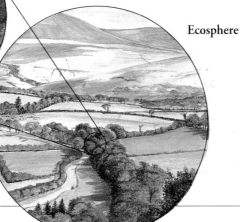

Ecosphere

A diagram of how populations of animals, communities and ecosystems are related to each other and how they form the ecosphere.

HOW IS THE SOIL AERATED?

AIR containing oxygen needs to be present in the soil so that plant roots can produce energy and grow. One of the main ways by which air penetrates deep into the soil is by the activity of creatures such as moles and earthworms. Smaller creatures such as mites help to break the soil into even smaller particles.

ARE THE WORLD'S DESERTS GETTING LARGER ?

THE land around the world's deserts receives little rainfall. As a result, the poor soil has little vegetation, and this is heavily grazed by animals. With the vegetation removed, the land suffers soil erosion and becomes desert itself. Unless steps are taken to halt this process, called desertification, the world's deserts could double in size within a century or so.

Existing deserts
Areas of desertification
At risk of desertification

This map shows the extent of the world's deserts today and how they might increase.

WHY ARE RHINOS ENDANGERED ?

RHINOS are endangered because they are illegally killed for their horns. Rhino-horn powder is valued by a small number of people, particularly in China, who mistakenly believe that it has healing properties. Black and white rhinos, both from Africa, are particularly endangered and just a few thousand of each are left in the wild.

White rhinos are killed illegally for their horns, which are sold for a high price to the Far East.

WHEN DID THE DODO BECOME EXTINCT ?

THE dodo was a large, flightless bird that lived on the island of Mauritius in the Indian Ocean. It thrived until human settlers came to the island in the 16th century and used the dodo as a convenient source of food. Not surprisingly, it became more and more scarce. The bird finally became extinct in 1680, its disappearance giving rise to the expression "dead as a dodo".

Without the ability to fly, the dodo was easy prey for humans.

WHAT IS CONSERVATION ?

MANY plants and animals are threatened by human activities such as hunting and habitat destruction. In an attempt to keep populations of these species healthy, many people help protect both the creatures and the environment. This is called conservation. Methods used by conservationists are varied and include such activities as habitat protection and restoration, and guarding nests of rare birds. Without conservation, many species would soon become extinct.

The koala suffers from habitat loss, the kakapo parrot is killed by humans, cats and rats, and the manatee is threatened by hunting.

Koala

Kakapo

Manatee

WHICH WHALE SPECIES IS MOST THREATENED ?

THE North Atlantic right whale is probably the most threatened whale species. Only a few hundred animals are left today. Whalers found them easy to kill because they spend a lot of time swimming slowly on the surface.

WHAT IS GLOBAL WARMING ?

MANY scientists believe the Earth's climate is getting warmer and this process is called global warming. Burning fossil fuels such as coal and using chemicals that affect the ozone layer in the atmosphere may be the cause.

WHAT IS OIL POLLUTION ?

MOST people in developed countries of the world use oil, or oil products such as petrol. These cause pollution when burned, but oil can also damage the environment when it is spilled at sea. Huge oil tankers transport millions of gallons of oil, and if the ship hits a rock the oil spills out into the sea. Oil pollution is harmful in many ways. When seabirds get coated in oil they soon die, and dolphins, fish and other marine life also suffer. Life on the seashore is destroyed when the oil gets washed on to a beach, and creatures on the sea bed die if the oil sinks.

In 1989 the Exxon Valdez *lost 11 million gallons of oil off the coast of Alaska. This polluted 1,700 km of coastline and caused an environmental disaster.*

WHY IS DDT HARMFUL ?

DDT is a chemical that was commonly used in the 1960s to kill insect pests on fruit farms. But it also contaminated the fruit, and thus the fruit-eating birds, which stored the chemical in their bodies. Many birds of prey became scarce after eating smaller birds contaminated by DDT.

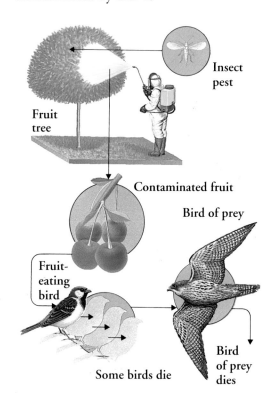

Insect pest

Fruit tree

Contaminated fruit

Bird of prey

Fruit-eating bird

Some birds die

Bird of prey dies

DDT sprayed onto a fruit tree can find its way into the body of a bird of prey.

WHY ARE RAINFORESTS UNDER THREAT ?

RAINFORESTS are being cut down in many parts of the world, either to provide timber or to create farmland. In the Amazon, scientists estimate that an area of rainforest the size of a football pitch is destroyed every minute.

WHAT IS OVERFISHING ?

OVERFISHING occurs when a fish species is caught at a faster rate than it can reproduce. When it is no longer profitable for trawlers to catch a particular species, they go elsewhere to fish. But it takes a long time for a fish population to recover after it has been overfished.

HOW IS AFRICAN WILDLIFE PROTECTED ?

SOME of Africa's most familiar animals only survive because they live in protected areas such as national parks. Among the most important are Lake Ichkeul in Tunisia, a haven for wetland birds, and the Masai Mara National Reserve in Kenya, which hosts the annual migration of millions of wildebeest. Kalahari Gemsbok National Park in southern Africa protects the gemsbok antelope, and the Okavango Delta is a wilderness for wetland birds and mammals.

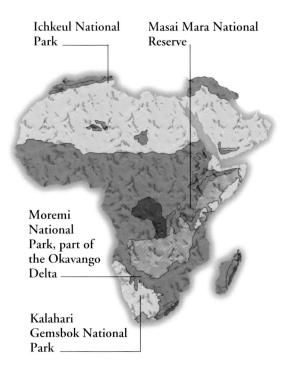

Ichkeul National Park

Masai Mara National Reserve

Moremi National Park, part of the Okavango Delta

Kalahari Gemsbok National Park

A map of Africa showing some of its most important protected areas for wildlife.

WHY IS THE PASSENGER PIGEON EXTINCT ?

IN THE early 1800s, billions of passenger pigeons could be found in North America. Over the next century the birds were killed in their millions by people. The last one died in a zoo in 1914.

WHY ARE SOME SPECIES ENDANGERED ?

SPECIES often become rare and endangered because they have been hunted by humans; this is the case with many whales. Others are threatened because their habitats are destroyed.

DO PENGUINS MAKE NESTS ?

PENGUINS live in the southern oceans and breed on ice floes or rocky shores. They do not make nests but lay their eggs on the ground. However, the parent birds still protect both eggs and young chicks from the freezing air and keep them warm. The egg rests on the penguin's foot and is kept snug in a special brood pouch. Inside the brood pouch, a bald area of skin supplies heat from the penguin's body to the egg or the chick.

A pair of king penguins with their new egg.

WHY DO SOME ANIMALS FIGHT ?

ANIMALS fight for a number of different reasons. Most will defend themselves against predators, but many also do battle with members of the same species. Some of these fights may take place to keep rivals out of a good feeding area. Fights between male deer at the start of the breeding season are not concerned with feeding, however. Two males lock antlers to see which is the strongest. The victor will then dominate the herd and earn the right to mate with the female deer.

Rival white-tailed deer stags battle to see which one is the strongest.

WHAT IS ANIMAL MIMICRY ?

MIMICRY happens when one species of animal looks or behaves like another. There are many good examples of mimicry among butter-flies. These creatures make tasty meals for birds, but some species avoid attack by being poisonous. They advertise the fact with bright colours so that birds learn to avoid them. Some non-poisonous butterflies mimic the colours and markings of the poisonous species so birds avoid them as well. They also mimic the behaviour and flight patterns of their poisonous look-alikes.

A poisonous butterfly (top) and its tasty look-alike (below).

A tiger ambushes a spotted deer and springs from cover to catch its prey.

WHY DO BIRDS SING ?

USUALLY it is the male birds that sing. They do so to attract mates and to advertise their territory. Each singing bird competes with nearby males to see who is the best songster. Birds with good songs stand the best chance of finding a mate.

WHY DO SOME ANIMALS HAVE TERRITORIES ?

AN ANIMAL may guard a territory to protect its supply of food from rivals or because it is a safe place to rear its young. Some species hold a territory throughout their lives, but many only have one during the breeding season.

HOW DOES A TIGER CATCH ITS PREY ?

TIGERS can sprint at speed, but cannot chase fast prey like deer for long distances. Instead, they use cunning behaviour to get close enough to launch an attack. The tiger creeps slowly forwards keeping low to the ground and using its striped coat to camouflage it in the vegetation. It also stalks from a downwind direction, because most prey animals have a good sense of smell and can detect danger. When the tiger is close enough, it springs from cover, killing the prey with a bite to the neck.

WHY DO HOWLER MONKEYS HOWL ?

HOWLER monkeys live in family groups in the rainforests of South America. They howl so that other monkey groups do not stray into their territories. The sound also helps group members stay in contact with each other.

DO ANIMALS USE TOOLS ?

APART from man, only a few other animals use tools. Chimps shape grass stems to extract insects called termites from their underground homes. A bird called the woodpecker finch uses cactus spines to help it remove insect grubs from plant stems.

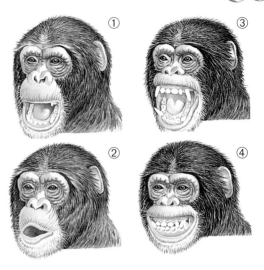

The four most common facial expressions seen in chimps.

An Arctic hare in its summer and winter coats.

WHAT IS SCENT MARKING ?

SOME animals use powerful smells to mark tree bark, twigs or even the ground, and this is known as scent marking. Scent marks are sometimes used to show the boundaries of a territory or to attract a mate. Animals that scent mark are often nocturnal or live in habitats with dense vegetation, where visual signals cannot easily be seen.

CAN CHIMPS SHOW THEIR MOODS ?

CHIMPS are good at showing their moods and do so using the expressions on their faces. The shape of the mouth and whether or not the teeth are bared are important signals. The chimps pictured above are showing: (1) a desire to play, (2) begging for food, (3) fear and (4) anxiety.

WHY DO ARCTIC HARES TURN WHITE IN WINTER ?

DURING the summer, an Arctic hare's coat is grey-brown. This blends in with the vegetation and helps it avoid predators such as eagles. If it kept this coat colour during the winter, when snow covers the landscape, it would stand out and make an easy target. So the hare moults in autumn and grows a pure white coat instead.

HOW DO HONEY BEES COMMUNICATE ?

HONEY bees live in colonial hives and gather pollen and nectar from nearby flowers for food. If a particularly good source of food is found, the bee that has discovered it performs a strange dance in the hive. The angle and intensity of its dance tells the other bees where to fly to find the right flowers.

The great shearwater breeds on the Falkland Islands and migrates to the north Atlantic and back.

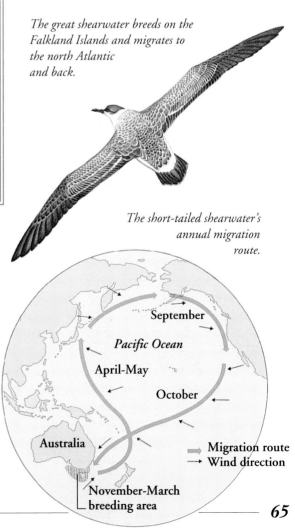

The short-tailed shearwater's annual migration route.

WHY DO SOME ANIMALS MIGRATE ?

ANIMALS breed at times of year when food is in good supply. Birds that can fly strongly often move to areas far away to find food. Some seabirds that nest on islands in the southern oceans, for example shearwaters, abandon their breeding areas after the brief Antarctic summer. They fly north to the Atlantic and Arctic oceans, where the feeding is better at that time of year. Each year, their journeys cover tens of thousands of kilometres.

September

Pacific Ocean

April-May

October

Australia

Migration route
Wind direction

November-March
breeding area

ARE THERE DIFFERENT TYPES OF GOLDFISH ?

GOLDFISH were originally bred from wild carp. They have been kept as pets for hundreds of years and there are now over 150 different types. The common form of the goldfish is golden-orange all over. Sometimes a fish with unusual colours or fins appears, however. By only allowing similar-looking fish to breed together, fish keepers are able to produce more of these unusual-looking goldfish.

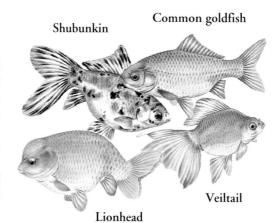

Shubunkin Common goldfish

Lionhead

Veiltail

Apart from the true goldfish, the best-known types are the shubunkin, the lionhead and the veiltail.

HOW DID THE PERSIAN CAT GET ITS NAME ?

PERSIAN cats were first bred in Europe in the 1800s from cats that were imported from Persia (now Iran) and from Angora in Turkey. It is the most popular and best-known breed of long-haired cat and is famous for its long, silky coat. The breed typically has rather short legs, a powerful body and a broad head. Persian cats are often black and white, but other colours are also popular among cat owners.

A black-and-white Persian cat.

ARE DOGS AND WOLVES RELATED ?

ALTHOUGH they may often look very different, wolves are thought to be the ancestors of domestic dogs. Thousands of years ago humans started to keep wolves for companionship and for guarding duties. Each time wolves were bred in captivity, their offspring behaved less like wolves and more like the dogs of today. They also became less aggressive and more dependent on humans.

WHAT IS DOMESTICATION ?

ALTHOUGH early people hunted wild animals, they also kept some types in captivity. Some of their animals were easy to tame, and they found that their offspring could be bred to be even more docile. This process is called domestication.

WHAT IS SELECTIVE BREEDING ?

SELECTIVE breeding is a method used by breeders to produce plants or animals with qualities favoured by humans. In selective breeding only specimens showing the desired qualities are allowed to breed, to ensure the qualities are passed on to the next generation.

DO PIGS HAVE WILD RELATIVES ?

WILD boars are the closest wild relatives of domestic pigs. They are large and aggressive animals that still roam the forests of parts of Europe and Asia. Male wild boars have sharp tusks with which to defend themselves.

Although related, wolves and toy dogs look completely different.

WHAT IS THE HEAVIEST HORSE ?

THE shire horse is the heaviest horse breed. A full-grown animal is more than 1.7 m tall at the shoulder. Shire horses were originally bred in England and used for ploughing and pulling heavy loads. Today, working shire horses have been replaced by machines. They are now kept mainly for show.

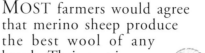

HOW LONG HAVE GOATS BEEN KEPT AS DOMESTIC ANIMALS?

GOATS have been kept as domestic animals for more than 9,000 years. They are important mainly for their milk, but goat meat, wool and skin can be used as well. Goats are particularly suited to stony, dry ground and can survive in areas where there is little rainfall. Goats were probably first domesticated in the Middle East, and their wild ancestors still live in parts of Europe and Asia.

The Nubian goat is particularly popular in North America.

WHICH CATTLE BREEDS ARE BEST FOR HOT CLIMATES?

MANY breeds of cattle do not like hot climates and only thrive in areas with cool summers. Two breeds are, however, perfectly suited to warmer regions. The Santa Gertrudis is a stocky breed with short horns. It is farmed for beef and is popular in Texas. The Kankrej is common in India and is used mainly for pulling loads. It has a large hump and long horns.

Santa Gertrudis and Kankrej cattle both thrive in hot climates.

Santa Gertrudis

Kankrej

WHAT IS A MERINO SHEEP?

MOST farmers would agree that merino sheep produce the best wool of any breeds. Their coat is very thick and the fleece is strong and fine. They are also hardy animals. The breed originated in Spain nearly 1,000 years ago. Today, merino sheep are found all over the world, and have also been crossed with other breeds.

An Arles merino sheep from the south of France, valued for its high-quality fleece.

WHAT IS A LOP RABBIT?

A LOP is a breed of rabbit known for its extremely long ears. Rather than standing upright, the ears droop and often touch the ground when the rabbit is resting. Rabbits have been kept as pets and for food for about 2,000 years.

WHY ARE PIGS IMPORTANT IN POOR COUNTRIES?

PIGS are extremely useful animals to keep in poor countries because they will eat almost anything edible. They can be fed with scraps from the kitchen, but will happily forage for themselves and eat plants and roots. Pigs are kept mainly for their meat, but almost every part of the animal can be used: the skin can be made into leather, the bristles make brushes and the fat can be used for cooking.

WHERE DO GUINEA PIGS COME FROM?

GUINEA pigs come from South America. They have been kept in captivity for hundreds of years and are no longer found in the wild. In South America they are kept for food and not as pets.

HOW DID FRIESIAN COWS GET THEIR NAME?

FRIESIAN cows were named after their place of origin, the Friesian Islands in the Netherlands. Friesian cows are a black-and-white breed and are prized for their milk production. A single cow can produce around 6,000 litres each year.

Nearly 800 million pigs are kept throughout the world.

WHO BUILT THE FIRST HOUSES?

EARLY humans built temporary shelters, but the first permanent houses were built by early farmers in the Middle East about 11,000 years ago. Around that time, at Zawi Chemi Shanidar in the Zagros Mountains, people used river boulders to build some of the earliest houses.

WHAT WERE HUNTER-GATHERERS?

HUNTER-GATHERERS were people who moved around hunting animals and gathering wild plants for food. People did not stay in one place until they learnt how to farm the land.

WHAT WERE ZIGGURATS?

ZIGGURATS were high towers made of brick. They were built from about 2100 BC in Mesopotamia as temples. The shape of a ziggurat was a series of progressively smaller, rectangular terraces, with a shrine at the top.

Villagers at Zawi Chemi Shanidar in about 9000 BC. This is one of the earliest settled communities ever found.

WHAT DID AN IRON AGE HILL FORT LOOK LIKE?

AN IRON Age hill fort was surrounded by up to four or five lines of banks and ditches. First a bank was built, then a ditch, and then a steep slope, which the attackers would have to cross to reach the fort.

Cadbury Castle in Britain was an Iron Age hill fort. It became one of the largest, strongest forts in Britain.

HOW DO WE KNOW ABOUT EARLY CIVILIZATIONS?

PEOPLE called archaeologists dig up places of historical interest and study the objects they find there. "Archaeology" means "the study of everything ancient".

WHEN DID PEOPLE START FARMING?

FARMING first began in the Middle East about 9000 BC. Later, it also developed separately in America and the Far East about 6000 BC.

WHAT WERE STAMP SEALS USED FOR?

FROM 5000 BC, a transportable object often had a piece of clay tied to it. This was stamped by the owner, while still damp, with his own mark.

WHEN WAS MONEY FIRST USED?

COINS as we know them developed about 2,500 years ago, but before that ancient societies used things like shells and stones to pay for goods, or they exchanged one item for another.

In this Celtic Iron Age hill fort, the cooking pot, weapons and horseshoes were all made of iron.

WHEN WAS THE IRON AGE?

THE Iron Age probably began in the Middle East about 4000 BC. The first iron objects were tools and weapons made from meteorites that fell to Earth from space. People first learnt how to extract iron from iron ore about 1500 BC, in the Middle East. In western Europe, the Celts became expert at working iron about 800 BC. Farm tools, weapons and iron cauldrons for cooking meat are just a few of the things they made from metal.

WHEN DID PEOPLE FIRST LEARN TO WRITE?

WRITING first developed in Mesopotamia about 3300 BC as a way of recording trade deals. At first pictures were used; then symbols were invented to represent the sounds of speech.

WHEN DID TRADE START ?

SOON after people began to live in settled communities they began to trade. Many items, like textiles and skins, have not survived, so the full extent of early trade is not known. But Jericho, an oasis town from 9000 BC, is thought to have been an early trading centre for salt and bitumen from the Dead Sea, cowrie shells from the Red Sea, and copper and turquoise from the Sinai Peninsula.

At Kanesh (in modern Turkey) merchants set up an important trading centre in 2000 BC.

WHAT SORT OF WEAPONS DID THE FIRST ARMIES HAVE ?

COPPER axes, spears and daggers were in use in Europe by about 4000 BC. Bronze weapons, used by the Sumerians in the Middle East, appeared about 3000 BC, and included spears and large rectangular shields. By about 1400 BC, the Egyptians, among others, were wearing an early form of body armour.

An Egyptian soldier wearing armour made from stiffened fabric.

The Babylonian king, Nebuchadnezzar, attended by his queen and servants. They are sitting in the beautiful Hanging Gardens of Babylon, part of his massive rebuilding programme.

WHEN DID CITIES DEVELOP ?

BY 6000 BC, Jericho and a few other places had developed into towns. But the main change from village to city life took place between 4300 and 3450 BC in Mesopotamia. About this time, large numbers of people began living closely together and many stopped being farmers.

WHO WERE THE BABYLONIANS ?

BABYLON, on the Euphrates River, was founded about 2000 BC by the Amorites from Syria. By the 18th century BC Babylon controlled a large empire in the heartland of early civilization, but in 1595 BC it was invaded and destroyed. Hundreds of years later, in the 7th century BC, Nabopolassar became king. He and his son Nebuchadnezzar made Babylon rich, powerful and famous again.

WHEN WAS THE PERSIAN EMPIRE ?

CYRUS, who became king of the Persians in 559 BC, founded the Persian empire, which was very powerful for the next 200 years. The Persians defeated Babylon in 539 BC and Egypt in 525 BC. They also conquered the Indus Valley region of present-day Pakistan. But they were finally defeated by the Greeks. In 331 BC the Persian empire was taken over by Alexander the Great.

The armies of Alexander the Great conquered the Persian empire, which was split up when Alexander died.

WHEN WAS THE ANCIENT EGYPTIAN CIVILIZATION?

ORIGINALLY, ancient Egypt was divided into two areas: Upper Egypt and Lower Egypt. The history of ancient Egypt begins when these two areas were united in about 3100 BC under one king, and lasts for nearly 3,000 years. Historians divide this long period into three main parts: the Old Kingdom, the Middle Kingdom and the New Kingdom.

WHAT IS A MUMMY?

A MUMMY is a body that has been preserved so that it will last forever. The ancient Egyptians believed that if a person's body was preserved, he or she would continue living in the next world. When a king died, surgeons cut open the body, removed the organs, and dried the body and preserved it with oils. It was then wrapped in bandages and placed in a coffin.

While the body was being wrapped in bandages, a priest dressed as the jackal god Anubis, god of the dead, said prayers.

The heart, lungs and kidneys were kept in pottery jars called canopic jars.

Finally the body was placed in a human-shaped coffin, which was put inside a large stone coffin called a sarcophagus.

WHAT ARE THE PYRAMIDS?

THE pyramids are enormous triangular-sided structures that were built as giant tombs for the mummified bodies of the Egyptian kings and queens. The first pyramids were built around 2630 BC, and pyramid building continued for about 1,000 years. Thousands of Egyptian workers had to drag the huge blocks of stone to the site on sledges. The kings and queens were buried with rich treasures in tombs deep inside the pyramids, reached only by secret passages that were later sealed shut.

The Great Pyramid at Giza, built for King Khufu in about 2500 BC, used more than 2 million blocks of stone.

WHAT IS THE SPHINX?

THE Sphinx is a huge, human-headed lion made of stone at the site of the Great Pyramid at Giza. It measures over 57 m long. Historians think it may be much older than the Great Pyramid, and was possibly intended to guard the entrance to the Nile.

WHAT WAS THE EASIEST WAY TO TRAVEL IN ANCIENT EGYPT?

THE Nile passed like a highway through the whole length of the country. There was no need for roads on land. All sorts of boats sailed up and down the river, from small passenger ferries to huge cargo barges.

WHY WERE THE PYRAMIDS BUILT IN THAT SHAPE?

THE kings were believed to be the sons of the Sun god, Re. The shape of the pyramids is thought to represent rays of the Sun, up which the dead kings would climb to reach the next world.

WHY DID THE EGYPTIANS LIVE NEAR THE RIVER NILE?

ALTHOUGH ancient Egypt was a very large country, most people lived along a narrow strip of land on either side of the River Nile, because this was where the good farmland was found. Every summer, monsoon rains falling on the mountains in Ethiopia, south of Egypt, flowed into the river, which flooded, making the land near its banks very fertile.

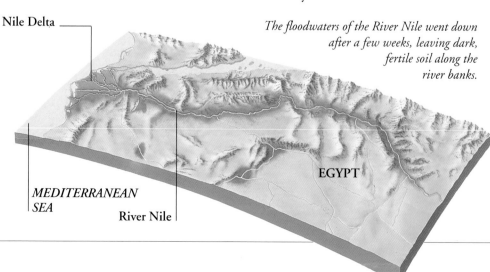

Nile Delta

The floodwaters of the River Nile went down after a few weeks, leaving dark, fertile soil along the river banks.

MEDITERRANEAN SEA

River Nile

EGYPT

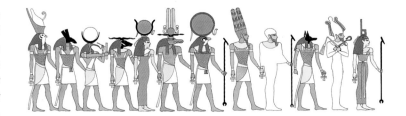

Many of the gods and goddesses were depicted with the heads of animals and birds.

WHAT WAS THE RELIGION OF ANCIENT EGYPT ?

THE Egyptians were very religious people and they had about 2,000 gods and goddesses, although not all of them were worshipped all over the country. There were gods of nature, such as water or air; and gods who looked after daily life, like farming or fishing. Some were fierce, others were gentle. The most important were Re, the Sun god; Isis, the fertility goddess; and Osiris, ruler of the Underworld.

The earliest Egyptian writing was carved on stone. Later, ink was used on paper made from papyrus reeds.

COULD EGYPTIANS WRITE ?

WRITING was very important to the Egyptians, but only people called scribes, who had been specially trained, could write. They used a method of writing, known as hieroglyphic, which had over 700 pictures or signs. These could be written from left to right, right to left or from top to bottom. Some stood for one letter, others for groups of letters or whole words.

WERE THERE ANY TEMPLES IN ANCIENT EGYPT ?

THE most important gods and goddesses were worshipped at temples all over Egypt. Sometimes a local god was linked to a national one; the most significant was Amun, god of invisibility, who was linked to Re, the Sun god, to become Amun-Re. His temple at Thebes became one of the most powerful in Egypt.

WHAT IS THE VALLEY OF THE KINGS ?

DURING the period of the New Kingdom, from 1552 BC, royal tombs were situated in the Valley of the Kings, a remote canyon on the west bank of the River Nile at Thebes. This was to prevent robbers from stealing the royal treasures, as they had done from the pyramids.

The pharaoh listened to the day's news from the vizier, his chief minister.

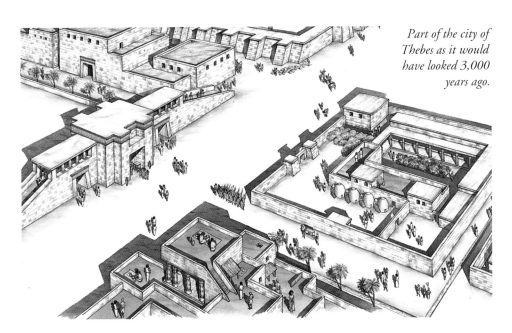

Part of the city of Thebes as it would have looked 3,000 years ago.

DID THE EGYPTIANS HAVE CITIES ?

ANCIENT Egypt had a few large cities. The most important were Thebes in the south and Memphis in the north. These were hot, dusty and crowded. The ordinary people lived in tall, mud-brick houses designed to keep out the Sun. Richer people had spacious houses with walled gardens. The cities' great temples were the centre of Egyptian life.

WHAT DID THE EGYPTIANS CALL THEIR RULERS ?

THE first Egyptian rulers were called kings. They were believed to be gods. After 1552 BC they were called pharaohs. The pharaoh was by far the most powerful person in the land. He was in charge of the government; he was commander of the army; and he was chief of all the priests. Only one of his wives could be queen.

WHO LIVED IN THE BIBLE LANDS?

MANY different groups of people lived in the Bible lands at different times. Some of the first were the Canaanites, who lived along the eastern shores of the Mediterranean Sea about 2000 BC. Around 1550–1150 BC, Canaan was dominated by Egypt. When the Egyptians withdrew, the Israelites and Philistines moved in. Merchants called Phoenicians also lived in the area. They set up colonies around the Mediterranean, including the city of Carthage in Tunisia, founded in 814 BC.

WHO WAS KING HEROD?

KING Herod, also known as Herod the Great, was appointed king of Judaea by the Roman senate in 37 BC. This was in return for his loyalty to Rome. Under Herod, Judaea remained part of the Roman empire. He reigned until his death in 4 BC.

WHAT WAS JERUSALEM LIKE WHEN JESUS WAS THERE?

THE city of Jerusalem has been in existence since at least 3000 BC. Herod the Great shaped the city as it is described in the Bible at the time of Jesus. The most important buildings in the city at that time were Herod's palace, the temple, the fortress where Jesus probably stood trial before Pontius Pilate, and the High Priest's house. The Garden of Gethsemane (where Jesus was arrested) and Golgotha (the crucifixion ground) were outside the city walls.

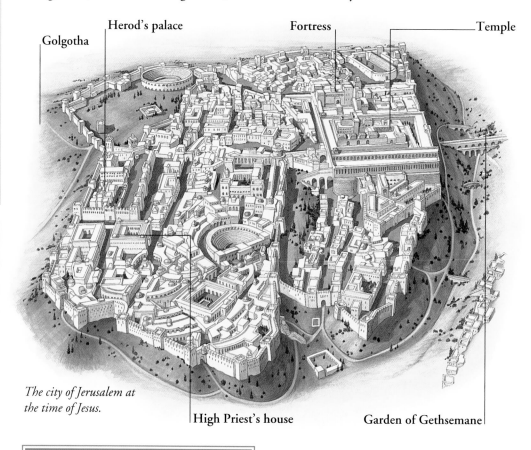

The city of Jerusalem at the time of Jesus.

HOW DID CHRISTIANITY BEGIN?

CHRISTIANITY was founded by the followers of Jesus of Nazareth, known as Jesus Christ, who lived in Palestine when it was part of the Roman empire. The new religion taught that Jesus was the Son of God. It promised everlasting life after death and forgiveness of people's sins. Early Christians were persecuted by the Romans, but in AD 394 Christianity became the empire's official religion.

On his many travels, St Paul preached to non-Jews all round the Mediterranean.

WHAT DO BC AND AD MEAN?

THESE letters are used with dates: BC means Before Christ was born, and AD means after the birth of Jesus (it stands for *Anno Domini*, Latin for "in the year of our Lord").

WHICH GODS DID THE CANAANITES WORSHIP?

THE Canaanites had many gods and goddesses. They made idols, which were supposed to look like these gods, and worshipped them in hilltop temples. One of the most important was Baal, god of fertility and weather. The Philistines inherited many of the Canaanite gods.

Two of the gods worshipped by the Canaanites: Baal on the right, and a bronze bull on the left.

WHO WAS KING DAVID?

DAVID became king of the Israelites in about 1000 BC. He defeated the Philistines and built up his kingdom into a powerful nation, with Jerusalem as its capital. The kingdom flourished under David's son, Solomon, but was divided after he died.

WERE JUDAH AND JUDAEA THE SAME PLACE?

AFTER King Solomon died, Israel was split into two parts: the northern part kept the name Israel, and the southern part was called Judah. Judah was called Judaea by the Romans, who entered Jerusalem in 63 BC.

WHERE WERE THE BIBLE LANDS?

MODERN Israel occupies the land called Palestine in the New Testament of the Bible. To the east lay the ancient cities of Ur and Babylon in an area then known as Mesopotamia, roughly where the modern country of Iraq is now. Further west lay Egypt, which was mentioned early in the Bible, and to the north lay Assyria.

WHO WERE THE ASSYRIANS?

THE Assyrians were some of the fiercest fighters of Biblical times. In the 9th century BC they began to expand their territory beyond their homeland in the valley of the River Tigris, and for the next 200 years they fought relentless battles against Syria, Phoenicia, Israel and Judah. They built large, strong-walled cities.

A map of the lands described in the Bible. They are known as the Bible lands.

The Assyrians attacked their enemies' cities with battering rams.

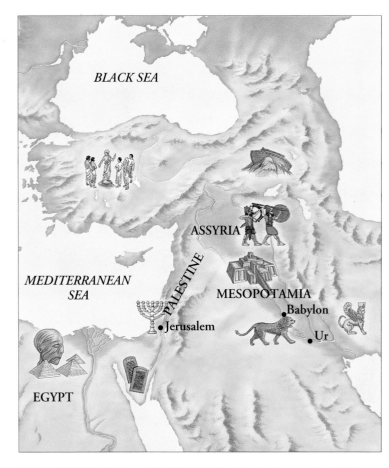

BLACK SEA

MEDITERRANEAN SEA

ASSYRIA

PALESTINE

MESOPOTAMIA

Babylon

Jerusalem

Ur

EGYPT

WAS FOOD PLENTIFUL IN BIBLICAL TIMES?

THE word "famine" occurs over a hundred times in the Bible. The rains often did not come, which meant that food crops like cereals could not be sown in the rock-hard ground after a dry summer. But fruit and vegetables were grown, and grapes were eaten fresh or pressed to make wine.

WHO WERE THE JEWS?

THE Israelites became known as the Jews from the 6th century BC, because they came from Judah. At first they had worshipped several gods and goddesses, but long before they became known as the Jews they were worshipping just one god, called Yahweh.

WHEN WAS THE BIBLE WRITTEN?

THE Bible is divided into two main parts. Most of the Old Testament was written between the 6th and 2nd centuries BC, although it was started much earlier. The New Testament was written in the 1st century AD.

Once the wheat was harvested, it was threshed to extract the grain. This was ground into flour to make bread.

WHAT WAS BUILT ON THE ACROPOLIS ?

THE Acropolis is a rocky hill overlooking the city of Athens. It was chosen as the site for temples, statues and ritual buildings, which were among the finest in ancient Greece. The largest building was the Parthenon, a magnificent, white marble temple built between 447 BC and 432 BC in honour of Athena, the goddess of Athens.

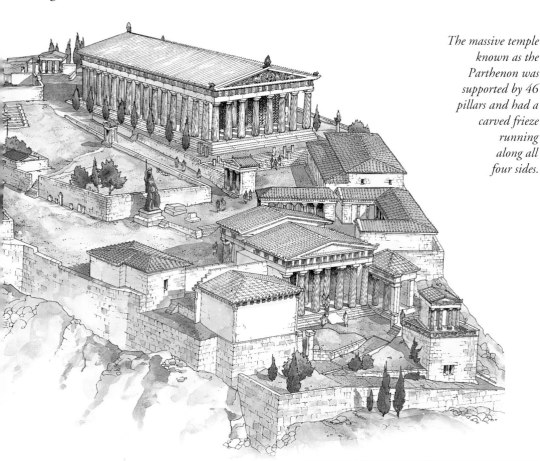

The massive temple known as the Parthenon was supported by 46 pillars and had a carved frieze running along all four sides.

The hoplite used his spear to attack his enemy until he was wounded, or turned and ran.

WHAT DID GREEK SOLDIERS WEAR ?

A GREEK foot soldier was called a hoplite. His uniform was a linen shirt with metal armour plates on the shoulders. A bronze breastplate covered his chest and stomach, and greaves (shin guards) covered his legs. On his head he wore a bronze helmet with a tall crest. He carried a shield, an iron-tipped spear, and a short sword for use in close combat.

WHAT EVENTS TOOK PLACE AT THE FIRST OLYMPIC GAMES ?

EVERY four years, from 776 BC, about 40,000 spectators would flock to Olympia to see the best Greek athletes compete in games held in honour of the god Zeus. Running races were held in the stadium; the track was up to 192 m long and the runners were naked. Wrestling was popular, and could be won by throwing your opponent three times. Javelin throwing was encouraged, too, because javelin or spear throwing was a useful skill in wartime. During the games, all wars were banned and personal feuds were forgotten.

There was no greater honour for an athlete than to win at Olympia.

WHO WERE THE FIRST GREEKS ?

THE first people to speak Greek were the Mycenaeans. They ruled southern Greece about 1600–1200 BC. Mycenae was their most important city. The Mycenaeans were fierce warriors, but they were also superb builders.

WHAT TYPE OF GODS DID THE GREEKS WORSHIP ?

THE Greeks worshipped more than a dozen gods and goddesses. They believed the gods had adventures like humans; they fought wars, quarrelled, and fell in love. The Greeks also believed that the gods could help or harm humans, so they built many temples where they prayed and offered sacrifices.

WERE GREEK NAVIES VERY POWERFUL ?

MUCH of Greece is surrounded by the sea, so the Greeks have always been shipbuilders and sailors. Wealthy trading cities such as Athens and Corinth built powerful navies to protect their merchant ships. The most important type of warship was the trireme, which was fast and easy to turn. It was a long, narrow ship rowed by 170 sailors sitting in three tiered rows. The main weapon was a ram at the front, which was used to smash holes in enemy ships.

The rowers in a trireme sat above each other and had to avoid hitting each other's oars.

WHAT HAPPENED AT THE BATTLE OF SALAMIS ?

IN 480 BC the Persian army invaded Greece with a large navy. The Greeks lured the enemy ships into the narrow stretch of water between the island of Salamis and the mainland. The Persians had no room to escape, and the Greeks were able to destroy them.

WHAT WAS GREEK POTTERY LIKE ?

THE Greeks made some of the finest pottery and sculpture ever. They learned their skills from the East, but they developed their own styles. In Athens, 200 potters and painters worked together to make the best pots in the world.

This large pot was used for mixing wine and water at parties. Fine pots were usually signed by the artist.

WHO WAS HERODOTUS ?

HERODOTUS was the world's first true historian. He was born about 484 BC at Halicarnassus, and is most famous for his account of the Persian Wars. He travelled widely around the Mediterranean, the Black Sea, Egypt and the Middle East, collecting information for his book, which has many anecdotes about the peoples involved in the wars.

HOW WERE GREEK CITIES RULED ?

MOST of the Greek cities were ruled by kings or nobles, but a few, such as Athens and Thebes, were ruled by democracy or "citizen power". The citizens elected leaders and voted on important issues. Foreigners, women and slaves were not citizens, so only about 10 percent of the population could vote.

Indian troops in the Punjab used elephants against Alexander's army in 326 BC. Alexander dreamed of conquering all of India, but his troops rebelled and forced him to go home.

DID GREEK CHILDREN GO TO SCHOOL ?

SCHOOL was only for boys. The main subjects were reading, writing and music. They wrote on wax tablets that could be smoothed over and written on again.

WHO WAS THE GREATEST GENERAL OF THE GREEK WORLD ?

IN 336 BC King Alexander of Macedonia, a kingdom north of Greece, conquered all the Greek cities except Sparta. He united them and led them to war against Persia. Over the next 10 years he conquered almost the entire known world, from Europe to India, and was considered to be the world's greatest general: Alexander the Great.

WHO WERE THE GREEK PHILOSOPHERS ?

PHILOSOPHER means "lover of wisdom", and many philosophers were early scientists. They held public discussions on questions such as: "What is a good man?" The most famous Greek philosophers were Socrates, Aristotle and Plato.

HOW BIG WAS THE ROMAN ARMY ?

WHEN the Roman empire was at its biggest there were 450,000 soldiers in the army. For hundreds of years it was one of the strongest armies in the world. It was organized into groups of different sizes. The smallest group had eight soldiers, and was called a contubernium. Eight of these formed a century. Centuries were grouped into cohorts, and eight of these made a legion. A centurion was in charge of a century and a legatus was in charge of a legion.

Rich Romans frequently enjoyed banquets, and were waited on by servants or slaves.

WHO WERE THE ROMANS ?

THE Romans were originally the people who lived in the city of Rome in Italy. In 396 BC, they captured the nearby city of Veii. Over the next 400 years they went on to build up a vast empire by conquering other countries. People who were loyal to the empire were rewarded with citizenship, and thought of themselves as Romans.

WAS THERE A KING OF ROME ?

BEFORE 509 BC the Romans were ruled by kings. But they were so unpopular that they were overthrown, and Rome became a republic run by politicians called senators. From 31 BC, a long line of emperors ruled the empire for many centuries.

WHAT WERE ROMAN CITIES LIKE ?

ROMAN cities often had grand public buildings: theatres, amphitheatres, a forum (public meeting place and market square), baths, temples and law courts. But most people lived in squalid slums.

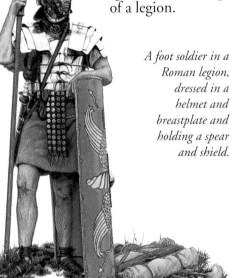

A foot soldier in a Roman legion, dressed in a helmet and breastplate and holding a spear and shield.

WERE THE ROMANS GOOD AT BUILDING ?

THE Romans were very skilled engineers. They built bridges, public baths, huge aqueducts for carrying water to their cities, and long, straight roads, many of which still exist today.

DID ROMAN CHILDREN GO TO SCHOOL ?

THE boys of rich families went to school from seven to eleven. They were taught reading, writing and numbers. Boys from poor families started work as young as five. Girls were taught how to run a household by their mothers.

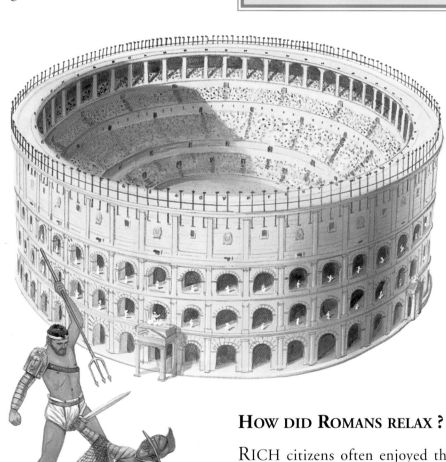

In the amphitheatre in Rome, called the Colosseum, gladiators fought to the death.

HOW DID ROMANS RELAX ?

RICH citizens often enjoyed themselves at parties, where they were entertained with music and readings of poetry. Plays, both tragedies and comedies, and pantomimes were performed in the theatres, and in the amphitheatres there were four-horse chariot races and gladiator shows. Gladiators fought each other armed with different kinds of weapons.

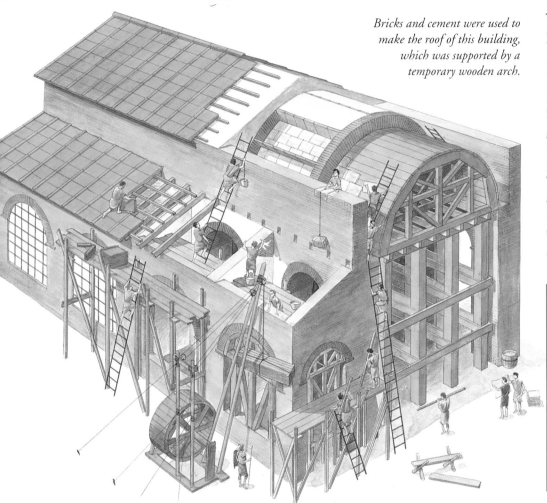

Bricks and cement were used to make the roof of this building, which was supported by a temporary wooden arch.

WHAT WERE THE NEW ROMAN BUILDING METHODS ?

ROMAN builders developed many new ideas and skills. Many of their public buildings were so well made that at least parts of them are still standing. They were the first people to become expert at using concrete, made from volcanic ash and small stones. This made the walls and roofs very strong. They developed the skill of making arches, which meant buildings could be larger than before. They also perfected the dome.

WHY DID THE ROMAN EMPIRE COLLAPSE ?

IN THE 5th century AD the Roman empire came under attack from Germanic barbarian tribesmen who wanted to live in the empire and share its wealth. The emperors, by now powerless, could not prevent them from taking over half the empire.

WHAT SORT OF HOUSES DID ROMANS LIVE IN ?

IN TOWNS and cities, most people lived in apartment blocks several storeys high. Richer people lived in the lower storeys. They often had a large country villa, too, with beautiful gardens and rooms with underfloor heating.

WHAT DID ROMANS EAT ?

MOST homes did not have kitchens, so many people ate cold meals or bought hot food from a takeaway! The rich had three good meals a day: bread and fruit for breakfast; cheese, cold meat or fish, and vegetables for lunch; and a three-course dinner.

DID ART PLAY AN IMPORTANT PART IN ROMAN LIFE ?

THE house of a wealthy Roman would have been elaborately decorated with wall paintings. Some copied famous Greek paintings; others portrayed the gods and goddesses of love. It would have been filled with silver, pottery and glass ornaments, and furniture of marble or bronze.

DID THE ROMANS WORSHIP MANY GODS ?

THERE were many Roman gods, each of which was believed to watch over a different activity of daily life. Sacrifices were made to keep them happy. Many of the gods and goddesses were the same as ancient Greek ones, but with different names. The most important was Jupiter (the Greek god, Zeus). As well as their own gods, the Romans often worshipped gods from the countries they conquered. In the late Roman empire, Christianity became the official religion.

Roman floors were often decorated with colourful mosaics made from tiny pieces of stone. This one shows a hunting scene.

Mars was the Roman god of war and the guardian of Rome. It was believed he would avenge any wrong.

WHO WAS THE FIRST EMPEROR OF CHINA?

UNTIL 221 BC China was divided into separate states ruled by kings who often fought each other. Then the most powerful state, Ch'in, conquered the others, and its king, Shih Huang-Ti, became first emperor of the whole of China.

Shih Huang-Ti, first ruler of the Ch'in dynasty.

WHAT DID THE ANCIENT CHINESE INVENT?

AMONG the great inventions of the ancient Chinese were: the first compass, gunpowder — which they used both in war and in fireworks — and the art of paper-making. But perhaps their most famous invention was silk. The Chinese were weaving delicate patterns in silk by about 1000 BC.

WHAT WAS THE SILK ROAD?

THIS was an ancient trade route that led from China to the Mediterranean Sea. It was named after the silk that was transported along it, but many other precious goods were carried back and forth along the Silk Road, too.

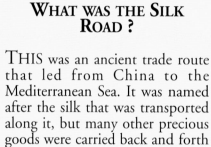

During the Ming dynasty (1368–1644), the Great Wall of China was built in stone, in the form that survives today.

WHEN WAS THE GREAT WALL OF CHINA BUILT?

THE Great Wall was started in about 300 BC, when the first separate parts, made of earth, were built by warring states to keep raiding tribes out of their lands. In 221 BC, Shih Huang-Ti, first emperor of a united China, ordered these short lengths to be joined to form a continuous wall. It took 300,000 slaves 20 years to complete the task.

The Chinese New Year is still celebrated with processions, dancing and music.

WHICH FESTIVALS WERE CELEBRATED BY THE ANCIENT CHINESE?

A BOOK called *The Spring and Autumn Annals*, which was written every year from 722 to 481 BC, records that village people danced to celebrate good harvests and healthy animals. The most important festival was held at New Year to mark the start of the farming year. It was celebrated with processions and kite-flying.

How old is Japanese Civilization?

THE first settled people were the Jomon. They were fishermen who lived in Japan between 7000 and 300 BC. Rice farming and metalworking were introduced by immigrants from Asia.

Did the Japanese build castles?

MANY castles were built in Japan by powerful warlords, especially between 1568 and 1600. The walls were made from enormous stones fitted together without cement. Inside, they were often beautifully painted. One of the finest surviving Japanese castles is Himeji-jo. The original building dated from the 14th century, but it was greatly enlarged about 1600.

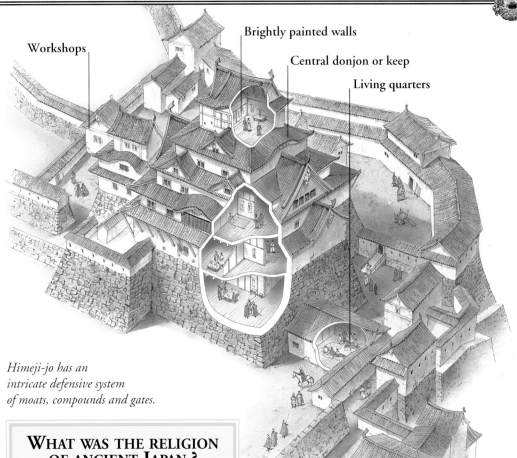

Workshops

Brightly painted walls

Central donjon or keep

Living quarters

Himeji-jo has an intricate defensive system of moats, compounds and gates.

Were there empresses as well as emperors?

WOMEN sometimes ruled in ancient Japan, but real power was held by male regents like Prince Shotoku, regent to Empress Suiko in about AD 600.

When was writing first used in Japan?

THE earliest people of Japan had no system for writing down their language. They first learnt to write it in Chinese characters from about AD 450 onwards.

What was a shogun?

THE first shogun was General Yoritomo, leader of a powerful clan in 12th-century Japan. He was given the title "shogun", which meant commander-in-chief, by the emperor. From then until the 19th century, shoguns had more power than the emperors.

What was the religion of ancient Japan?

THE religion of ancient Japan began about AD 400. It is known as Shinto, and is still practised. Believers see higher spirits, called *kami*, in all aspects of nature. Offerings to these spirits are made at shrines, in the hope that the person will be rewarded. Buddhism was introduced from China in 552.

What did the people eat in ancient Japan?

THE early people of Japan lived mainly on fish. Rice was first grown in about 500 BC. When the rice was harvested, it was stored in special granaries on stilts to keep out the damp.

Who were the samurai?

ORIGINALLY the samurai were guards, but by the 12th century they were highly respected warriors who formed the strongest part of society. They fought for the nobles, and were famed for their loyalty. In return they were rewarded with land and riches. The samurai fought hand-to-hand battles and carried razor-sharp swords. The sword was the symbol of a samurai's honour. The strict training that a samurai received was passed on from one generation to the next.

Around 1560, samurai armour was made from plates of metal tied together with silk threads.

WHAT WAS THE INDUS VALLEY CIVILIZATION ?

INDIA'S first major civilization flourished for 1,000 years from about 2500 BC along the Indus Valley. Its great cities, Mohenjo-daro and Harappa, were ruled by priests rather than kings. It is thought that the cities were eventually abandoned because of environmental changes.

The map shows the extent of Hinduism today. Hindu pilgrims bathe in the River Ganges.

HOW DID HINDUISM BEGIN ?

HINDUISM developed from the religion that the Aryans brought to India with them in about 1500 BC. Its beliefs and practices are based on the Vedas, a collection of hymns (thought to refer to actual historical events) that Aryan scholars had completed by about 800 BC. Hinduism is concerned with living a good life in the hope of being rewarded in the next.

WHAT IS SANSKRIT ?

SANSKRIT is the ancient language originally spoken by the Aryans, and in which the early Hindu literature (including the Vedas) was written. From the 5th century BC it came to be understood throughout India. It is still sometimes used for writing poetry and drama.

WHO WERE THE ARYANS ?

THE Aryan people were nomadic herdsmen, probably from central Asia, who invaded India from the north in about 1500 BC. They occupied the valleys of the Indus and then the Ganges rivers, and forced the original inhabitants, the Dravidians, to move south.

WHEN WAS INDIA FIRST UNITED BY ONE EMPIRE ?

IN 321 BC the empire of Chandragupta Maurya came to power. From its capital in present-day Patna, it spread across northern India. Chandragupta's grandson, Ashoka, hugely extended the empire until it unified the subcontinent, stretching for about 1,600 km from north to south, and 3,200 km from east to west.

WHAT ARE STUPAS ?

STUPAS are circular monuments of the Buddhist faith found all over India. The original ones contained relics of the Buddha.

In Sri Lanka a great procession is held every year to honour a holy relic, the Sacred Tooth of the Buddha; it is carried on the back of an elephant.

Rang Mahal, the Painted Palace

WHO WAS THE BUDDHA ?

A YOUNG Indian prince called Siddhartha Gautama lived 2,500 years ago. He was so upset by the poverty of his people that he decided to give up his riches, live simply and search for the inner meaning of life. He became known as the Buddha, which means the "Enlightened One", and set about teaching what he had learnt. He called his teaching the "Middle Way", but it has become known as Buddhism.

Diwan-i-Am, Hall of Public Audience

Moti Masjid, the Pearl Mosque

The emerald-canopied Peacock throne

Diwan-i-Khas, Hall of Private Audience

The Red Fort in Delhi, a magnificent example of Mogul architecture, contains decorated pavilions, marble palaces, courtyards and galleries within its 30-m high, red-sandstone walls.

WHO WERE THE MOGULS?

THE Moguls were Muslim warriors from Afghanistan who invaded northern India in 1526. The empire they established lasted for more than 300 years. The first Mogul emperor was called Babur. Under later emperors the Moguls conquered all of India.

The magnificent Taj Mahal in Agra was built by the Mogul emperor Shah Jahan in 1631.

HOW LONG DID THE BRITISH RULE INDIA?

BY THE early 19th century India was effectively under British control. India gained independence in 1947.

WHAT DID THE MOGULS BUILD?

THE Moguls built some of the most magnificent palaces, fortresses and mosques in the world. One of the most famous examples is the deserted city of Fatehpur Sikri, near Agra, which was built in 1570 by the Emperor Akbar as his new capital at the height of the empire's splendour. It was occupied for only 16 years. Equally impressive is the Red Fort in Delhi, built by Emperor Shah Jahan about 1638. He moved his capital to Delhi from Agra. The palace is surrounded by a great fortified citadel.

WHAT IS THE CASTE SYSTEM?

THE Indian caste system is Hindu in origin and has been part of the culture since about 1500 BC. It divides society into ranks, each with its own rules of behaviour. A person is born into the same caste as their parents.

WHAT WAS THE RAJ?

IN 1876 Britain's Queen Victoria became Empress of India. The British government of India was called the Raj, and was based first in Calcutta, then New Delhi.

DID HINDUS ALWAYS HAVE LOTS OF GODS?

THERE have always been lots of Hindu gods and goddesses, but they all represent different parts of one all-powerful god. Stories of adventures developed around the gods, who were sometimes said to come to Earth.

Ganesh is the Hindu elephant-headed god, the son of the god Shiva and his wife Parvati.

WHO ARE THE TUAREG?

THE people north of the Sahara are relatives of Middle Eastern people. They can be divided into three main groups: the Berbers, the Egyptians and the Cushites of the Red Sea Coast. One group related to the Berbers is the Tuareg. Traditionally they lived in the west and central Sahara Desert in hand-woven tents, and herded goats. Today many Tuareg live in towns.

A man of the Tuareg people of northern Africa. His face is covered and he wears loose cotton clothes against the heat of the Sun.

WHAT WAS THE NOK CULTURE?

THE Nok culture belonged to the village communities of central Nigeria. By 400 BC they had developed the ability to smelt iron, and they also produced magnificent terracotta sculptures of men and animals.

WAS ONE LANGUAGE EVER SPOKEN ALL OVER AFRICA?

THERE have always been hundreds of languages in Africa. Some developed sounds, such as clicking noises, used only in Africa, and many existed for centuries without being written down.

WHAT WERE THE TRADITIONAL RELIGIONS?

BEFORE missionaries took Christianity and Islam to Africa, most people worshipped many gods and the spirits of their ancestors. Animals were sometimes sacrificed to the gods.

WHERE WAS CARTHAGE?

CARTHAGE was a city on the north African coast, near modern Tunis. In the 3rd century BC it was powerful enough to fight major battles with the Romans. After 146 BC it was defeated and taken over by Rome.

From the late 15th century, the Portuguese dominated trade with the Arabs on Africa's east coast.

WHAT WAS THE EAST COAST TRADE?

EARLY traders came to the east coast of Africa from many parts of the world to buy gold and ivory, ostrich feathers, wild animals and rare woods like ebony. They also came to buy human slaves. The east coast was an important trading area for the Romans, and it continued to be important until the 17th century.

WHAT WERE EARLY AFRICAN VILLAGES LIKE?

IN MANY parts of rural Africa, village houses look the same today as they have always looked. Wooden poles are bound together to make a circular structure. The walls are made of mud, and the roofs thatched with grass. In some villages the houses are long and rectangular, and the flat roofs are covered with earth. The outsides of the walls are often decorated with bright colours.

The women of the village would pound the local grain to make flour.

The high stone walls of Great Zimbabwe were decorated with posts carved with creatures.

WHAT WAS GREAT ZIMBABWE?

DURING the 7th century AD, kingdoms grew up in a rich gold-mining area around the Zambezi River. In the eastern part (modern Zimbabwe and Mozambique), many stone-walled enclosures, or "royal courts", were built for the kings. They were called *zimbabwes*. The most famous is Great Zimbabwe in Zimbabwe, built by the Shona people. Work began in the early 11th century and went on for some 400 years. The palace was surrounded by a huge stone wall. Outside, a city with a population of about 10,000 people developed. It is not known why the city was abandoned in the 15th century, but it may have been because the soil could no longer maintain the population.

WHAT EARLY AFRICAN BUILDINGS HAVE SURVIVED?

AT KILWA, on the east coast, some 14th-century buildings have been excavated. These rare finds survived because they were made from locally cut coral, rather than wood, earth and grass.

WHAT IS A KINSHIP GROUP?

AFRICAN society is organized into kinship groups, called lineages. These consist of all the descendants of one original common ancestor.

WHO CARVED CHURCHES OUT OF SOLID ROCK?

AT THE town of Roha (now Lalibela) in Ethiopia, the 12th-century King Lalibela built thirteen beautiful churches cut from solid rock. They stand below ground level, some at 12 m high.

WHO WAS SHAKA?

SHAKA was king of the Zulu people of South Africa. During the early 19th century, his strong army conquered the neighboring peoples, creating a large empire.

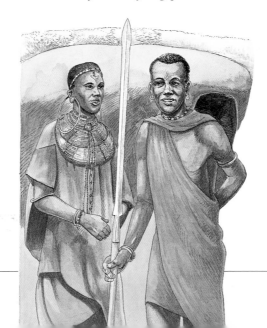

Masai warriors of Kenya still dress in the traditional way and carry long spears.

WHAT WAS THE AXUMITE EMPIRE?

THE Axumite empire, which stretched from the Red Sea inland across northern Ethiopia to the River Nile, was a major trading power from the 1st to the 7th centuries AD. The kings erected over 100 tall, solid-granite monoliths, called stelae, above the royal tombs as symbols of their power. Some were over 30 m high.

The 23-m tall stele of King Ezana in Axum is carved with a door and nine windows.

WHAT WAS THE KINGDOM OF BENIN FAMOUS FOR?

THE kingdom of Benin, in West Africa, was at the height of its power in the 14th and 15th centuries. It was famous for casting beautiful bronze and brass statues. Most of its bronzes were for ceremonial use.

WHEN WAS CHRISTIANITY FIRST INTRODUCED?

THERE have been Christians in Africa since shortly after the death of Christ. By the 2nd century AD, the Christian Coptic Church in Egypt was strong, and it has continued up to the present day.

DID ALL AFRICANS COME FROM ONE GROUP OF PEOPLES?

THERE have always been many different peoples in Africa, just like in Europe. Some are really tall, for example the Masai of Kenya, the Dinka of Sudan and the Tutsi of Rwanda. The Mbuti, whose origins are unknown, are some of Africa's smallest people. The peoples all have their own histories and cultures.

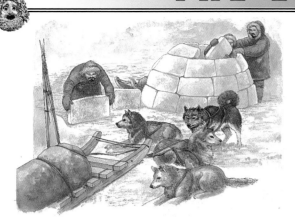

The early Inuit arrived about 2500–1800 BC. They were nomadic hunters who used blocks of packed ice to build snow houses as temporary shelters.

WHERE DID THE FIRST PEOPLE TO LIVE IN AMERICA COME FROM ?

THE first people to live in America originally came from Asia about 15,000 years ago, when large parts of the Earth's surface were covered in ice. At this time, Asia and America were joined together by a bridge of land and ice that people could walk across.

WHAT DID THE INUIT WEAR ?

IN THE frozen north, warm clothing was essential for survival. The Inuit wore sealskins in summer and caribou skins in winter, stitched with gut thread.

The early Americans hunted with stone-tipped spears, and made their tents and clothes from animal skins.

WHY DID PEOPLE MIGRATE TO AMERICA ?

THE first people to arrive in America across the land bridge from Asia were hunters, who probably went there following herds of animals. They hunted large animals called mammoths and mastodons, which were adapted to the cold weather. They also caught and ate fish, and picked wild plants such as herbs, nuts and berries.

DID NATIVE AMERICANS LIVE IN GROUPS ?

NATIVE North Americans lived in groups, but the size varied a lot from people to people. The Inuit people who lived in the far north stayed in small family groups of about 10 to 20 people. Other groups, like those living on the Great Plains of North America, had thousands of members. They were ruled by chiefs chosen because they were brave or clever.

A warrior from the Great Plains of North America. He is dressed in full battle clothes and is carrying his weapons.

WHO WERE MEDICINE MEN ?

IF A Native American was sick, a high-ranking man of the community, called a medicine man, would call upon the spirits to heal the person. He also made medicines from plants and herbs.

WHAT GAMES DID THE NATIVE AMERICANS PLAY ?

ALL sorts of games were popular, including archery, running races, wrestling and a hoop and pole game. The latter involved two men rolling a hoop covered with a net along the ground. They threw darts at the hoop, scoring points according to where they hit the hoop or net.

DID EARLY NORTH AND SOUTH AMERICANS WRITE ?

MOST early Americans did not write using letters, but Native Americans of North America and the Maya and Aztecs of Central America used a form of picture-writing, called "glyphs". The Incas of Peru, in South America, tied knots in strings called "quipu" to make messages and to count.

WHO WERE THE BURIAL-MOUND BUILDERS?

FROM about 1000 BC, a group of Native Americans settled around the Mississippi River in North America. As well as gathering wild plants for food, they also grew crops on the fertile land, and their culture prospered. They built huge earthworks, some as enclosures and some for important ceremonies. From AD 800, Mississippian settlements were larger than any built before. Temples and houses were built on top of the mounds, and important people were buried under the temple floors.

The ordinary people of the Mississippian cities were buried in cemeteries. Pottery, shell and copper ornaments were put in the graves.

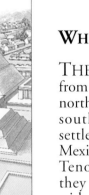

WHEN DID EUROPEANS FIRST VISIT AMERICA?

THE first Europeans to reach America were the Vikings, who sailed there from Greenland about 1,000 years ago.

WHO WERE THE MAIN AZTEC GODS?

HUITZILOPOCHTLI was god of the Sun and of war; Tlaloc was the rain god; and Quetzalcoatl was the god of wind and fertility.

WHO WERE THE AZTECS?

THE Aztecs claimed to be descended from a nomadic group of people from northern Mexico. These people moved south in the 12th century AD and settled in an area of lakes in central Mexico, where they built their capital, Tenochtitlan. By the 15th century they had created a powerful empire with a strong army. All boys over the age of 15 had to train to be warriors.

Large, stone pyramid-temples dominated the Aztec city of Tenochtitlan. Sacrificial heads were displayed on a skull rack (bottom right).

The ruins of the Inca city of Machu Picchu occupy a rocky ridge surrounded by mountains.

WHY DID THE AZTECS MAKE HUMAN SACRIFICES?

THE Aztecs believed that the world would end unless their gods were given human blood. They usually sacrificed people they had taken captive in war. Offerings to the rain god included human sacrifice.

WHO WERE THE INCAS?

THE Incas lived in the mountains of Peru in South America. From Cuzco, the capital, they conquered the surrounding lands and created a huge empire that lasted from about AD 1400 to 1533. They were highly skilled architects, engineers and stonemasons. Machu Picchu, a city high in the mountains to the northwest of Cuzco, consisted of 300 stone buildings arranged around a central plaza; a stone aqueduct supplied it with fresh water. A network of bridges and roads linked all parts of the empire. The emperor was so powerful that his people believed he was descended from their Sun god.

WHAT IS ISLAM ?

ISLAM is a religion that was founded in Arabia in the 7th century AD by the Prophet Mohammed (c.570–632). The word "Islam" means "surrender to the will of Allah [God]". Its followers are called Muslims. The many different Muslim groups within the religion are bound together by their faith in one God. After Mohammed's death, the Muslims swept out of Arabia and conquered a huge empire.

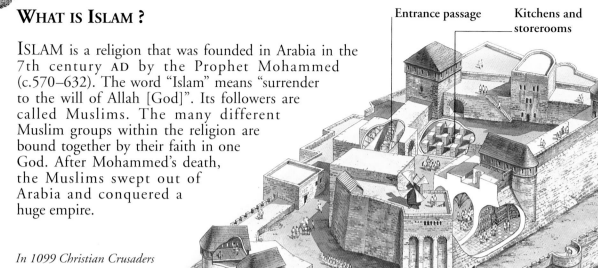

Entrance passage   Kitchens and storerooms   Aqueduct

In 1099 Christian Crusaders recaptured the Holy Land from the Muslims. Krak des Chevaliers was one of many castles built to hold off Muslim counterattacks.

These are the areas of Islamic faith today. Islam's holiest cities are Mecca, Medina and Jerusalem.

HOW BIG WAS THE ISLAMIC EMPIRE AT ITS GREATEST ?

FROM the 7th century, Muslim armies conquered the eastern part of the old Roman empire and defeated the old empire of Persia. They went on to conquer North Africa and northern India. At its greatest, the Islamic empire stretched from Spain in the west to the borders of China in the east. Today, there are many Islamic countries, and over 1,300 million Muslims in the world.

WHO WERE THE SELJUKS ?

THIS Turkish dynasty controlled most of Central Asia and Iraq from the 11th to the 13th centuries. Two of their great capitals were Isfahan and Baghdad. In Iraq they assumed the title of Sultan, or sovereign of a Muslim territory.

WHAT SORT OF ARMOUR DID ISLAMIC SOLDIERS WEAR ?

EARLY Islamic soldiers adopted the same armour as their Persian enemies: chain mail coats and lamellar armour made from numerous small, pierced iron plates that were laced together. Simple conical iron helmets and hardened leather shields gave extra protection. From the 14th century, mail-and-plate armour was worn on the body, arms and legs.

WHAT IS A JIHAD ?

THE word jihad comes from the Arabic word for conflict, and is used to mean a holy war waged by Muslims against people who do not believe in Islam.

A 15th-century Turkish horseman would have been heavily armed. He and his horse wore mail-and-plate armour.

WHERE IS MECCA?

THE city of Mecca is in western Saudi Arabia. It lies in a narrow valley about 65 km from the Red Sea coast. Mecca was the birthplace of Mohammed, and is the holiest of all Muslim cities.

WHERE DO MUSLIMS PRAY?

MUSLIMS usually pray in holy buildings called mosques. They pray facing towards Mecca. The largest mosques have an open court surrounded by covered arches, and a well or fountain in the middle to provide water for washing before prayer. They also have a tower called a minaret, from which the people are called to prayer five times a day.

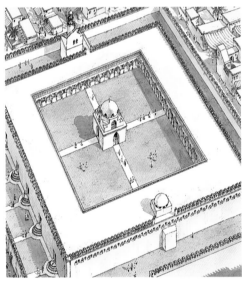

The mosque stands in a courtyard where pupils are taught the Koran. Near the entrance is a minaret.

WHAT DO ISLAMIC DESIGNS LOOK LIKE?

THE larger mosques are often decorated on the outside with elaborate designs that do not include people or animals. The intricate intertwining leaves, flowers and geometrical designs are described as arabesques. Passages from the Koran are often written around the walls of mosques, too, painted on brightly coloured ceramic tiles.

WHO WERE THE MAMLUKS?

THE Mamluks were two dynasties of freed slaves in Egypt and Syria, reigning from 1250 to 1517. They controlled Mecca and Medina, and were probably the greatest builders of any Islamic dynasty.

WHAT IS THE HAJJ?

ALL Muslim men must try to make the "Hajj", or pilgrimage to Mecca, at least once in their lifetime. When they reach Mecca's Grand Mosque, they pass seven times around the Ka'aba, a chamber with a holy black stone in one corner. It culminates in the Feast of Sacrifices, in which every Muslim family that can afford to slaughters a sheep.

WHAT IS THE KORAN?

THE Koran is the Muslims' Holy Book. Its 114 chapters contain the teachings of Mohammed as revealed to him by God. The most important teaching is that there is only one God.

Islamic designs are made up of beautiful swirling patterns, colours and lines.

These are letters in the Arabic alphabet. Arabic is written from right to left.

WHAT IS THE LANGUAGE OF THE KORAN?

BECAUSE the Islamic empire was so big, many different languages were spoken. But the most important was Arabic. This was the language spoken by Mohammed and the one in which the Koran was written. The Koran was not allowed to be translated into other languages, so all Muslims had to learn how to speak Arabic.

WHAT WERE EMIRS AND VIZIERS?

EMIR was the title given to great military commanders, particularly under the Seljuks and Mamluks. They governed large provinces and held high positions at court. The government was carried out by the vizier and his staff.

WHAT WAS A SIEGE ?

IF AN army was unable to take an enemy castle quickly by force, it might try to starve the people inside into surrendering. This was known as a siege. Because the risk of a siege was great in the Middle Ages, many castles had their own wells (for water) and plentiful stores of food so that they could hold out for a long time if necessary. If the siege failed, the attacking army might resort to force again.

After unsuccessfully laying siege to a castle, this army is preparing to take it by force.

WHO WERE KNIGHTS ?

KNIGHTS were soldiers on horseback who fought for a king or a prince. At first anyone could become a knight, but gradually it became an honour given to the rich. Only wealthy men could afford chain mail, a sword and a trained war horse.

WHY WERE CASTLES BUILT ?

CASTLES were great strongholds built to give protection from enemy armies. They were often built on hilltops that gave a commanding view all round. From the battlements soldiers could shower the heads of their attackers with deadly weapons. Castles also served as homes for kings, princes or great lords and their families and servants. Larger castles sometimes had so many people living inside that they were like small towns.

A cross section of Rochester Castle, England, with its strong outer wall surrounding the main castle, or keep.

WHAT DID SOLDIERS WEAR ?

HISTORIANS know from the Bayeux Tapestry, which chronicles the Norman invasion of Britain in 1066, that Norman knights wore long chain mail shirts. These were made from hundreds of small iron rings linked together. Gradually steel plates were added to armour for greater protection, and by 1400 knights were covered from head to foot in plate armour.

This German knight of about 1480 is wearing full battle armour, which weighed about 20 kg.

WHEN WERE THE MIDDLE AGES ?

THE Middle Ages was a period in the history of Europe and the Middle East that lasted for over 1,000 years, from about AD 500 to 1500. Things that were made in, or belong to, the Middle Ages are called "medieval".

WHAT IS THE BAYEUX TAPESTRY ?

IN 1066 William the Conqueror invaded England. The Bayeux Tapestry records his victory in pictures and words on a piece of linen over 70 m long and 50 cm wide. The tapestry is kept in a museum at Bayeux, France.

DID EVERYONE GO TO SCHOOL ?

IN THE Middle Ages only a few schools existed, run by the Church. Learning was mostly restricted to boys who were going to become monks or priests. Most people, rich and poor, could not read or write.

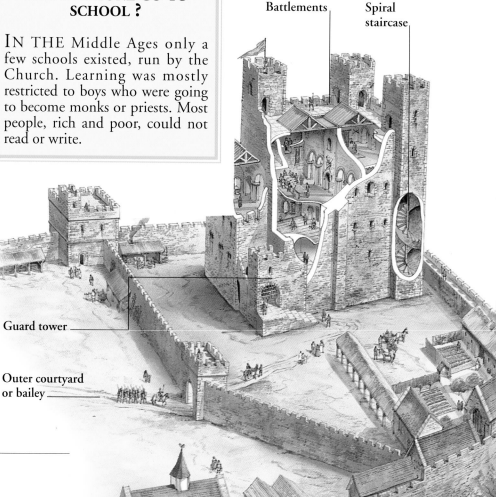

Battlements

Spiral staircase

Guard tower

Outer courtyard or bailey

WHAT WERE THE CRUSADES ?

THE Crusades were religious wars fought between the Muslims of the Middle East and Christian Crusaders from Europe. They began in 1096 and lasted for about 200 years. The Crusaders tried to capture the Holy Land from the Muslims, but they were eventually defeated.

WHAT WAS A JOUST ?

IN THE 1100s, tournaments were held as a form of rehearsal for war. Mounted knights would take part in mock battles. Later there were jousts, in which two knights, one on each side of a barrier, tried to knock the other one off his horse using a lance.

WHAT DID PEOPLE EAT ?

MOST people lived in the country and grew their own food: for example, apples, oats, peas, beans and barley. Poor people ate mostly vegetables and bread. Meat was too expensive. The rich ate mostly meat. Fish was always eaten on Fridays, and salted meat was eaten in winter. Fresh meat like chicken, beef, wild deer and pork was eaten in the summer. Everyone, including children, drank beer.

Country people brought eggs, cheese, fruit, vegetables and livestock to town to sell at market.

In the Middle Ages many of the big towns and cities, such as Paris, were built on rivers.

WHAT WERE THE TOWNS LIKE ?

TOWNS were usually very crowded, dirty, smelly and unhealthy. In the centre stood the marketplace, the main church or cathedral and other important buildings. Small shops opened onto the streets, and craftsmen sat and worked in full view of the passers-by. The houses were tall and narrow, with the top floors jutting out over the streets below. Rotting heaps of rubbish filled the streets.

WHO WERE THE TEMPLARS ?

THE Templars were the Knights of the Temple of Solomon, a Christian order founded about 1120 by some French knights. They became a fighting force and took part in the Crusades.

WHO WAS MARCO POLO ?

MARCO Polo (1254–1324) was an Italian traveller. When he was 17, he journeyed with his father and uncle to the court of Kublai Khan, ruler of the Mongols. Polo was the first European to travel across the entire width of Asia.

WHAT WAS THE DOMESDAY BOOK ?

THIS book was a great survey of England ordered by William the Conqueror. Completed in 1086, it included details of the estates of the king's tenants, and was used to collect taxes.

WHAT WAS THE RENAISSANCE ?

THE Renaissance, which literally means "rebirth", is generally thought to have begun in Italy during the 14th century and to have ended in the late 16th century. The word is also applied to the new cultural styles in art, architecture and learning that developed during this time, and which were greatly influenced by ancient Greece and Rome. The Renaissance was also a time of exploration and of scientific discovery.

King Henry VIII of England spent vast sums of money on new palaces.

HOW DID THE RENAISSANCE RULERS DISPLAY THEIR POWER ?

MANY of Europe's rulers became extremely powerful during the Renaissance. Some countries, like England, were kingdoms ruled by kings and queens. In Italy and Germany, nobles ruled over small, separate states. The power and riches of these kings, princes and nobles drew many people to their courts. Rulers all over Europe tried to outshine each other by building elaborate palaces, collecting works of art and holding pageants. The more beautiful his palaces and cities, the more powerful and magnificent a prince or king was thought to be.

WHO INVENTED PRINTING ?

IN 1453 a German goldsmith called Johannes Gutenberg invented the printing press. Until then, all books had been written by hand. The printing press could produce thousands of books quickly and cheaply.

WHY WAS UNDERSTANDING PERSPECTIVE IMPORTANT ?

PERSPECTIVE is a method of representing objects on a two-dimensional surface so that they appear three-dimensional. Once artists had grasped the rules of perspective, it was possible for them to reproduce accurately landscapes and buildings. Many Renaissance artists wanted to convey the perfection of God by portraying the perfect proportions of a building or the human form.

WHY WERE PRINTED BOOKS SO IMPORTANT ?

PRINTED books spread the new ideas of the time to ordinary people, and gave scholars access to books not previously available.

WHO WERE THE GREAT RENAISSANCE ARTISTS ?

BOTTICELLI, Michelangelo, Leonardo da Vinci, Raphael and Titian were just a few of the great artists of the time.

HOW WERE PEOPLE EDUCATED ?

IN RICH homes, boys (and only rarely girls) were taught by visiting teachers. Boys could go on to study at university.

WHAT WAS A RENAISSANCE PALACE LIKE ?

THE rulers of Renaissance Europe lived in magnificent palaces. In Italy, which had been the centre of the Roman empire, there were many ancient buildings still standing. Renaissance architects studied them and began to design new buildings using columns, domes and rounded arches. The new classical style of architecture was copied all over Europe.

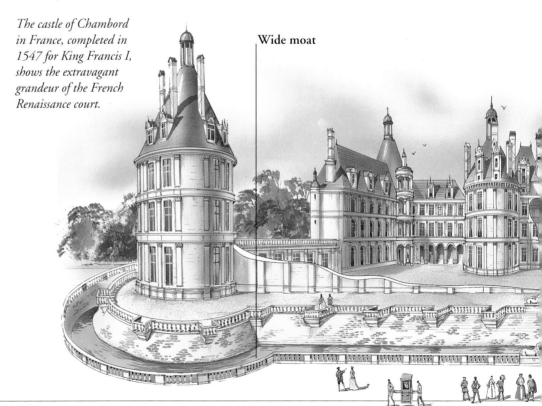

The castle of Chambord in France, completed in 1547 for King Francis I, shows the extravagant grandeur of the French Renaissance court.

Wide moat

WHO WERE THE GREAT EXPLORERS OF THE AGE?

EARLY in the 15th century, explorers from Europe went to look for new opportunities for trade. The Portuguese, including Vasco da Gama, sailed east, exploring the west coast of Africa and then rounding the southern tip of Africa on route to India. The Spanish, or those in the employment of Spain, sailed west to America: Christopher Columbus in 1492 and Amerigo Vespucci in 1499. The Italian navigator John Cabot sailed from England in 1497 and reached Newfoundland. The first circumnavigation of the Earth was made by a Portuguese, Ferdinand Magellan, in the service of Spain (1519–21).

In 1497 John and Sebastian Cabot set sail from England in the Matthew *and landed in Newfoundland, North America.*

WERE MANY RENAISSANCE CHURCHES BUILT?

CHURCHES were built all over Europe at this time. Some medieval churches were pulled down and rebuilt in the new classical style. One of the first new churches was Florence Cathedral, Italy. Its huge dome was designed by an architect called Brunelleschi.

As well as designing Florence Cathedral, Brunelleschi also built this chapel there, with its beautiful internal dome.

WHEN WERE THE ITALIAN WARS?

IN 1494, a large French army crossed into Italy to claim Naples. This began a series of power struggles, called the Italian Wars, which lasted until 1559 and involved Spain, Germany, Switzerland and the Italian states. Italian influences, brought back by returning armies, came to dominate French cultural life.

WHO WERE THE MEDICI?

THE Medici were the leading family of Florence, the richest of the cities of northern Italy. As well as ruling the city, they established banks all over Europe and lent money to kings and princes to pay for art, buildings, trade and wars.

WHAT WAS THE REFORMATION?

IN THE early 16th century a religious movement began. It was called the Reformation because people wanted to reform the Roman Catholic Church. They began to criticize the popes for their wealth, pleasure-seeking and power. A German priest named Martin Luther accused the Catholic Church of corruption and wickedness. The people who protested against the beliefs of the Catholic Church established their own Church, later known as the Protestant Church.

John Calvin was a Frenchman who carried on the reforming work of Martin Luther.

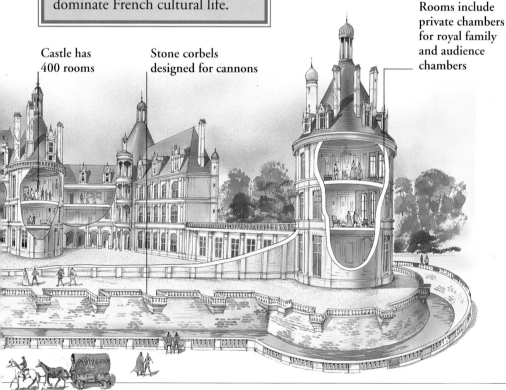

Castle has 400 rooms

Stone corbels designed for cannons

Rooms include private chambers for royal family and audience chambers

WHAT CAUSED THE ENGLISH CIVIL WAR?

THIS was a war between King Charles I of England and his parliament. For many years before war broke out there was a growing struggle between the king and parliament. Charles believed that it should not try to take away his powers. But some members of parliament began to demand a greater part in running the country. This power struggle led to civil war breaking out in 1642. In 1649 Charles was executed. Parliament won the war in 1651.

Parliamentarian soldiers on horseback confront supporters of the king, called Royalists.

WHO WAS OLIVER CROMWELL?

DURING the English Civil War (1642–51), Oliver Cromwell led parliament's army against King Charles. After he won, he set up a republic called the Commonwealth, which ended in 1660.

WHEN WAS THE FRENCH REVOLUTION?

THE French Revolution started in 1789. It began as a movement to change the way the king of France ruled. But it quickly became a bloody revolution against the nobles of France.

WHO WAS NAPOLEON BONAPARTE?

NAPOLEON Bonaparte was a soldier during the French Revolution. He became a general in 1796 and rose quickly to power. Napoleon made himself Emperor of France in 1804 and rapidly conquered most of Europe. He was finally defeated by the Duke of Wellington at the Battle of Waterloo in 1815. The British exiled him to the island of St Helena, where he died in 1821.

Napoleon Bonaparte led his army into battle with the tricolore, the "three-coloured" French flag, created during the French Revolution.

WHEN WAS THE AMERICAN WAR OF INDEPENDENCE?

THE United States became an independent nation in 1783. Until then it had been part of the British empire. Large ports on the east coast of North America, like New York and Boston, were growing very rich from trade, and the British government taxed the American people. They resented these taxes, and sometimes attacked the British tax collectors. War broke out between the two sides in 1775. In 1781 the British were defeated at the Battle of Yorktown and they surrendered.

A Rattlesnake flag of the American rebels carried the warning "Don't tread on me".

The American War of Independence started at Lexington, Massachusetts, when 70 American soldiers faced 700 British redcoats.

WHAT WAS THE DECLARATION OF INDEPENDENCE?

THIS document of 1776 listed the Americans' complaints against King George III of Britain. It states that all people are born equal and that governments must ensure their freedom and safety. If governments fail to do this, the people can overthrow them.

WHAT WAS THE AMERICAN CIVIL WAR?

IN THE middle of the 19th century, tensions grew between the northern and southern states of America. The industrialized north was rich, while the south depended on cotton-growing and slavery. Many people in the north were against slavery, and bitter arguments broke out between the two sides. War started in 1861, when the southern states broke away from the rest of the country to form the Confederate States of America. The Confederates were defeated in 1865 by the northern Unionists.

A Unionist soldier, carrying the flag of the United States, defends his flag from attack by the southern Confederates.

WHEN WAS THE RUSSIAN REVOLUTION?

THE Russian Revolution broke out in March 1917 because the people were desperate for change. Many Russians were being killed during the First World War, and many more people at home were starving. Both the army and the people turned against their emperor, Tsar Nicholas II, whom they blamed. A large crowd demonstrated against him in Petrograd (St Petersburg). The army refused to crush this rebellion, and the tsar was forced to give up his throne. In November 1917, the Communists seized power and Nicholas II and his family were shot.

On November 7th (October 25th in the old Russian calendar), armed workers attacked the government buildings in Petrograd.

WHO WAS ABRAHAM LINCOLN?

ABRAHAM Lincoln became President of the United States in 1861, the same year that the American Civil War started. He is famous for bringing in a law that freed all slaves. He was assassinated at the end of the war, a few days after the surrender of the Confederates.

WHO WAS JOSEF STALIN?

AFTER the death of Vladimir Lenin, Russia's first Communist leader, Josef Stalin seized power. He was leader of the Soviet Union until his death in 1953. His secret police force arrested, tortured and executed millions of people whom he suspected of being anti-Communist.

WHO WAS MAO ZEDONG?

MAO ZEDONG was a founder of the Chinese Communist Party, and its leader from 1936. He organized the war of liberation (1937–49), which his army won. From 1949 he ruled the People's Republic of China through the Communist Party.

The red flag of the People's Republic of China was based on the Red Flag of the former Soviet Union.

WHAT IS COMMUNISM?

COMMUNISM is a set of beliefs based on the ideas of a German called Karl Marx, who was born in 1818. It states that there should be equality in society, with no social classes or private ownership, and that all means of production (industries) should be owned by the workers.

WHAT WAS THE INDUSTRIAL REVOLUTION ?

IN THE early 1700s in Britain, most people lived and worked on farms in the countryside. But over the next hundred years, Britain was transformed from a farming to an industrial nation using new machinery. From Britain the Industrial Revolution spread to the rest of Europe and across the world. It was called the Industrial Revolution because people's working lives were completely changed or "revolutionized".

Steam provided the power for many of the new machines. The Rocket *was the first commercial steam train.*

WHY WERE CANALS MADE ?

IN THE 1700s, the cheapest way to transport heavy goods was by barge. But there wasn't always a suitable river connecting the inland towns with the ports, so canals (artificial waterways) were made instead.

DID CHILDREN WORK THE NEW MACHINES ?

YOUNG children from poor families often worked long days in terrible conditions to earn a little money. They operated many of the machines and pulled heavy coal trucks out of mines.

One of the new farming inventions was the seed drill, which planted grain seeds much more quickly than a person could by hand.

WHAT POWERED THE NEW MACHINES ?

THE early machines were powered by running water. Then a Scotsman called James Watt discovered how to make steam engines to drive the machines of the Industrial Revolution.

WHO WAS JETHRO TULL ?

JETHRO Tull was an English agriculturalist. In 1701 he developed a drill that mechanically sowed seeds. He contributed to the Agricultural Revolution, which enabled farmers to produce food more cheaply and efficiently. New machines, better crops and special animal breeding all helped revolutionize farming methods in the 18th century.

WHAT DID THE MACHINES MAKE ?

NEW machines were invented that helped spinners and weavers to make cloth much more quickly and cheaply. This meant that people could now wear cheaper wool and cotton clothes. In 1709 an inventor called Abraham Darby discovered a new, cheap way to make good-quality iron. Iron was used to make everything from saucepans to machines, bridges, steam ships and railways. Iron and, later, steel were also used to make guns. This fast and cheap way of making goods is called mass production.

Cheap clothing, iron and weapons were just some of the products of the Industrial Revolution.

WHO WERE THE LUDDITES ?

THE Luddites were a group of workers from northern England. They set about destroying the machinery introduced during the Industrial Revolution, because the new machines had put them out of work. When caught, they were hanged or sent to the penal colony of Australia.

WHAT WAS COAL USED FOR ?

PEOPLE had used coal to heat their homes for a very long time. But during the Industrial Revolution, more of it was needed to heat water to make steam, which ran the new engines. A type of coal called coke was also used for making iron. Deep mines were dug to extract the coal.

The new factories and workers' houses were mostly built of red brick.

WHO WORKED IN THE NEW CLOTH FACTORIES ?

BEFORE the Industrial Revolution, cloth was woven on hand looms by villagers. The new mechanized looms were too big for people's homes, so huge factories were built for them. The villagers were forced to work in the factories because they could not compete at home.

WHERE DID THE FACTORY WORKERS LIVE ?

TOWNS grew up around the factories so that the factory workers could live close to their work. They lived in small, brick houses built in terraces. The backyards of one street backed straight on to the backyards of the next, and were often in the shadow of the factories' smoking chimneys.

WAS THERE A REVOLUTION IN TRANSPORT ?

AS THE Industrial Revolution progressed, iron was used in place of wood to build ships, and in 1802 the first working steam ship, the *Charlotte Dundas*, was launched. But the greatest change came with the invention of the steam train in 1804; eventually there was a network of railways across Europe and beyond.

WHAT WERE TRADE UNIONS ?

TRADE unions were organized groups of factory workers who came together to demand better working conditions. They were often forced to work up to 16 hours a day for low wages, using dangerous machinery.

WHAT WERE THE TOWNS LIKE ?

THE towns were overcrowded and dirty, and the air and rivers were polluted by the factories. Disease spread quickly. Gradually new laws were introduced to improve working conditions, and hospitals were built.

The Great Britain, *built in 1843, was the first really large ship to be made wholly from iron. She was powered by steam.*

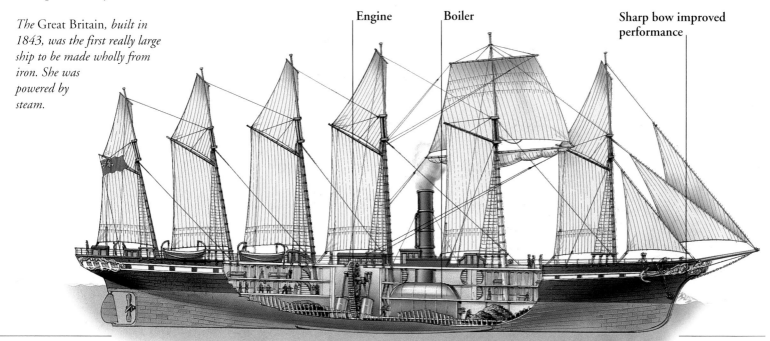

Engine   Boiler   Sharp bow improved performance

WHICH COUNTRIES FOUGHT IN THE FIRST WORLD WAR ?

IN 1914, France, Britain and Russia (the Allies) formed an alliance against Germany and Austria-Hungary (the Central Powers). Other countries decided to join one side or the other, depending on which they thought would benefit them the most. Germany was joined by Turkey and Bulgaria. The Allies were joined by Italy, Japan, Greece, Portugal and Romania. Later on, in 1917, America entered the war on the side of the Allies.

A German Albatross and a French Spad in a dogfight in 1918. Pilots who shot down many aircraft were called "Aces".

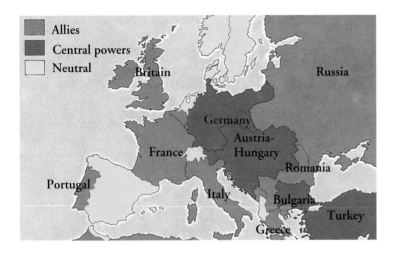

Allies
Central powers
Neutral

Britain
Russia
Germany
France
Austria-Hungary
Romania
Portugal
Italy
Bulgaria
Turkey
Greece

Spain, Switzerland, Albania, the Netherlands, Denmark, Norway and Sweden all remained neutral in the First World War.

WHAT FIGHTING METHODS WERE USED IN THE FIRST WORLD WAR ?

FAST fighter planes like the Sopwith Camel were invented; these attacked enemy planes using machine guns, which could fire hundreds of bullets a minute. Battles in the air were known as dogfights. Tanks armed with guns were also used for the first time. Soldiers on land fought with rifles fixed with bayonets.

WHAT WAS A ZEPPELIN ?

A ZEPPELIN was a huge airship, filled with hydrogen to make it rise. The first zeppelin was built in Germany in 1900. From 1915, they were used by the German army to make bombing raids on England.

WHEN DID THE FIRST WORLD WAR END ?

EACH side tried to wear the other down with constant attacks. By 1918 Germany was running out of men and supplies. It realized it could not win and surrendered on November 11th.

HOW MANY SOLDIERS LOST THEIR LIVES IN THE FIRST WORLD WAR ?

OVER 70 million men were mobilized, or assembled, to fight in the war. The total number of soldiers who died on active service is estimated at over 9 million.

WHAT WAS TRENCH WARFARE ?

TRENCH warfare was a new form of fighting that took place during the First World War. Soldiers on both sides dug deep ditches called trenches. Inside, they were protected from enemy machine-gun fire, and could fire at the other side as they advanced, charging across the open ground between the trenches.

The main area of fighting in France and Belgium was called the Western Front, where soldiers fought from trenches.

WERE THE WORLD WARS FOUGHT AT SEA ?

BEFORE the First World War started, Germany and Britain both built up their navies in an "arms race". The British built a battleship called the *Dreadnought* in 1905, the world's most powerful ship. Submarines were also built. From 1915, the Germans used submarines called U-boats to sink British ships in the Atlantic Ocean. During the Second World War, they sank thousands of tonnes of merchant shipping, preventing vital supplies from reaching Britain.

A Second World War German U-boat, armed with torpedoes.

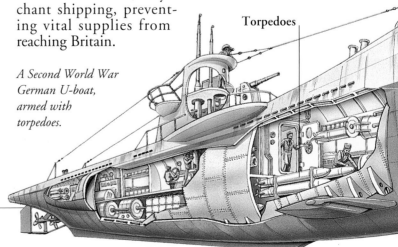

Torpedoes

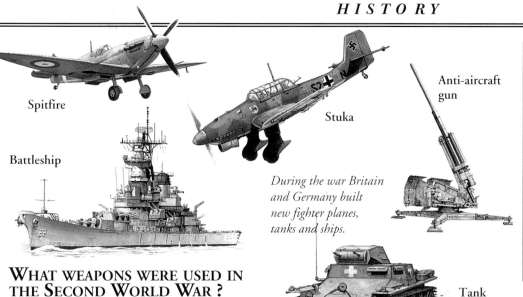

Spitfire

Stuka

Anti-aircraft gun

Battleship

During the war Britain and Germany built new fighter planes, tanks and ships.

Tank

WHAT WEAPONS WERE USED IN THE SECOND WORLD WAR?

DURING the 1930s, Britain and Germany built huge new battleships and armed them with powerful guns that could fire shells great distances. These were gradually replaced during the course of the Second World War with aircraft carriers, which enabled aircraft to attack from the sea. Aircraft also played a decisive role in battles over land, while armoured tanks broke through enemy lines. Anti-aircraft guns were used to protect those on the ground from air attack.

WHAT HAPPENED AT PEARL HARBOR?

ON DECEMBER 7th, 1941, Japanese planes attacked the American naval base at Pearl Harbor, Hawaii. Five US battleships were sunk or crippled, another 14 warships were hit, and over 2,000 naval officers and men were killed. Following this attack, America joined the Allies in the Second World War.

WHO WAS ADOLF HITLER?

IN 1933, a Fascist leader called Adolf Hitler became Chancellor of Germany. He wanted to make the country powerful again. He built up the army throughout the 1930s and led the country to war in 1939. He set up concentration camps to exterminate Jews and other groups of people. When Germany was defeated in 1945, he committed suicide.

WHO WAS WINSTON CHURCHILL?

IN MAY 1940 Winston Churchill was appointed British Prime Minister. He led Britain to victory over Adolf Hitler. During the war he bolstered British morale and won American support.

WHAT WAS FASCISM?

THE modern Fascist movement was founded in Italy in 1919 by the charismatic dictator Benito Mussolini. Fascists believed that the needs of their country were more important than people's rights or freedom.

WHEN WAS THE ATOMIC BOMB DROPPED?

TWO atomic bombs, the most deadly weapon yet developed, were dropped on Japan in August 1945, killing thousands of people. This forced Japan to surrender, ending the Second World War.

DID WOMEN FIGHT IN THE SECOND WORLD WAR?

WOMEN did not fight on the front line, but many women joined the women's air, army and naval forces. They also played an important part working in factories and on farms.

HOW LONG WAS THE SECOND WORLD WAR?

THE Second World War lasted nearly six years. It began in September 1939, when Germany invaded Poland. Two days later Britain and France declared war on Germany, but could not save the Poles. In 1940 Germany invaded Denmark, Norway, the Netherlands, Belgium and France, using a terrifying tactic called *Blitzkrieg* ("lightning war"). Italy then joined Germany, but Britain and her allies (Australia, Canada, New Zealand and South Africa) fought on. In 1941 Germany attacked Russia, while Japan attacked America. On June 6th, 1944 (D-Day), Allied forces crossed the English Channel and landed on the beaches of Normandy in France, while the Russians advanced from the east. Germany surrendered in May 1945, and Japan in August.

On D-Day, troops arrived by sea in special landing craft.

20th-CENTURY ACHIEVEMENTS

WHAT IS A MAGLEV TRAIN?

MAGLEV trains are the trains of the future. They have no wheels. Instead, they use the principle of magnetic levitation to raise them off the track. With friction almost eliminated, they can be propelled forward at speeds of up to 400 km/h. Prototypes have already been built in Germany and Japan. In the future it is anticipated that they will reach speeds of up to 800 km/h.

In 1996 a Maglev train opened at Disney World in Florida.

WHO DISCOVERED DNA'S STRUCTURE?

THE letters DNA stand for deoxyribonucleic acid. This is a chemical substance that is found in all living things. The information that controls the way plants, animals and humans look and how their bodies work is passed from each generation to the next in DNA. Two scientists working in England, called Francis Crick and James Watson, worked out the structure of DNA in 1953. They built a model of the DNA molecule to show how it divides to form two identical copies of itself, passing the characteristics of the parents to their offspring.

DNA consists of two strands shaped in a double helix, like a twisted ladder. It divides to form two copies of itself.

WHAT IS THE UNITED NATIONS?

THE United Nations (UN) was set up in 1945 at the end of the Second World War to keep worldwide peace and security, and to promote international cooperation. All the member countries of the UN provide soldiers who act as peacekeepers in any country that comes under attack. During the 1990s, UN peacekeeping forces were involved in many countries, from Africa and the Middle East to the former Yugoslavia.

The flag of the United Nations.

HOW HAS TELEVISION CHANGED OUR LIVES?

SINCE its invention in 1926, the television has become the most widely used form of mass communication. It is the main source of home entertainment, and can show us "live" pictures from the other side of the world. More than 500 million homes worldwide have a TV set.

WHICH DISEASE WAS WIPED OUT?

SMALLPOX is a virus that once killed one in three of those who caught it. Survivors were left with permanently scarred skin. The World Health Organization declared war on smallpox in 1967. By 1980 the world was virtually free of the disease.

HOW POWERFUL IS THE MOST POWERFUL LASER?

THE world's most powerful laser has ten arms that deliver laser pulses on to a target. For a fraction of a second, the power they generate is two hundred times greater than the combined output of all the electrical generating plants in America.

WHAT IS THE WORLD'S MOST ACCURATE CLOCK ?

THE world's most accurate time keeper is an atomic clock that was produced in America in 1990. It is about the size of a desktop computer, and is accurate to 1 second in 1.6 million years.

WHO ORGANIZES INTERNATIONAL AID ?

AID agencies are organizations that provide money, food and medical supplies in emergency situations. Both the World Health Organization (WHO) and the United Nations International Children's Emergency Fund (UNICEF) have brought help to developing countries that have suffered because of underdeveloped economies, crop failure or civil war.

WHAT ADVANCES HAVE THERE BEEN IN MEDICINE ?

THIS century, organ transplants have been made possible; microsurgery can repair delicate nerves and tissues; and a revolution has begun in genetic engineering.

WHAT HAS PRECISION ENGINEERING ACHIEVED ?

DURING the course of the 20th century, scientists have built machines that can cut glass to a thickness of 0.035 mm; cut a human hair lengthways 3,000 times; and make a television with a screen 30.5 mm wide.

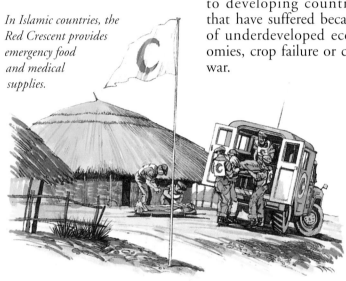

In Islamic countries, the Red Crescent provides emergency food and medical supplies.

WHAT IS THE "GREEN" MOVEMENT ?

THE world is waking up to the threats that the planet is facing from pollution and habitat destruction. By being environmentally aware, or "Green", people can begin to manage the planet better for the future.

WHAT DID NELSON MANDELA DO ?

NELSON Mandela became the first black president of South Africa. He was imprisoned in 1964 for his campaign against apartheid, which kept whites and blacks separate, and was only released in 1990.

Tenzing Norgay and Edmund Hillary finally reach the top of Mount Everest.

WHAT DID MARTIN LUTHER KING DO ?

MARTIN Luther King was an American clergyman who led the civil rights movement in America. Many black Americans had died for their country during the Second World War, but they were still regarded as second class citizens. During the 1960s, King led peaceful protests and gave speeches that inspired many people to follow him. When he was shot dead in 1968, America went into national mourning.

Martin Luther King protested against the unfair treatment of black Americans and against war and poverty among all people.

WHO FIRST CLIMBED MOUNT EVEREST ?

THE climb to the final summit of Mount Everest — the world's highest mountain at 8,848 m — was made by a New Zealander called Edmund Hillary and Tenzing Norgay of Nepal. Their final obstacle was a vertical band of rock 12 m high and covered in ice. But the two mountaineers found their way over it and on May 29th, 1953, they were the first people to stand at the top of the world.

Ramapithecus *was an early ape-like creature that lived about 15 million years ago.*

ARE HUMANS DESCENDED FROM APES ?

THE structure of the human body is similar to that of the apes (gorillas, chimpanzees, orang-utans and gibbons) which are alive today. But this does not mean that humans are directly descended from any of these creatures. Most scientists believe that humans and apes had a common ancestor millions of years ago. Then humans and apes evolved, or developed and changed, in quite different ways.

WHO WERE THE FIRST HUMAN-LIKE CREATURES ?

A HUMAN-LIKE creature that we call *Australopithecus*, meaning "southern ape", lived in Africa from about 4 million years ago. These creatures were similar enough to humans to be thought of as closely related to us, and they are known as hominids. A trail of fossil footprints was found in Africa, showing that *Australopithecus* walked upright on two legs.

Groups of Australopithecus *travelled across open country in parts of Africa.*

WHAT IS PREHISTORY ?

PREHISTORY means "before history", and we use the term to refer to the time before writing was invented. It was only when people started to write things down about 5,000 years ago that history could be recorded. A great deal of what we know about prehistory comes from fossils.

WHO WAS "LUCY" ?

"LUCY" was the name given to the remains of an *Australopithecus* (early human-like creature) discovered in 1974 in Ethiopia. Leg and arm bones were found, as well as ribs, a hip and parts of her skull. "Lucy" lived about 3 million years ago.

WHAT DID PREHISTORIC PEOPLE EAT ?

MOST prehistoric people were hunters and gatherers. They lived by hunting large animals such as bison, mammoths and woolly rhinoceroses. They also gathered fruits, berries and seeds.

WHO WAS THE "HANDY MAN" ?

HUMANS belong to the genus *Homo*, which means "man". An early species lived in east Africa nearly 2 million years ago, and was given the name *Homo habilis*, meaning "handy man", because it made tools. Scientists think that it was the first creature to make tools for specific purposes, rather than simply picking up sticks and stones and using them. It made stone tools by hitting one piece of flint against another.

Homo habilis *may have used stone tools to cut up animals.*

WHEN WAS THE STONE AGE ?

THE Old Stone Age lasted from when people first used stones as tools, about 3 million years ago, to about 12,000 years ago. Next came the Middle Stone Age, up to about 5,000 years ago, followed by the New Stone Age, when people started to farm.

We think that Homo erectus *built campfires and may have made simple ovens with hot stones.*

WHEN DID HUMANS FIRST USE FIRE ?

HOMO erectus or "upright man", who lived from about 1.5 million years ago in Africa, was the first creature to stand fully upright. By about 500,000 years ago, these early humans had spread to southern Asia and Europe. They were probably the first to use fire. This was useful for cooking food, keeping warm and scaring animals away from shelters.

DID PEOPLE REALLY LIVE IN CAVES ?

PREHISTORIC people did find shelter in caves. One of the most famous sets of fossils of *Homo erectus* were of "Peking Man", found in a cave in China. These showed that early humans had lived in the cave for some time.

WHEN WERE THE FIRST WORKS OF ART MADE ?

CAVE paintings and small sculptures made about 30,000 years ago have been found. Creating art is a uniquely human activity.

HAVE HUMAN BRAINS GOT BIGGER ?

MODERN human brains are about 1,400 cc; *Homo habilis* (the first toolmakers) had brains of 650-800 cc; and *Australopithecus* had brains of 450-500 cc.

WHO WAS "PILTDOWN MAN" ?

IN 1912 remains were found in a gravel pit on Piltdown Common, in Sussex, England. They appeared to be of a prehistoric hominid (human-like creature) with an ape-like jaw. Over 40 years later, new techniques showed that Piltdown Man was a hoax. The skull was a man's, and the jaw was from an orang-utan.

We know from remains that Neanderthals buried their dead.

WHO WERE THE FIRST MODERN HUMANS ?

WE CALL modern humans like ourselves *Homo sapiens*, meaning "wise" or "thinking man". There were once two subspecies: *Homo sapiens neanderthalensis*, which evolved about 250,000 years ago and died out about 30,000 years ago, and their cousins, *Homo sapiens sapiens*, which evolved a little later. Remains of this later group were discovered in 1868 at a site called Cro-Magnon in France. The Cro-Magnon people developed farming, kept animals and made cave paintings.

As well as being skilful hunters, Cro-Magnons sewed skins for clothes and made bone fish-hooks.

WHERE WERE THE "NEANDERTHALS" FOUND ?

THE remains of *Homo sapiens neanderthalensis* were first found in the Neander valley near Düsseldorf in Germany, in 1856, and it is from this that scientists gave the subspecies its name. These early humans were very strong, with broad heads and jutting brows.

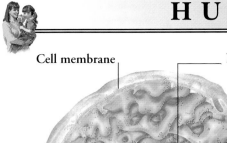

Cell membrane — — Nucleus

— Cytoplasm

Body cells are designed to perform specific tasks. They reproduce by dividing into two.

WHAT ARE CELLS ?

CELLS are the basic building blocks of life, and almost all living things are made up of them. The human body contains billions of tiny cells. Cells have three main parts. In the middle is the nucleus, which is the cell's control centre. This is surrounded by a fluid called cytoplasm, where energy is made. Around the outside is the cell membrane, which allows certain substances to enter and leave the cell.

WHY IS BLOOD RED ?

BLOOD is made up of red cells and colourless cells (called white cells), as well as colourless plate-lets, which make blood clot, and plasma. The red cells get their colour from the iron in haemo-globin, which is the chemical in the blood that carries oxygen and exchanges it for carbon dioxide. In a given quantity of blood, there are a thousand times more red blood cells than white ones.

WHAT ARE VEINS AND ARTERIES ?

BLOOD is pumped by the heart along vessels called arteries and veins. It leaves the heart through arteries, and carries oxygen to all the cells of the body. When it has delivered its oxygen, blood flows back to the heart through vessels called veins.

HOW DO WE MOVE ?

ALL the body's movements, from blinking or smiling to running and jumping, are made by muscles. Muscles move our bones, to which they are connected by tendons, by contracting or becoming shorter. They need energy to work, and this is supplied by oxygen and nutrients in the blood. The human body has about 620 muscles, and they are all controlled by the body's nervous system.

Heart

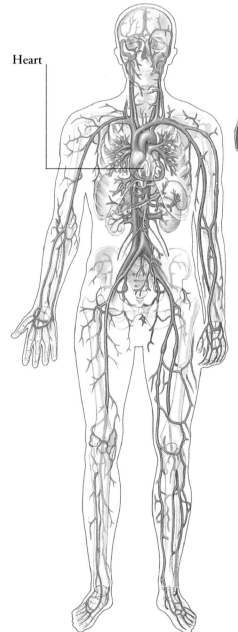

Blood is bright red when it is carrying oxygen. Here arteries are shown as red and veins as blue.

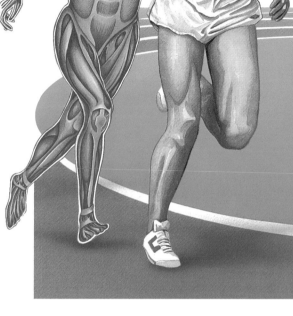

Muscles make the body move. Blood carries oxygen to our muscles through arteries.

WHAT IS THE CENTRAL NERVOUS SYSTEM ?

THE central nervous system controls everything that we do. It is made up of the brain and the spinal cord. Nerves run to and from the spinal cord all over the body. These nerves carry messages from the brain to the body, and from the body's sense organs to the brain.

HOW IS FOOD DIGESTED ?

WHEN we swallow food, it travels down the oesophagus into the stomach. There, muscles churn it into a soup-like mixture. This passes into the small intes-tine, where soluble food sub-stances pass into the bloodstream, to be delivered all over the body.

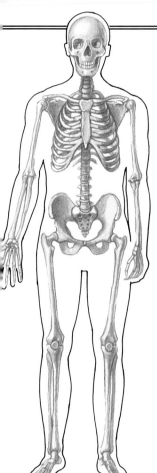

The bones of the skeleton form a frame for the body.

WHY DO WE NEED A SKELETON ?

THE skeleton is the body's framework. It is made of bones, which provide a firm surface for muscles to attach to, so that they can move. Without a skeleton, we would not be able to move at all. The skeleton also supports the body and protects our internal organs. The heart and lungs are protected by the rib cage, and the brain is surrounded by the bones of the skull. The nerves leading from the brain are protected by the backbone.

HOW MANY BONES DO WE HAVE ?

AN ADULT person has 206 bones. Babies are born with as many as 270 small, soft bones, but as a child grows, some of the bones join together. The largest bone is the femur, or thigh bone, which can be 50 cm long in a tall man. The smallest bone, the stapes, is in the middle ear and is about 3 mm long.

HOW DOES A BABY DEVELOP ?

A BABY'S life begins when a male sperm joins a female egg, inside a woman's body. The sperm joins with the egg to form a single cell, which divides to make more cells. After about a week, it has multiplied to become more than 100 cells. The developing baby is called a foetus. After two weeks blood cells start to form, and after four weeks the heart is beating. At eight weeks, the foetus is about 4 cm long and has all the major organs. After nine months the baby is ready to be born.

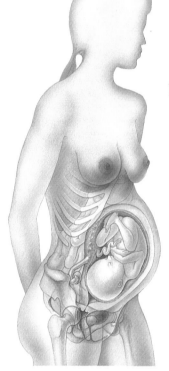

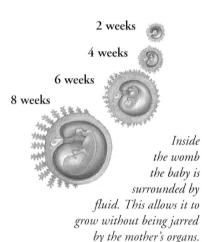

2 weeks
4 weeks
6 weeks
8 weeks

Inside the womb the baby is surrounded by fluid. This allows it to grow without being jarred by the mother's organs.

WHAT ARE THE BODY'S CHEMICAL MESSENGERS ?

HORMONES are chemical substances carried in the blood. They are produced by glands. Most hormones cause part of the body to be more active. When a person is in danger, for example, glands release a hormone called adrenalin, which prepares the body for quick action.

HOW FAST DOES OUR HAIR GROW ?

HAIR on the scalp normally grows about 1.25 cm a month. Most adults have about 120,000 hairs on their head, but they do not all grow all the time. Every six months or so hairs go into a resting phase; up to 10 percent of our scalp hairs are resting at any one time.

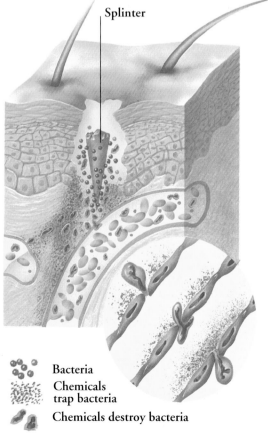

Splinter

Bacteria
Chemicals trap bacteria
Chemicals destroy bacteria

Chemicals and special cells deal with any infection beneath the outer layer of the skin.

WHY DO WE SWEAT ?

WE SWEAT when the outside temperature is high and the body needs to cool down. Glands in the skin produce the salty liquid we call sweat, which moves through pores (narrow openings) in the surface of the skin. The sweat spreads over the warm skin and evaporates, causing the body to cool down.

WHAT IS BENEATH THE SKIN ?

THE skin is made up of two layers of tissue. The thin outer layer, called the epidermis, protects the tissue beneath. The deep inner layer, called the dermis, contains blood vessels and fat. Hairs pass through the epidermis to the surface of the skin. If cells beneath the epidermis become infected, they release chemicals to trap the infection. Other cells try to destroy the bacteria causing the infection.

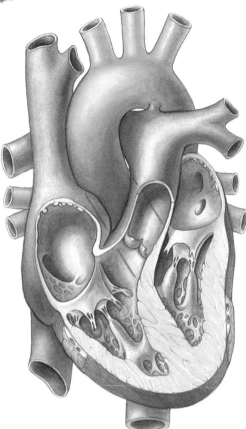

Each side of the heart has an upper and lower chamber. Blood comes into the upper chambers and is pumped out from the lower chambers.

Our two kidneys, each about 10 cm long, lie on either side of the spine below the diaphragm.

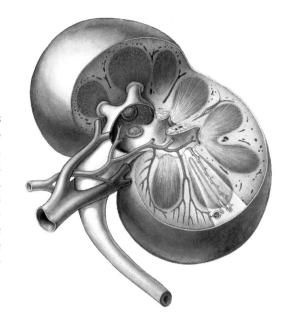

WHY DO WE NEED KIDNEYS ?

THE kidneys remove waste products from our blood. Inside each of the two kidneys there are about a million clumps of tiny blood vessels called capillaries. There are tiny tubes around the clumps, and as blood flows through the capillaries, waste substances pass into the tubes. The waste products travel from the kidneys to the bladder, where they are stored in urine until we pass it out of the body.

WHAT ARE THE SENSES ?

OUR senses tell us what is going on in the world around us. We have five main senses: sight, hearing, smell, taste and touch. The body's sense receptors send messages through nerves to the brain. Messages are received and interpreted in different parts of the brain.

WHAT IS AN ORGAN ?

THE body's organs are parts that do one (or more) special job. The heart, lungs, stomach and brain are all important organs. Groups of organs work together as a system. The nose, throat, windpipe and lungs make up the respiratory, or breathing, system.

WHAT DOES THE HEART DO ?

THE heart pumps blood around the body. It is made of a special type of muscle that does not become fatigued. Each heartbeat that we feel in our chest is one complete contraction and relaxation of the heart muscle. The right side of the heart collects blood carrying waste carbon dioxide from the body, and pumps it to the lungs. The left side collects blood with fresh oxygen from the lungs and pumps it around the body.

HOW DO WE BREATHE ?

BENEATH the lungs is a large dome of muscle called the diaphragm. This is the main muscle for breathing. When we breathe in, the diaphragm contracts, along with smaller muscles between the ribs. This makes the space inside the chest larger. Our lungs expand and air rushes into them from the windpipe. In the lungs, oxygen from the air is passed into the bloodstream. Then the diaphragm and chest muscles relax and we breathe out. Our breathing is controlled by the brain.

HOW OFTEN DOES THE HEART BEAT ?

WHEN we are sitting quietly, our heart might beat about 70 times a minute. But when we are moving about, our cells need more oxygen and nutrients, so the heart beats faster. If you run fast, your heart may beat more than 150 times a minute.

The windpipe runs down from the throat and branches into two tubes, called bronchi, one for each lung.

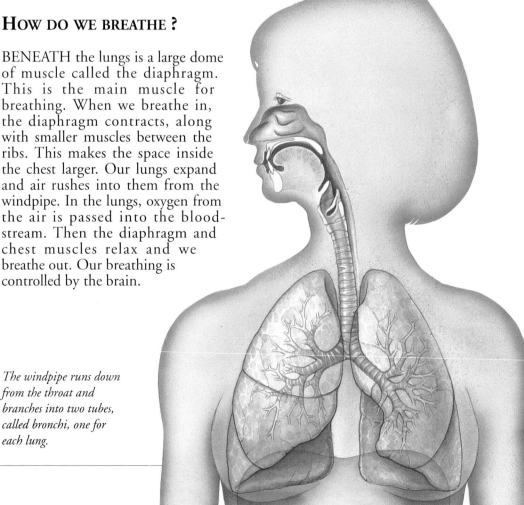

HOW DO OUR EYES WORK ?

LIGHT enters a small opening in the centre of the eye, called the pupil, which is covered by a clear, protective shield. Muscles in the coloured iris around the pupil change its size and control the amount of light that enters the eye. The light passes through a lens, which focuses an image on the retina at the back of the eye. The retina contains nerve cells that send messages to the brain through the optic nerve.

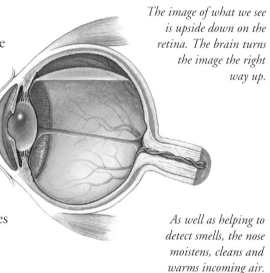

The image of what we see is upside down on the retina. The brain turns the image the right way up.

As well as helping to detect smells, the nose moistens, cleans and warms incoming air.

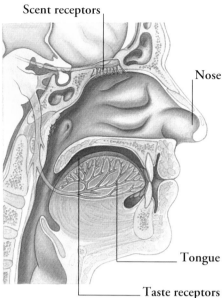

Scent receptors

Nose

Tongue

Taste receptors

WHAT DOES THE LIVER DO ?

THE liver does many important jobs for the body. It makes a substance called bile, which helps digestion, and other substances needed by the body to fight disease. The liver also removes certain types of poisons and wastes. It lies in the upper part of the abdomen.

WHAT ARE THE MAIN PARTS OF THE BRAIN ?

THE human brain may consist of about 10 billion nerve cells. It has three main parts: the cerebrum is the largest part and is where learning and memory take place; the cerebellum coordinates muscular activity such as walking; and the brain stem controls involuntary activity such as breathing.

HOW DO WE TASTE AND SMELL ?

THE tongue is covered with thousands of taste receptors, which we call taste buds. These are grouped together in special areas on the tongue. We taste sweetness at the front, bitterness at the back, and sourness and saltiness at the sides of the tongue. When we sniff, tiny particles in the air are carried to scent receptors in the nose. Taste and smell receptors send messages to the brain.

WHAT ARE ALVEOLI ?

ALVEOLI are the tiny air sacs at the end of the smallest air passages in the lungs. There are millions of alveoli in each lung. Oxygen particles from the air seep through the walls of the alveoli into blood vessels, to be taken to the heart. The blood also passes carbon dioxide to the alveoli, to be breathed out.

Each of our lungs has about 300 million alveoli. Oxygen passes from the alveoli into the bloodstream.

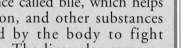

WHERE IS THE VOICE BOX ?

OUR voice box, or larynx, is in the lower part of the throat. Here soft folds, called vocal cords, open and close. As air is forced through the gap between the cords it makes them vibrate. This makes the sounds of our voice.

WHAT HAPPENS INSIDE THE EAR ?

WHEN sound waves enter the ear, they pass along a short canal to the eardrum, which is a thin sheet of skin that vibrates when it is hit by the sound waves. The vibration moves three tiny bones on the other side of the eardrum. This movement sets in motion a fluid in a spiral tube (the cochlea) in the inner ear. Nerve cells connected to tiny hairs in the cochlea send signals to the brain.

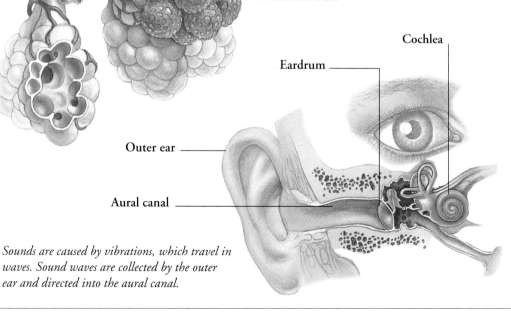

Cochlea

Eardrum

Outer ear

Aural canal

Sounds are caused by vibrations, which travel in waves. Sound waves are collected by the outer ear and directed into the aural canal.

WHAT IS RAMADAN ?

RAMADAN is a time of fasting for Muslims, followers of the religion of Islam. During Ramadan is the "night of power", which commemorates the first revelation of the Qu'ran (Koran) to the prophet Mohammed. Ramadan lasts for a month, and for those 30 days Muslims may not eat food during the hours of daylight. Children usually learn to fast by not eating for half a day at first.

A Muslim family celebrates the end of Ramadan, which is marked by the Islamic festival of Eid al-Fitr.

WHAT DOES PURIM CELEBRATE ?

THIS Jewish festival celebrates the rescue of Persian Jews many centuries ago from a plot to destroy them. In the 5th century BC, the prime minister of Persia, a man named Haman, ordered all Jews in the kingdom to be killed because one of the Jewish leaders had refused to bow down to him. The Jews were saved by Queen Esther, the Jewish wife of the Persian king, who persuaded her husband to overrule the order.

Children enjoy fancy-dress parades, plays and parties at the festival of Purim.

WHAT IS BUDDHISM ?

BUDDHISM is one of the world's major religions. It is based on the teachings of an Indian prince who gave up his riches and became a religious teacher. He lived over 2,500 years ago and was known as the Buddha, or Enlightened One. He founded the Buddhist order of monks and his teachings soon spread throughout Asia.

WHAT IS SHINTO ?

Shinto means "the way of the gods" and is the ancient religion of Japan. Each Shinto shrine has a wooden "torii" or "bird-perch", because in Japanese legend it was birdsong that persuaded the Sun Goddess to come out of her cave and light up the world. When Shinto began, the Japanese thought their islands were the only inhabited parts of the world.

A Swedish girl wears a headdress of shining candles, celebrating light on Saint Lucia's day.

WHO IS THE SAINT OF LIGHT ?

LUCIA is the Christian saint of light and brightness. She lived about 1,700 years ago on the Italian island of Sicily. According to legend, Lucia gave all her riches to the poor. She was persecuted and killed by the Romans because of her Christian beliefs. Her saint's day is December 13th. On this day, not long before the shortest day of the year, people celebrate light and look forward to Christmas.

WHY DO PEOPLE MAKE PANCAKES ON SHROVE TUESDAY?

SHROVE Tuesday is the last day before Lent, a 40-day period of fasting before the Christian celebration of Easter. Traditionally, people did not eat eggs or fat during Lent. Making pancakes was a good way of using up these foods before Lent started.

WHAT DOES HALLOWEEN MEAN?

HALLOWEEN is a shortening of All Hallows Eve, or "the day before the feast of All Saints". All Saints' Day, on November 1st, commemorates all people who have been honoured as Christian saints. It is followed by All Souls Day, which commemorates all other Christian people who have died. Before Christianity, people believed that the souls of the dead visited their homes at this time. This is the origin of Halloween ghosts and witches.

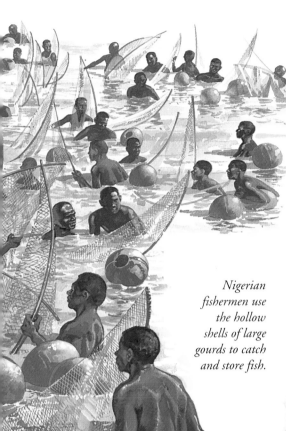

Nigerian fishermen use the hollow shells of large gourds to catch and store fish.

WHY DO PEOPLE DANCE ROUND A MAYPOLE?

DANCING round a maypole is part of a traditional festival held on May Day, May 1st. Since the Middle Ages, this is the day people in northern Europe have celebrated the coming of spring. Merrymakers hold streamers as they dance round the maypole.

English children in medieval costume weave their streamers round the maypole as they dance.

WHERE IS THERE AN ANNUAL FISHING FESTIVAL?

AN EXCITING fishing festival takes place each February at Argungu, in the West African country of Nigeria. The two-day festival marks the beginning of the fishing season in the region. Crowds line the banks of the River Sokoto to watch men and boys wade into the water with nets. They drive big fish into shallow waters, making them easier to catch. There are canoe races at the festival, too.

WHERE IS THE WORLD'S GREATEST CARNIVAL?

A SPECTACULAR carnival is held every year in Rio de Janeiro, Brazil. The carnival lasts for four days and nights, during which there are street parades, fancy-dress parties and outdoor dancing.

WHO FOUNDED CONFUCIANISM?

CONFUCIANISM is a religion and philosophy based on the teachings of K'ung Fu-Tzu, or Confucius. This famous Chinese philosopher lived from 551 to 479 BC.

WHO IS THE PATRON SAINT OF CHILDREN?

ST NICHOLAS, also called Santa Claus, is the patron saint of children. He was a bishop who lived in Asia Minor, in present-day Turkey, over 1,600 years ago. Stories about how he gave gifts of gold to poor children started the legend of Father Christmas.

WHEN DO HINDUS PLAY TRICKS?

THE Hindus of India and Nepal like to play tricks during their spring festival of Holi. One of their favourite tricks is to stain each other with dye. People run through the streets and throw coloured powder and water over each other. Holi celebrations go on for up to five days during March or April, in honour of the Hindu god Krishna.

Everyone is soon stained with coloured powder and water during Holi.

The Great Pyramid was built as a tomb for King Khufu by free men (not slaves), who laboured in honour of their king.

WHAT WAS THE FORUM IN ANCIENT ROME ?

THE Forum was an open public square in the middle of the ancient city of Rome. It was originally a market place, and then became the centre of public business. Roman orators came to make speeches, and citizens gathered there to discuss the important questions of the day. It was also used for imperial ceremonies.

The Forum was dominated by the Temple of Julius and the Temple of Castor and Pollux.

HOW WAS THE GREAT PYRAMID AT GIZA BUILT ?

THE Great Pyramid is one of three vast pyramids at Giza, near Cairo in Egypt. It probably took 100,000 men 20 years to build, and it was finished in about 2565 BC. The pyramid was made from more than 2 million blocks of stone, most weighing 2.5 tonnes or more. These were dragged to the site on sledges, and then hauled up a huge earth ramp, which was made higher for each layer of blocks.

WHAT ARE THE SEVEN WONDERS OF THE ANCIENT WORLD ?

THESE great structures, listed by a Greek poet over 2,000 years ago, were: the Great Pyramid at Giza, the Hanging Gardens of Babylon, the Temple of Artemis at Ephesus, the Statue of Zeus at Olympia, the Mausoleum at Halicarnassus, the Colossus of Rhodes and the Pharos of Alexandria.

HOW TALL IS THE EMPIRE STATE BUILDING ?

THE Empire State Building in New York is 381 m high and has 102 storeys. On the top is a radio and TV mast. The building took 15 months to complete, and was opened on May 1st, 1931. At that time it was the tallest skyscraper in the world. There are 1,860 steps from ground level to the top floor, but there are 73 lifts, too, including an express lift to the observation platform on the 86th floor.

The steel-framed Empire State Building weighs 308,000 tonnes.

The Sears Tower (5), built in 1974, was the world's tallest building until the Petronas Towers (6) overtook it in 1996.

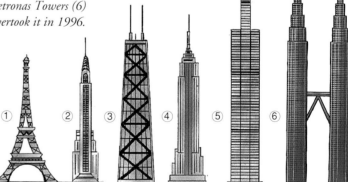

WHICH ARE THE WORLD'S TALLEST BUILDINGS ?

THE tallest buildings in the world are the twin Petronas Towers (6, above) in Kuala Lumpur, Malaysia. Each of the towers is 452 m high, and they are linked by a bridge. Some other very tall buildings are: (1) the Eiffel Tower in Paris, at 300 m; (2) the Chrysler Building, New York, at 319 m; (3) the John Hancock Center, Chicago, at 343 m; (4) the Empire State Building, New York, at 381 m; and (5) the Sears Tower, Chicago, at 443 m.

WHERE IS THE LONGEST WALL IN THE WORLD?

THE Great Wall of China runs all the way from the mountains of northwest China to the Pacific coast, following the hilltops and high ground. Its main length and side branches give a total of more than 6,000 km.

WHICH INTERNATIONAL AIRPORT IS ON A MANMADE ISLAND?

KANSAI International Airport stands on an entirely manmade island in Osaka Bay, Japan, 5 km off the coast. The island was made by piling sand, earth and rock on to the sea bed.

WHAT IS THE WORLD'S TALLEST STRUCTURE?

THE world's tallest free-standing structure is the CN Tower in Toronto, Canada, which rises to 553 m. A restaurant revolves in the Sky Pod, 351 m above the ground, and from there you can see hills 120 km away.

WHICH IS THE WORLD'S WIDEST LONG-SPAN BRIDGE?

THE world's widest long-span bridge is Sydney Harbour Bridge, in Australia. It is 48.8 m wide and carries eight road lanes, two electric railway tracks, a cycle track and a pedestrian walkway. The bridge, which is 509 m long, took five years to build. It opened in 1932.

The deck of Sydney Harbour Bridge is suspended from steel girders.

WHO BUILT THE TAJ MAHAL?

THE Taj Mahal was built in Agra, India, on the orders of Shah Jahan, a Mogul ruler. He had the beautiful marble structure built as a tomb for his wife, and it was completed in about 1648.

WHY DOES THE LEANING TOWER OF PISA LEAN?

THE Leaning Tower — the bell tower of Pisa's cathedral — leans because the ground has subsided. Work has been done to prevent it from leaning further.

The Eiffel Tower is still the most famous landmark in Paris, France.

WHY WAS THE EIFFEL TOWER BUILT?

THE Eiffel Tower was built as a focal point for the Paris International Exposition (public exhibition) of 1889, which was held to celebrate the centenary of the French Revolution. The organisers held a competition to find the best design of a tower; it was won by the French engineer, Alexandre Gustave Eiffel. Unpopular at first, it has become a great attraction.

Liberty's torch shines out across New York Harbour at night.

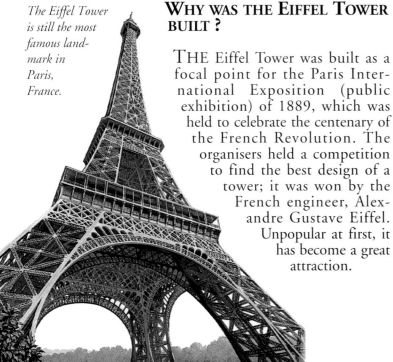

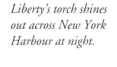

WHO DESIGNED THE STATUE OF LIBERTY?

THE internal framework of the Statue of Liberty was designed by Alexandre Gustave Eiffel, who later designed the Eiffel Tower in Paris. The outer skin, made from sheets of copper, was the work of the French sculptor Frédéric Auguste Bartholdi. First built in France, it was taken apart and shipped to New York in 1885.

HOW BIG IS A SOCCER PITCH?

EVERY full-sized soccer pitch must be between 91 and 119 m long, and between 46 and 91 m wide. However, a pitch cannot be 91 sq m because the rules say that it must be longer than it is wide. These dimensions mean that the biggest allowable pitch can be over 2.5 times the area of the smallest. The size of the goals, goal areas and penalty areas have to be the same for every pitch, otherwise goals might be scored too easily!

A soccer goal is always 7.3 m wide and 2.4 m high.

The trumpet, double bass, drums and a singer are a typical line-up for a jazz band.

WHAT IS A TRIATHLON?

A TRIATHLON is a three-part endurance race. First the competitors must swim for 1,500 m, usually in the sea. Then they cycle for a distance of 40 km. Finally the triathletes run for another 10 km. Men and women compete in separate races.

WHAT WAS THE FIRST FULL-LENGTH ANIMATED FILM?

WALT Disney's first feature film was *Snow White and the Seven Dwarfs*, which was released in the United States in 1937. Before computer animation, every image had to be drawn by hand.

WHERE WAS JAZZ MUSIC FIRST PLAYED?

JAZZ was first played in the United States, at the start of the 20th century. It became popular among black Americans, especially in New Orleans. In the 1920s jazz spread to other big cities, such as New York and Chicago. This new music mixed European harmony and melody with rhythms from Africa.

In ancient Greek theatres the audience sat on stone steps. Large theatres could seat up to 14,000 people.

WHO BUILT THE EARLIEST THEATRES?

THE ancient Greeks were the first people to build permanent stone theatres. The oldest is the Theatre of Dionysus, in Athens, which was built about 2,300 years ago. Greek theatres were built into hillsides. A chanting chorus stood in the "orchestra", a circular or semi-circular space in front of the stage. The actors, who were men, wore masks.

WHERE IS THE GREATEST CYCLE RACE HELD?

THE Tour de France is the longest and most famous of the world's cycle races. The course through the French countryside covers 4,000 km or more and takes up to 25 days to complete.

WHEN WERE THE FIRST OLYMPIC GAMES HELD?

THE present-day Olympics are based on Games that were held long ago at Olympia, a sacred site in ancient Greece. The Olympic Games were first held in 776 BC. The Games took place at four-yearly intervals until AD 393, when they were banned by the Romans. The first modern Olympic Games were held in Athens in 1896.

Competitors from all over the world parade around the stadium at the opening ceremony of the Olympic Games.

WHAT DOES THE CHEQUERED FLAG STAND FOR?

IN MOTOR racing, the chequered flag signals the end of a race. It is waved at the side of the track to the winning driver, to let him know that he has completed the right number of laps of the track. Other coloured flags are used to warn drivers or to tell them to stop.

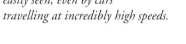

The chequered flag is easily seen, even by cars travelling at incredibly high speeds.

WHO HAS WON MOST WIMBLEDON TITLES?

BILLIE-JEAN King (USA) won twenty Wimbledon tennis titles between 1961 and 1979. She won six singles, ten women's doubles and four mixed doubles titles. The record-holder for singles is Martina Navratilova (USA), winner of nine Wimbledon singles finals between 1978 and 1990.

HOW DID THE MARATHON RACE GET ITS NAME?

THE marathon is named in honour of the defeat of the Persian army by the Athenians at Marathon, near Athens, in 490 BC. Pheidippides, a Greek runner, ran to give the news to the people of Athens, but died as he did so. The first modern marathon was run in honour of this event at the 1896 Athens Olympics.

WHERE WAS CHESS INVENTED?

CHESS was played in India and Persia more than 1,300 years ago. A slightly different form may be even older. It probably reached Europe in the 10th century. The word "chess" comes from the Persian word *shah*, meaning "king".

WHO ARE HEPTATHLETES?

HEPTATHLETES are women who take part in a seven-part athletic event. There are three races (100-m hurdles, and 200-m and 800-m flat races), two jumps (high and long) and two throws (shot put and javelin).

WHAT EQUIPMENT DO ROCK CLIMBERS USE?

ROCK climbers need equipment that is both lightweight and strong. They wear a helmet to protect against rock falls, sturdy shoes to grip the rock face and tight clothes that will not catch on the rocks. They drive spikes into the rock and attach ropes to them using clips called karabiners.

Rock-climbing equipment must be chosen with safety in mind.

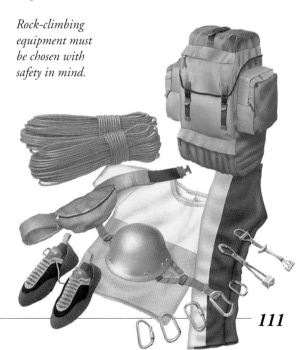

WHICH IS THE LARGEST COUNTRY IN THE WORLD ?

THE Republic of the Russian Federation, called Russia for short, is the world's largest country. With an area of just over 17 million sq km, it covers over 10 percent of the world's land area. It stretches from Europe in the west to the Pacific Ocean in the east, and from the Arctic Ocean in the north to the Mongolian grasslands in the south. The Ural Mountains cross it from north to south, forming the border between Europe and Asia. Russia has fewer than nine people per sq km, compared with 122 in China, the world's third largest country.

WHAT WAS THE SOVIET UNION ?

THE Soviet Union, or Union of Soviet Socialist Republics (USSR), was a country made up of 15 republics, the biggest of which was Russia. The Soviet Union was formed in 1922, five years after the Communist Revolution. It split up into 15 separate countries in 1991.

Since Roman times, Jews have gathered at the Wailing Wall to mourn and to pray.

This region of extremes goes from hot desert in the Arabian Peninsula to cold desert above the Arctic Circle.

Israel's emblem is the Star of David, a symbol of Judaism.

Kuwait's flag is in the pan-Arab colours of red, white, green and black.

WHERE IS THE WAILING WALL ?

THE Wailing Wall is a wall of huge limestone blocks in Jerusalem, the capital of Israel. It is actually the Western Wall, the last remaining part of the Temple of Jerusalem. The first Temple was built by King Solomon around 950 BC and has been destroyed and rebuilt twice. The Wailing Wall is one of the most important places of prayer in Jerusalem for Jews.

WHEN WAS ISRAEL FOUNDED ?

IN 1947 the United Nations voted to establish a Jewish state in the region then called Palestine. The modern State of Israel was founded the following year. The link between the Jewish people and the land of Israel dates back at least 4,000 years, but the area had been ruled in turn by Romans, Arabs, Crusaders, Turks and the British.

WHAT MADE THE GULF STATES RICH ?

THE nations around the Persian Gulf — Iran, Iraq, Kuwait, Saudi Arabia, Bahrain, Qatar, United Arab Emirates and Oman — are rich in oil and natural gas. It was the discovery of oil that brought enormous wealth to these Gulf States. Saudi Arabia is the second biggest producer of crude oil in the world, after Russia.

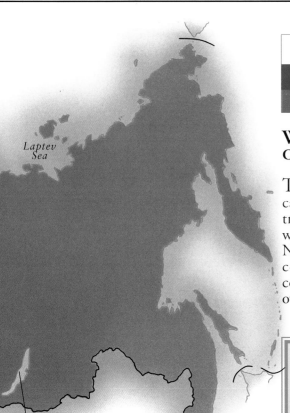

Laptev Sea

Lake Baikal

Russia's flag was introduced by Peter the Great, but was not used during the Soviet Union years.

WHICH FAMOUS RAILWAY CROSSES RUSSIA?

THE longest railway track that you can travel along without changing trains is the Trans-Siberian Railway, which crosses Russia from Moscow to Nachodka and Vladivostok on the coast of the Pacific Ocean. The complete railway journey takes just over eight days and covers 9,438 km.

WHICH IS THE WORLD'S DEEPEST LAKE?

LAKE Baikal, in southeastern Russia, is the world's deepest lake. It contains more water than any other freshwater lake. Baikal has 336 rivers flowing into it, but just one outlet, the River Angara. It has a greatest depth of 1,620 m.

Kyrgyzstan's emblem is a traditional yurt, or round tent.

WHERE IS THE "LAND OF THE NOMADS"?

THE name Kyrgyzstan means "Land of the Nomads", and the country has called itself by this name since it gained independence from the former Soviet Union in 1991. Much of the Republic of Kyrgyzstan lies within the Tien Shan mountains. Some Kyrgyz people lead a nomadic life, living in felt tents called yurts. The Kyrgyz keep horses, yaks and bactrian camels.

WHICH COUNTRY FORMS A BRIDGE BETWEEN EUROPE AND ASIA?

TURKEY has land on both these continents. The small European region of the country, called Thrace, is bordered by Bulgaria and Greece. The much larger Asian region, called Anatolia, lies between the Mediterranean and the Black Sea.

WHAT IS THE TAIGA?

THE taiga is a huge belt of forest that stretches right across the northern part of this region, from the Baltic Sea to the Pacific coast of Siberia. It contains evergreen trees, such as fir, pine and larch. The taiga is very cold during the long, dark winters, while summers are short and usually cool.

Inside the walls of the Kremlin fortress are churches and palaces.

WHAT IS THE KREMLIN?

MOSCOW, Russia's capital, lies on the Moskva River, from which it takes its name. It was founded in 1147, and nine years later a Russian prince built a wooden stockade or fort, called a kremlin, there. In 1712 Peter the Great moved the capital to St Petersburg, but the Communists made Moscow the capital again in 1918, when the Kremlin became the seat of the Soviet government.

WHICH RIVERS FLOW RIGHT ACROSS RUSSIA?

THREE river systems flow from Russia's southern border, across Siberia, to the Arctic Ocean in the north. The longest is the Yenisei, which flows for 5,540 km from near the Mongolian border. The Ob-Irtysh runs from the China–Mongolia border. The Lena starts near Lake Baikal.

WHERE IS THE EMPTY QUARTER?

THE Rub' al Khali, or Empty Quarter, is in Saudi Arabia. It is one of the largest stretches of sand in the world, and forms part of the Arabian Desert. It is so hot and dry in the Rub' al Khali region that few people ever go there, though Bedouin nomads wander across its edges.

WHY IS THE ARAL SEA SHRINKING?

THE Aral Sea lies between Kazakhstan and Uzbekistan. In recent years this salt lake has dropped from fourth-largest to sixth-largest lake in the world. It is shrinking because water from the rivers that feed the lake has been diverted into canals and used for the irrigation of crops.

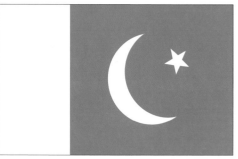

The flag of Pakistan, which features a crescent moon, is based on that of the Muslim League.

On India's flag orange stands for Hinduism, green for Islam, and the wheel for Buddhism.

WHEN WAS PAKISTAN FOUNDED?

IN 1947 India gained independence from Britain and divided into two countries, India and Pakistan. Pakistan was mainly Muslim (India mainly Hindu), and was made up of two areas, West Pakistan and East Pakistan, which were 1,600 km apart. In 1971 East Pakistan declared its own independence and became Bangladesh.

WHAT IS THE NAME OF INDIA'S HOLY RIVER?

TO HINDUS, the River Ganges is called Ganga Mai, or "Mother Ganges", and is sacred. Ancient Hindu writings say that the Ganges sprang from the feet of the god Vishnu. Hindus come from all over India, and beyond, to bathe in the river. They believe its waters will wash away their sins and purify their soul. They also place their relatives' ashes on the water.

WHICH RAILWAY CLIMBS THE HIMALAYAN FOOTHILLS?

SINCE 1881, a narrow-gauge railway has run from Siliguri on the Indian plains up to Darjeeling in the Himalayan foothills near the border with Nepal. The Darjeeling-Himalayan Railway is 82 km long and climbs more than 1,800 m. Locomotives pull loads of 50 tonnes up the steep slopes.

WHAT IS THE LARGEST CITY IN ASIA?

INCLUDING all its suburbs and surrounding built-up areas, Tokyo has a population of about 25 million people. This makes it the largest city in Asia. Japan's capital was founded in 1457.

A man at the front of the train throws sand on to the rails when they are wet to improve the wheels' grip.

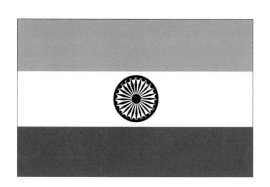

WHERE ARE THE "MOUTHS OF THE GANGES"?

MOST of the so-called "Mouths of the Ganges" are in Bangladesh. The mouths of this river form part of the world's largest delta. A delta is a fan-shaped area where a river's main flow splits up into many smaller channels.

WHERE IS THE WORLD'S HIGHEST MOUNTAIN?

MOUNT Everest, the world's highest mountain, lies on the border between Nepal and Tibet, a region of China. The figure usually given for its height is 8,848 m above sea level, though satellite surveys have measured Everest at 8,863 m.

WHICH PORT CITY BECAME CHINESE IN 1997?

HONG Kong, a port and island on the coast of China, became a British crown colony in 1842. On July 1st, 1997, it was returned to China as a special administrative region of the country.

WHAT WAS THE CULTURAL REVOLUTION?

THE Cultural Revolution was launched in China in the 1960s by Mao Zedong. Millions of people were sent to the countryside to be "re-educated" by doing manual work. It ended in 1976.

HOW DID THE PHILIPPINES GET THEIR NAME?

THE Spanish explorer Ruy López de Villalobos sailed to these islands in 1543 and named them Las Filipinas — the Philippines — in honour of Prince Philip of Asturias.

On the Japanese flag the red sun represents sincerity and passion, and the white background purity and honesty.

WHERE IS THE "LAND OF THE RISING SUN"?

THIS is a name for Japan. An ancient legend tells how the immortal being Izanagi dipped his spear into the ocean and formed the islands of Japan from shining drops of water. The Sun goddess, Amaterasu, promised that she and her descendants would always look after these sparkling islands.

WHERE DO GIANT PANDAS COME FROM?

PANDAS live only in the forests of the Sichuan province of China. They spend most of their waking hours eating. About 99 percent of a giant panda's diet is made up of bamboo, and it cannot survive without this food. They feed on different parts of the bamboo plant, which is a type of giant grass, at different times of the year.

A giant panda can eat up to 18 kg of bamboo a day.

WHICH COUNTRY IS MADE UP OF 3,900 ISLANDS?

JAPAN consists of over 3,900 islands. The biggest, Honshu, makes up 61 percent of Japan's land area, and 80 percent of the Japanese people live there. The other three large islands are Hokkaido, Kyushu and Shikoku.

WHERE IS THE GOBI DESERT?

THE Gobi Desert straddles the borders of China and Mongolia in central Asia, and lies on a plateau between 900 and 1,500 m high. It has scorchingly hot summers and bitterly cold winters.

WHICH COUNTRY HAS MOST PEOPLE?

WITH about 1.2 billion people, China has the largest population of any country. The world's total population is rapidly growing towards 6 billion, which means that roughly one in five of the world's people is Chinese. At least 40 Chinese cities have populations of more than a million.

RUSSIA

MONGOLIA

AFGHANISTAN

KOREA (North)

Sea of Japan

KOREA (South)

CHINA

PAKISTAN

Yellow Sea

JAPAN

BHUTAN

NEPAL

BANGLADESH

INDIA

MYANMAR

LAOS

East China Sea

PACIFIC OCEAN

TAIWAN

PHILIPPINES

VIETNAM

THAILAND

CAMBODIA

Bay of Bengal

South China Sea

SRI LANKA

BRUNEI

MALDIVES

MALAYSIA

MALAYSIA

INDIAN OCEAN

SINGAPORE

INDONESIA

Java Sea

Asia is bounded to the west by Europe. Together they form the world's largest land mass.

On the Organization of African Unity flag, the continent of Africa sits inside a laurel wreath.

WHAT IS THE ORGANIZATION OF AFRICAN UNITY ?

THE OAU is an organization that represents the interests of all the independent African countries. It was founded in 1963 to promote African unity and to make it easier for countries to help each other.

WHICH IS THE LONGEST AFRICAN RIVER ?

THE River Nile is the longest river in both Africa and the world. It has two main branches: the White Nile and the Blue Nile. Its total length is 6,670 km.

WHO ARE THE SMALLEST AFRICANS ?

THE Mbuti pygmies are thought to be the world's shortest people. They live mostly in the Dem. Rep. of the Congo. The average man is about 1.45 m in height. Some women are just 1.24 m tall.

WHY WAS THE SUEZ CANAL BUILT ?

THE Suez Canal was built to shorten the sailing route from Europe to Asia. Before it opened in 1869, European ships had to sail round the southern tip of Africa to reach the Indian Ocean. The Canal links the Mediterranean with the Red Sea. It is 173 km long, and 17,000 vessels pass through it each year.

WHERE IS THE WORLD'S LARGEST DESERT ?

THE Sahara in northern Africa is by far the largest desert in the world. It covers more than a quarter of the area of Africa, stretching over 5,000 km from the Atlantic Ocean to the Red Sea.

Africa is bounded by the Atlantic Ocean to the west, the Indian Ocean to the east, and the Mediterranean Sea to the north.

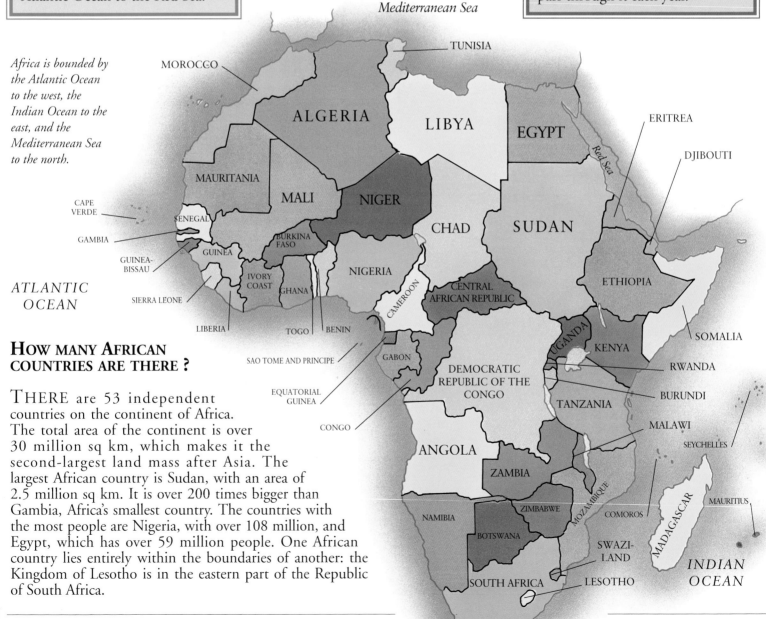

HOW MANY AFRICAN COUNTRIES ARE THERE ?

THERE are 53 independent countries on the continent of Africa. The total area of the continent is over 30 million sq km, which makes it the second-largest land mass after Asia. The largest African country is Sudan, with an area of 2.5 million sq km. It is over 200 times bigger than Gambia, Africa's smallest country. The countries with the most people are Nigeria, with over 108 million, and Egypt, which has over 59 million people. One African country lies entirely within the boundaries of another: the Kingdom of Lesotho is in the eastern part of the Republic of South Africa.

Sudan gained independence from Britain and Egypt in 1956. Its flag shows the Arab colours.

HOW MANY LANGUAGES ARE SPOKEN IN SUDAN ?

OVER half the Sudanese people speak the official language, Arabic, but altogether there are 115 languages spoken by the 570 different peoples. The northern Sudanese are mainly Arab Muslims; the black Africans of the south follow their own religions.

WHO ARE THE MALAGASY PEOPLE ?

THE people of Madagascar, the fourth largest island in the world, are called the Malagasy. The earliest settlers, the Merina, arrived more than 1,500 years ago from southeast Asia. Then came settlers from the African mainland.

WHEN WAS PRESIDENT MANDELA ELECTED ?

NELSON Mandela became president of the Republic of South Africa on May 10th, 1994, after the country's first multiracial elections.

WHERE IS THERE SNOW NEAR THE EQUATOR ?

TWO snowcapped African mountains lie near the equator. Mount Kenya rises to 5,199 m just south of the equator in Kenya. It is also called Kirinyaga, or "mountain of whiteness". At 5,895 m, Mount Kilimanjaro in Tanzania is Africa's highest mountain.

WHERE ARE AFRICA'S NATIONAL PARKS ?

THERE are national parks and wildlife reserves all over the continent. Leopards hunt gazelles in the Masai Mara National Reserve, in Kenya. Leopards live on the savannah (grassy plains with scattered trees). African elephants roam more wooded areas, where they are protected from poachers. The Serengeti, in Tanzania, and South Africa's Kalahari Gemsbok National Park are both famous for their herds of wildebeest and antelope.

A leopard can reach 60 km/h when chasing its prey.

WHAT IS THE GREAT RIFT VALLEY ?

THE Great Rift Valley is a huge depression that runs thousands of kilometres from the Red Sea to Mozambique. It is made from a series of faults in the Earth's crust, caused by earthquakes. Parts of the rift valley have become deep lakes, such as Lake Malawi.

WHERE WAS THE GOLD COAST ?

THE British colony of the Gold Coast, in west Africa, was established in 1874. It gained independence in 1957 and changed its name to Ghana. In the 18th century the region's Ashanti people had an independent kingdom. The gold they found in the area brought them great power. A famous golden stool was a symbol of the king and the Ashanti people.

WHERE IS THE HORN OF AFRICA ?

THE Horn of Africa is the area that juts out into the Indian Ocean, and includes Somalia and eastern Ethiopia. In recent years, the people there have suffered from drought and civil war.

The Ashanti king appears before his people wearing a golden crown and gold ornaments.

WHICH COUNTRIES MAKE UP THE UNITED KINGDOM?

THE official name of the country is the United Kingdom of Great Britain and Northern Ireland. Great Britain, the eighth-largest island in the world, is made up of England, Scotland and Wales. The name has been used since 1603, when King James of Scotland also became king of England and Wales. The whole of Ireland was part of the Kingdom until 1922, when it was separated from Northern Ireland and became an independent state.

The Union Jack (5) is made up of the crosses of (1) St George, England, (2) St Patrick, Northern Ireland and (3) St Andrew, Scotland. The flag of Wales (4) has a dragon.

HOW BIG IS EUROPE?

EUROPE is the second smallest of the seven continents: only Australasia is smaller. Europe has an area of 10.5 million sq km, which is less than a quarter the size of Asia. This map does not include the parts of Russia and Turkey that geographically form part of Europe. An imaginary line running through Russia from the Ural mountains to the Caspian Sea separates Europe from Asia.

The continent of Europe has a rugged coastline, full of peninsulas and dotted with islands.

WHAT IS SCANDINAVIA?

SCANDINAVIA is the name for a region in northern Europe that is made up of Norway, Sweden, Denmark and Finland. The island of Iceland is usually considered to be part of Scandinavia, too. From the 8th to the 11th century AD, the Scandinavian countries were the home of the Vikings, and the Scandinavian people share their history and mythology.

WHICH IS THE HIGHEST MOUNTAIN IN EUROPE?

AT 5,642 m high, Mount Elbrus, on the Russian border, is Europe's highest peak. It is in the Caucasus mountains, which form part of the boundary between Europe and Asia. The highest mountain in the Alps is Mont Blanc at 4,807 m.

WHERE IN EUROPE IS THE "MOUNTAIN IN THE SEA"?

THIS is the name sometimes used by the French for the island of Corsica, which lies in the Mediterranean Sea, north of Sardinia.

WHEN DID BOSNIA AND HERZEGOVINA GAIN INDEPENDENCE?

BOSNIA and Herzegovina were united under Turkish rule in the 15th century. The republic declared independence from former Yugoslavia in 1991. Civil war followed between the Bosnian Muslims, and the Serbian and Croatian Christians living in Bosnia.

The flag of Bosnia and Herzegovina shows the shield of a medieval king of Bosnia.

WHICH EUROPEAN CITY HAS MOST PEOPLE?

THE largest European city is Paris. Paris was founded in Roman times. In 1900 it was the third-largest city in the world after London and New York. Now, with a population of over 9 million people, it is the fifteenth-largest city in the world.

Paris is famous for its monuments, like the Eiffel Tower, and its museums, art galleries and cafés.

WHAT IS THE EUROPEAN UNION?

THE European Union (EU) is a union of 15 countries. Its aim is to make trade between the member countries cheaper and easier. The countries that belong to it are: Belgium, France, Germany, Italy, Luxembourg, the Netherlands, Denmark, Ireland, the United Kingdom, Greece, Portugal, Spain, Austria, Finland and Sweden.

WHAT IS THE IBERIAN PENINSULA?

THE Iberian Peninsula is the large piece of land occupied by Spain and Portugal.

WHICH IS THE WORLD'S BUSIEST PORT?

ROTTERDAM, the largest city in the Netherlands, is the busiest port in the world. Over 30,000 ships visit it each year, and in that time the port handles 300 million tonnes of goods. It was founded in the 13th century as a fishing village on the Rotte River, where it flows into the Rhine delta.

WHEN DID EAST AND WEST GERMANY REUNIFY?

GERMANY was divided into a western Federal Republic and an eastern Democratic Republic after the Second World War. The two parts reunified in 1990.

WHAT IS THE THAMES BARRIER?

THE Thames Barrier is a flood defence system across the River Thames to the east of central London. Building started in 1974 and took eight years to complete. When there is a flood alert from the North Sea, steel gates are raised to hold the waters back. The gates form a wall 520 m wide.

The shell-like structures of the Thames Barrier cover the machinery that raises and lowers the gates.

WHICH IS THE WORLD'S SMALLEST COUNTRY?

THE State of the Vatican City in Rome, Italy, has an area of just 0.44 sq km and is the smallest independent state in the world. It is the headquarters of the Roman Catholic Church.

WHICH MOUNTAINS SEPARATE FRANCE AND SPAIN?

THE Pyrenees stretch for about 500 km from the Bay of Biscay in the Atlantic Ocean to the Mediterranean Sea. This mountain range forms a natural boundary between France and Spain. The highest point in the Pyrenees is Pico d'Aneto at 3,404 m.

The Canadian flag's maple leaf design was adopted in 1965.

WHICH IS THE LARGEST NORTH AMERICAN COUNTRY ?

CANADA is the biggest country in North America and the second-biggest country in the world, after Russia. It has an area of almost 10 million sq km. All the North American countries are large; the United States is the fourth-largest country in the world (China is the third), and Mexico is the fourteenth largest.

WHICH IS NEW YORK'S TALLEST BUILDING ?

THE tallest skyscraper in New York is the twin-towered World Trade Center. Each tower has 110 storeys and rises to 412 m, and the gleaming twins dominate the skyline of Manhattan. The south tower, called number two, has observation areas that give wonderful views over the city.

WHOSE NATIONAL SYMBOL IS THE BALD EAGLE ?

THE bald eagle is the national emblem of the United States of America. In 1782 it was included in the design for the country's Great Seal, symbolizing the authority of the US government, and it appears on official documents. The bird's white head feathers gave it its name.

Bald eagles are very good at catching fish with their talons.

WHERE IS THE BIGGEST DESERT IN THE REGION ?

NORTH America's biggest desert is the Sonoran, which runs across the border between the United States and Mexico. It covers parts of Arizona and California, and three Mexican states.

WHICH IS THE WORLD'S LARGEST ISLAND ?

GREENLAND is the largest island in the world, with an area of over 2 million sq km. The island belongs to Denmark, but the 55,500 inhabitants govern themselves.

WHERE DO THE BIGGEST BROWN BEARS LIVE ?

THE world's largest brown bears (at over 3 m tall) live on Kodiak Island and neighbouring islands off the coast of Alaska.

WHY IS THE MAPLE LEAF CANADA'S NATIONAL SYMBOL ?

THE maple tree is widespread in the southeast, and is an important part of Canadian culture. In the autumn, tourists flock to the woods of Ontario to see the brilliant reds and yellows of the leaves. The most famous kind is the sugar maple. The sap is used to make maple syrup, traditionally put on pancakes.

WHERE DO THE INUIT LIVE ?

MANY Inuit people live in the Northwest Territories of Canada. They were the original settlers of this region. Inuit also live in Greenland and Alaska. They are sometimes called Eskimos, but they prefer the word Inuit.

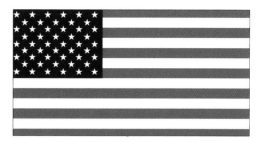

The US flag is known as the Stars and Stripes, the Star-Spangled Banner or Old Glory.

WHAT DO THE STARS AND STRIPES STAND FOR ?

THE 50 white stars on the American flag stand for the individual states that make up the country. The seven red and six white stripes stand for the thirteen original states that made up the United States when the flag was adopted in 1777, the year after the Declaration of Independence. The first flag had 13 stars and 13 stripes. Additional stars were added as new states joined the Union.

A large maple tree can produce up to 115 litres of sap in a single spring. The sap is made into maple sugar, used in sweets and flavourings.

WHAT ARE THE GREAT LAKES ?

THE Great Lakes are five large lakes in North America, four of which — Superior, Huron, Erie and Ontario — lie on the border between the United States and Canada. The fifth, Lake Michigan, lies totally within the United States. Lake Superior is the largest freshwater lake in the world.

WHO WERE THE MAYA ?

THE Maya were a Native American people who settled on the Yucatan peninsula of Mexico by 800 BC. They built pyramids and temples, had an observatory, and devised a complex calendar. It is a mystery why their great empire collapsed around AD 900.

The symbol on the Mexican flag is based on the Aztec legend of the founding of their capital city.

WHO FOUNDED MEXICO CITY ?

THE modern capital of the Republic of Mexico was built on the ruins of the capital of the Aztec empire. According to legend, a god told the Aztec Indians to settle where they saw an eagle grasp a snake. In 1325 they saw this, and built the city of Tenochtitlan. Their city was destroyed by Spanish conquerors 200 years later.

(1) Alabama, (2) Alaska, (3) Arizona, (4) Arkansas, (5) California, (6) Colorado, (7) Connecticut, (8) Delaware, (9) Florida, (10) Georgia, (11) Hawaii, (12) Idaho, (13) Illinois, (14) Indiana, (15) Iowa, (16) Kansas, (17) Kentucky, (18) Louisiana, (19) Maine, (20) Maryland, (21) Massachusetts, (22) Michigan, (23) Minnesota, (24) Mississippi, (25) Missouri, (26) Montana, (27) Nebraska, (28) Nevada, (29) New Hampshire, (30) New Jersey, (31) New Mexico, (32) New York, (33) North Carolina, (34) North Dakota, (35) Ohio, (36) Oklahoma, (37) Oregon, (38) Pennsylvania, (39) Rhode Island, (40) South Carolina, (41) South Dakota, (42) Tennessee, (43) Texas, (44) Utah, (45) Vermont, (46) Virginia, (47) Washington, (48) West Virginia, (49) Wisconsin, (50) Wyoming

WHAT SEPARATES NORTH AMERICA FROM ASIA ?

THE northwestern tip of North America is separated from northeast Asia by the Bering Strait. This stretch of water is just 88 km wide, leading from the Bering Sea to the Arctic Ocean. The strait is also shallow, with a greatest depth of 52 m. Tens of thousands of years ago, the sea level fell and there was a land bridge between the two continents. Hunters crossed from Asia in search of food. These were the ancestors of all the Native American peoples.

HOW FAR DO THE ROCKIES STRETCH ?

THE Rocky Mountains, also called the Rockies, stretch for 4,800 km down the western side of North America. This is the second-longest mountain range in the world, after the Andes.

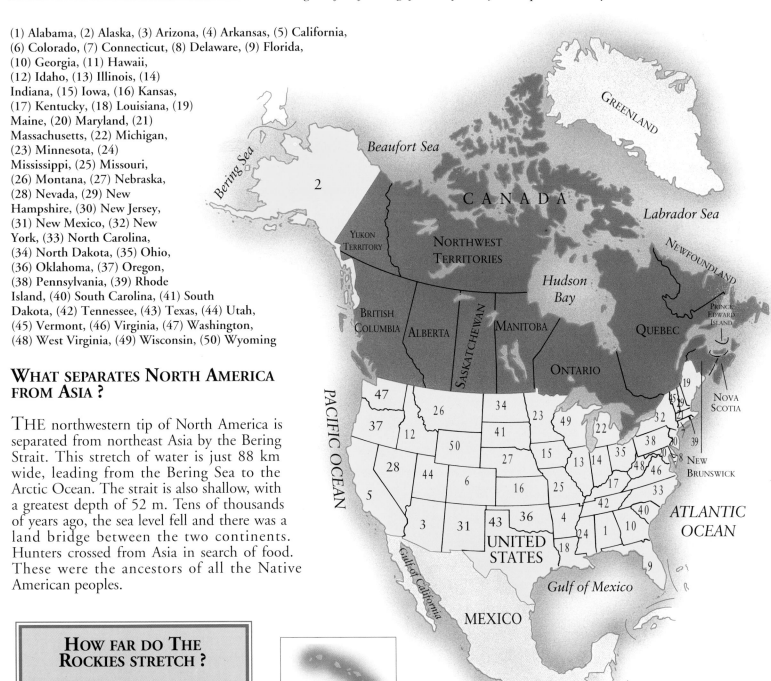

The 50 states of the United States include Alaska, separated from the rest by Canada, and Hawaii in the central Pacific Ocean.

WHICH IS THE LARGEST SOUTH AMERICAN COUNTRY?

SOUTH America's largest country is Brazil, which covers nearly half the continent. It has an area of over 8.5 million sq km. It is almost a hundred times bigger than the smallest South American country, French Guiana, which belongs to France.

Four new stars were added to the Brazilian flag in 1992. These stand for four new federal states.

WHERE IS THE WORLD'S HIGHEST WATERFALL?

THE Angel Falls plunge down 979 m in the Guiana Highlands of Venezuela, making them the highest waterfall in the world. They are named after an American pilot called Jimmy Angel, who spotted them in 1935.

WHERE IS SUGAR LOAF MOUNTAIN?

THIS 400-m high mountain, which Brazilians call Pão de Açúcar, is a famous landmark in Rio de Janeiro. It is a cone-shaped rock that juts into Guanabara Bay, a deepwater inlet of the Atlantic Ocean. A cable-car trip to the top gives visitors a wonderful view of the city and Copacabana beach. Nearby is another mountain, called Corcovado, or "Hunchback", with a huge statue of Christ at the top.

Rio de Janeiro means "River of January", named by Portuguese explorers in January 1503.

WHAT JOINS NORTH AND SOUTH AMERICA?

A NARROW strip of land, called an isthmus, forms the southern tip of the continent of North America. This region is known as Central America. It stretches from the southern border of Mexico to Colombia, in South America. The narrowest part of the isthmus is in Panama, where at one point only 58 km of land separate the Caribbean Sea from the Pacific Ocean.

Although the isthmus is narrow, it is extremely mountainous. The highest peak in Panama is Chiriquí, at 3,478 m.

HOW LONG IS THE ANDES MOUNTAIN RANGE?

THE Andes mountain range stretches for 7,200 km, forming part of seven countries. The northern end is in Venezuela and the southern in Chile. It is the longest range in the world.

WHERE IS THE DRIEST PLACE IN THE WORLD?

THE Atacama Desert, in Chile, is thought to be the driest region on Earth. The desert stretches for almost 1,000 km along the Pacific coast. There is scarcely ever any rainfall here at all.

HOW HIGH IS LAKE TITICACA?

LAKE Titicaca lies high in the Andes mountains on the border between Peru and Bolivia, at an altitude of 3,811 m. People have lived on the bleak, treeless plateau around the lake for over 10,000 years. Today it is home to the Aymara people.

HOW MANY SPECIES LIVE IN THE RAINFOREST?

THERE are over 1 million plant and animal species in the Amazon rainforest. A 10-sq km area may contain 1,500 species of flowering plants, 750 tree species and 150 butterfly species alone.

WHERE IS THE REGION'S LARGEST POWER PLANT?

THE hydroelectric power plant formed by a dam across the Paraná River is the largest in both South America and the world. The Itaipú Dam, on the border between Brazil and Paraguay, began making electricity in 1991.

WHICH IS THE LONGEST SOUTH AMERICAN RIVER ?

THE Amazon is the longest river in South America and the second longest in the world, after the Nile. The river begins high in the Andes mountains, and flows for 6,500 km across Brazil to the Atlantic Ocean. A fifth of all the world's river water flows down it.

Inca chiefs were carried in litters by their bearers, along roads that were a triumph of engineering. Deep ravines were crossed by suspension bridges made of twisted plant fibres.

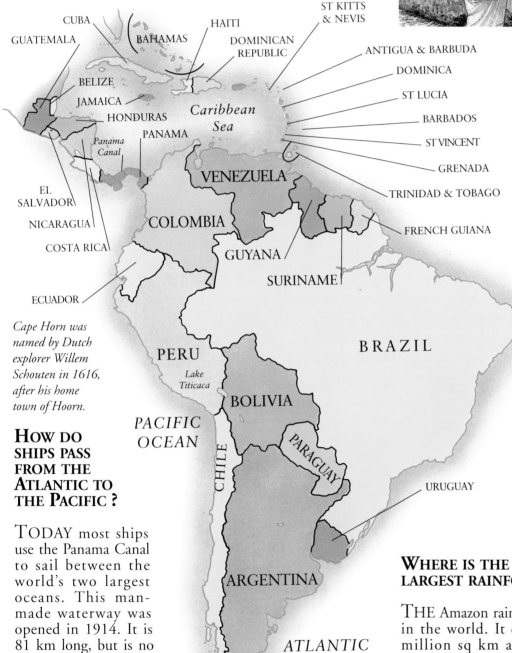

CUBA
GUATEMALA
BAHAMAS
HAITI
BELIZE
DOMINICAN REPUBLIC
JAMAICA
HONDURAS
PANAMA
Panama Canal
Caribbean Sea
ST KITTS & NEVIS
ANTIGUA & BARBUDA
DOMINICA
ST LUCIA
BARBADOS
ST VINCENT
GRENADA
TRINIDAD & TOBAGO
EL SALVADOR
NICARAGUA
COSTA RICA
VENEZUELA
COLOMBIA
GUYANA
SURINAME
FRENCH GUIANA
ECUADOR
PERU
Lake Titicaca
BRAZIL
BOLIVIA
PACIFIC OCEAN
CHILE
PARAGUAY
URUGUAY
ARGENTINA
ATLANTIC OCEAN
Cape Horn

Cape Horn was named by Dutch explorer Willem Schouten in 1616, after his home town of Hoorn.

HOW DO SHIPS PASS FROM THE ATLANTIC TO THE PACIFIC ?

TODAY most ships use the Panama Canal to sail between the world's two largest oceans. This man-made waterway was opened in 1914. It is 81 km long, but is no longer wide enough for some of the world's biggest ships to pass through. Before the canal was built, ships had to sail around Cape Horn, the southern tip of South America, where it is very cold and stormy.

WHERE DID THE INCA PEOPLE LIVE ?

THE empire of the Incas extended for about 3,500 km along the Pacific coast and Andes mountains, covering much of modern Ecuador, Peru, Bolivia and Chile. Their capital was Cuzco in southern Peru.

WHAT LANGUAGES DO SOUTH AMERICANS SPEAK ?

SPANISH is the main language in South America. But in the region's largest country, Brazil, people speak Portuguese. As well as these European languages, native Americans also speak hundreds of Indian languages.

The tendrils of this passion flower enable it to festoon the rainforest trees of Brazil.

WHERE IS THE WORLD'S LARGEST RAINFOREST ?

THE Amazon rainforest is the biggest in the world. It covers about 6 million sq km and stretches across Brazil and parts of Bolivia, Peru, Ecuador, Colombia, Venezuela, Guyana, Suriname and French Guiana. Most of the rainforest is just south of the equator; here it is always warm, and it rains nearly every day of the year.

The tail of the honey possum is longer than its head and body together.

The duck-billed platypus uses its large, flat bill to probe for food on river beds.

A kangaroo can go for weeks, or even months, without drinking, so long as it has moist vegetation to eat.

WHICH ANIMALS LIVE ONLY IN AUSTRALIA?

AUSTRALIA is famous for having a number of animals that live nowhere else in the world. The honey possum is a small, shrew-like animal that uses its long tail to grip on to branches. The duck-billed platypus is a mammal, but is unusual in that it lays eggs. The kangaroo is a marsupial, which means that the females carry their newborn young in a pouch.

WHAT DO THE FEATURES ON AUSTRALIA'S FLAG REPRESENT?

THE Union Jack on the Australian flag shows Australia's connection with Britain; it was once part of the British Empire. The large star is the Commonwealth Star. The group of five stars represents the constellation of the Southern Cross.

The Southern Cross, shown on Australia's flag, is visible at night only in the southern hemisphere.

WHAT IS FIJI'S MAIN CROP?

FIJI'S main crop is sugar cane, and sugar is the largest export. Most of the sugar cane is grown on small plots and is refined on the islands.

WHY DOES LAKE EYRE USUALLY HAVE NO WATER?

LAKE Eyre is in such a hot, dry place that it is usually no more than mud covered with salt. It only has water when it rains.

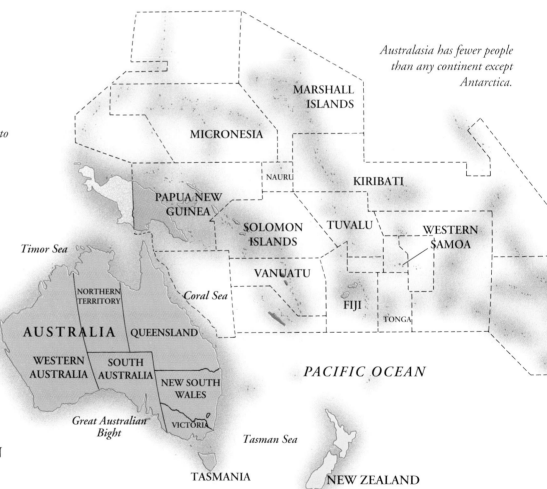

Australasia has fewer people than any continent except Antarctica.

WHAT IS OCEANIA?

AUSTRALASIA is made up of Australia, New Zealand, Papua New Guinea and thousands of small islands in the south Pacific Ocean. This whole region is one of the seven continents, and is sometimes called Oceania. It is the smallest continent in land area. Within Oceania there are three main regions of Pacific islands. Micronesia, which means "small islands", contains thousands of tiny islands. Melanesia, which means "black islands", includes Fiji and the Solomon Islands. Polynesia, meaning "many islands", includes Tonga and Samoa.

For dance festivals, Aborigines wear ceremonial body paint, as they have done for thousands of years.

WHAT IS THE OUTBACK ?

THE outback, or "bush", is a name for the desert areas of Australia that have a few shrubs and some trees. More than a third of Australia is desert, but it gets slightly more rainfall than most desert areas. The light rain creates a thin cover of vegetation, hence the name "bush".

The New Zealand flag shows part of the Southern Cross on the British Blue Ensign.

WHO WERE THE FIRST PEOPLE OF NEW ZEALAND ?

NEW Zealand lies about 1,600 km to the southeast of Australia. Its original inhabitants were the Maori people. Historians believe that they sailed there from the Polynesian islands in the Pacific about a thousand years ago. According to a Maori legend that has been handed down through the ages, they travelled across the seas in just seven canoes. Their traditional handicraft is wood carving, and today most of their work is done for tourists. About 15 percent of New Zealand's population are Maori.

WHERE DOES THE BIRD OF PARADISE LIVE ?

ALMOST all the different kinds of birds of paradise live in the forests of New Guinea and the neighbouring islands. Just a few inhabit the mountain forests of northeastern Australia. The males have brilliantly coloured feathers, some long and elegant, some fluffy and others like long wires on the head or tail. They use their plumage to attract females.

WHAT IS A DIDGERIDOO ?

A DIDGERIDOO is a long, thick wooden pipe that is played by the Aborigines of Australia. When blown, it plays a deep note; sometimes the player rests it against a hole in the ground to increase the sound. Didgeridoo music is played at Aboriginal sacred festivals called corroborees. Many of the Aborigines' dances at these festivals are based on stories about animal spirits.

WHICH IS THE WORLD'S LARGEST OCEAN ?

THE Pacific Ocean is by far the biggest in the world. Stretching from the Arctic Ocean in the north to Antarctica in the south, the Pacific covers more than a third of the Earth's surface. It is also the deepest ocean and contains more than half the world's sea water.

WHAT IS ULURU ?

ULURU is the Aborigines' name for Ayers Rock, which is one of the largest monoliths, or free-standing blocks of rock, in the world. It lies in Australia's Northern Territory, rising 348 m above the surrounding plain. There are Aboriginal paintings in the caves at its base, and the site is sacred to the Aborigines.

A kiwi is covered in thin feathers that look more like hair. It has no visible wings or tail.

WHY ARE KIWIS ENDANGERED ?

THE kiwis of New Zealand are becoming scarce because the forests they live in are being chopped down, both for wood and to clear the land for development. Forest clearance is a problem for many animals and plants all over the world. The kiwi is a large, flightless bird. It lives in a burrow and comes out at night to feed on worms and insects on the damp forest floor. Kiwis have very good hearing and a very sensitive bill.

WHERE IS THE GREAT BARRIER REEF ?

THE Great Barrier Reef lies in the Pacific Ocean off the coast of Queensland, Australia. It is made of thousands of coral reefs and islands, and stretches over 2,000 km. The Reef forms a barrier between the shallow coastal waters and the open sea. Since corals belong to the animal kingdom, the Great Barrier Reef is the largest living structure in the world.

A polar bear's big feet act like snowshoes, spreading the animal's weight on the ice.

WHERE DO POLAR BEARS LIVE ?

POLAR bears live in the huge area of frozen sea around the North Pole, and in the Arctic regions of Alaska, northern Canada and Greenland. They live mainly at the edge of the ice.

ARE THERE VOLCANOES IN ANTARCTICA ?

MOUNT Erebus is an active volcano on Antarctica's Ross Island. It is 3,743 m high, and when it erupts it spews lava bombs from a lake of molten rock.

WHICH BIRD FLIES FROM ONE POLE TO THE OTHER ?

ARCTIC terns raise their young during the Arctic summer. Then they fly south to the Antarctic, where summer is just beginning. In the autumn they fly north again, making a round trip of 36,000 km!

The Arctic tern sees more daylight each year than any other creature.

HOW BIG IS THE ARCTIC OCEAN ?

THE Arctic Ocean covers an area of over 13 million sq km, which makes it the smallest of the world's four oceans. It is covered in thick ice, which spreads over a wider area in winter.

IS THE NORTH POLE REALLY IN THE NORTH ?

THE North Pole marks the exact centre of the northern hemisphere; it is at the topmost point of the Earth's vertical axis. This point is about 11° away from "magnetic north", the direction in which a compass needle points.

WHO WAS THE FIRST PERSON TO REACH THE NORTH POLE ?

AN AMERICAN explorer, Robert Peary, reached the North Pole on April 6th, 1909, together with a colleague and four Inuit helpers. He announced his success in a message from his base camp: "Stars and Stripes nailed to the Pole".

The flag Peary planted at the North Pole was hand-sewn by his wife.

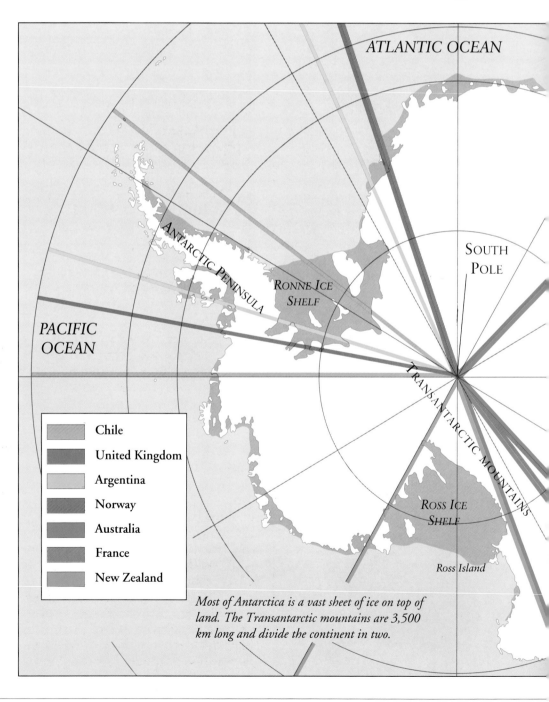

ATLANTIC OCEAN

ANTARCTIC PENINSULA

PACIFIC OCEAN

RONNE ICE SHELF

SOUTH POLE

TRANSANTARCTIC MOUNTAINS

ROSS ICE SHELF

Ross Island

Chile

United Kingdom

Argentina

Norway

Australia

France

New Zealand

Most of Antarctica is a vast sheet of ice on top of land. The Transantarctic mountains are 3,500 km long and divide the continent in two.

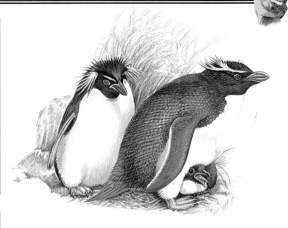

WHICH IS THE WORLD'S MOST COMMON SEAL?

THE most common seal is the crab-eater seal, whose numbers are estimated to be between 15 and 40 million. This is equal to the number of all other pinnipeds (seals, sealions and walruses) put together. Crab-eater seals have special teeth designed for eating tiny sea creatures called krill, although they also eat fish.

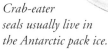

Crab-eater seals usually live in the Antarctic pack ice.

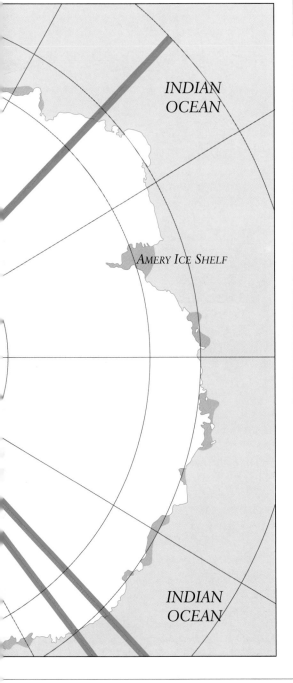

INDIAN OCEAN

AMERY ICE SHELF

INDIAN OCEAN

WHAT ARE THE ARCTIC AND ANTARCTIC CIRCLES?

THESE circles are imaginary lines around the Earth, like the equator. North of the Arctic and south of the Antarctic Circles, the Sun never sets in mid-summer and does not rise in mid-winter.

WHERE IS THE WORLD'S LONGEST GLACIER?

THE Lambert Glacier flows over the Prince Charles Mountains at the edge of Antarctica. With its extension, the Amery Ice Shelf, it is 700 km long, and is the world's longest glacier.

WHO ARE THE LAPPS?

THE Lapps, also known as the Sami people, live at the edge of the Arctic in northern Norway, Sweden, Finland and Russia. Their region is known as Lapland. Their traditional way of life is to herd reindeer.

WHAT ARE ICEBERGS?

ICEBERGS are huge chunks of floating freshwater ice that have broken off from glaciers and ice shelves and have floated out to sea. Most of the ice in an iceberg is below sea level.

HOW COLD IS ANTARCTICA?

ANTARCTICA is the coldest of the continents. In some parts the average temperature over a whole year is as low as -58°C. Winds can reach up to 320 km/h. Nearly all the land is covered by ice, which on average is about 2,000 m deep. Scientists think that the Earth's climate is getting warmer, and there are signs that this is happening in Antarctica. Glaciers are beginning to move faster and melt more quickly.

Rockhopper penguins from the Antarctic coast are easily recognized by their feathery crests.

WHAT DO PENGUINS EAT?

PENGUINS mainly eat fish and squid. There are 18 different species of these flightless birds, and 6 species live in the Antarctic. The rest are scattered around the coasts of the cold southern seas. The furthest north that penguins live is the Galápagos Islands, just south of the equator. There are no penguins in the Arctic region.

WHO WON THE RACE TO THE SOUTH POLE?

THE Norwegian explorer Roald Amundsen was the first person to reach the South Pole, on December 14th, 1911. British explorer Robert Scott left his base camp ten days after Amundsen, and finally reached the Pole on January 17th, 1912. There he found Amundsen's Norwegian flag already flying.

Amundsen journeyed to the South Pole with four men and sledges pulled by dogs.

HOW DOES SALT DISSOLVE IN WATER ?

COMMON salt, the sort we put on food, is a chemical compound called sodium chloride. Salt crystals are made up of molecules of sodium chloride. Each molecule has one atom of sodium chemically bonded to one atom of chlorine. The atoms take the form of ions, which have an electric charge. Sodium ions have a positive charge and chloride atoms have a negative charge. When salt dissolves in water, the ions separate and become surrounded by molecules of water.

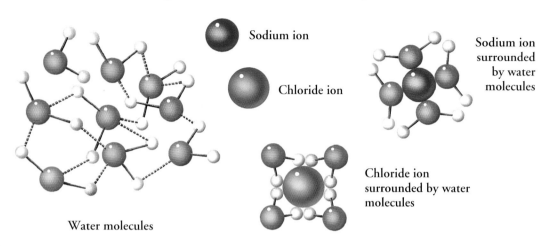

Sodium ion

Chloride ion

Sodium ion surrounded by water molecules

Chloride ion surrounded by water molecules

Water molecules

Salt dissolves quickly in warm water, and as it does so its ions separate.

HOW BIG IS AN ATOM ?

ATOMS vary in size, but a carbon atom, for example, is so small that there are 1,000 million of them in the ink in the full stop at the end of this sentence.

WHAT IS A MOLECULE ?

A MOLECULE is the smallest particle of a chemical compound that can take part in a reaction. Most molecules consist of two or more atoms held together by chemical bonds. Some molecules contain thousands of atoms.

HOW DOES FILM PROCESSING WORK ?

CAMERA film is a plastic sheet coated with grains of silver salts that are sensitive to light. When film is exposed in a camera, the silver grains are affected by light. During processing, developer converts the grains back to silver, forming a negative image. The negative is made into a positive print by projecting it on to a sheet of paper coated with similar silver salts. After development, light areas on the negative become dark areas on the print and dark areas become light.

Exposed film

Film is developed to produce a negative, which is enlarged to make a print.

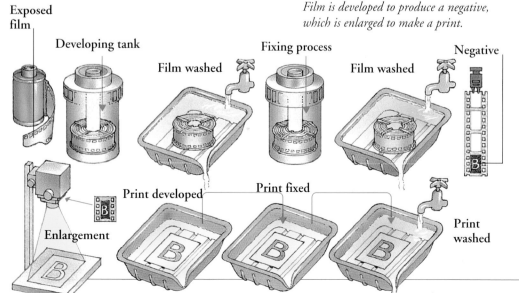

Developing tank

Film washed

Fixing process

Film washed

Negative

Print developed

Print fixed

Enlargement

Print washed

WHERE DO DYES COME FROM ?

ORIGINALLY, dyes were made from animals and plants. A sea snail named murex yields a rare expensive dye called tyrian purple. The blue dye that ancient Britons used to paint their bodies comes from the woad plant. The yellow dye, saffron, comes from the autumn crocus. And the madder plant yields an orange-red dye called madder. Today most dyes are made by chemists in the laboratory.

Madder plant

WHAT IS THE DIFFERENCE BETWEEN A MIXTURE AND A COMPOUND ?

A MIXTURE contains two or more substances that can be separated by physical means. For example, a mixture of iron nails and pebbles can be separated using a magnet. In a compound, two or more elements are bound together chemically and cannot be separated except by chemical processes.

HOW DO DETERGENTS WORK ?

MOLECULES of detergents are long and thin, like a match. The head end dissolves in water and the tail dissolves in grease. Usually grease holds dirt on to cloth. When dirty cloth is washed in detergent, the grease-soluble tails plug themselves into globules of grease. They surround it and form ball-shaped micelles, which float off the cloth, with the grease, into the water.

In a washing machine, detergent molecules attach themselves to large grease globules and lift them off the cloth.

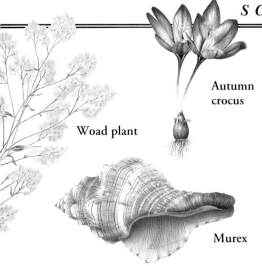

Autumn
crocus

Woad plant

Murex

Natural dyes can be made from animals and plants, such as those shown here.

HOW MANY ELEMENTS ARE THERE ?

THERE are about 106 known chemical elements. Just over 90 of them occur naturally on Earth. The remainder have been made artificially by scientists. About three-quarters of all elements are metals. The rest are gases and five non-metallic solids.

WHICH IS THE MOST COMMON ELEMENT ?

THE most common element on Earth is oxygen. It makes up 47 percent of the rocks and 21 percent of the atmosphere. The water in the oceans is 89 percent oxygen. However, the most common element in the universe is hydrogen.

WHAT IS INSIDE A FIRE EXTINGUISHER ?

THERE are various kinds of fire extinguishers designed to fight different types of fire. Electrical fires and those involving flammable liquids need a carbon dioxide (CO_2) extinguisher (1). It releases a blanket of CO_2 gas that keeps air from the fire. A dry powder extinguisher (2) contains sodium bicarbonate, which smothers a fire. A soda-acid extinguisher (3) contains sodium carbonate and a flask of acid. If the flask is broken, a chemical reaction releases a stream of frothy water.

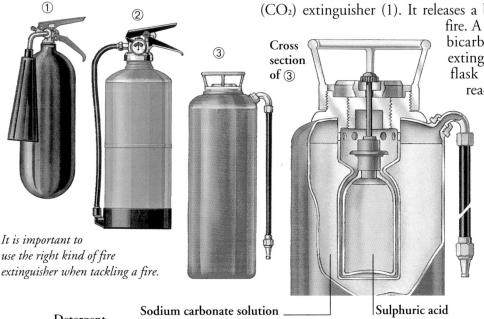

Cross section of ③

It is important to use the right kind of fire extinguisher when tackling a fire.

Sodium carbonate solution

Sulphuric acid

WHAT IS A POLYMER ?

A POLYMER is a large molecule (also called a macromolecule), which is made by joining together many small molecules. Natural polymers include cellulose, starch and rubber. Artificial polymers include rayon (artificial silk) and all plastics.

Detergent molecule

Grease

Cloth

WHAT ARE ACIDS USED FOR ?

STRONG acids are highly corrosive and must be handled with care. In industry they are used, for example, to etch fine patterns on to silicon chips. Weak acids, such as vinegar and lemon juice, are used to flavour foods.

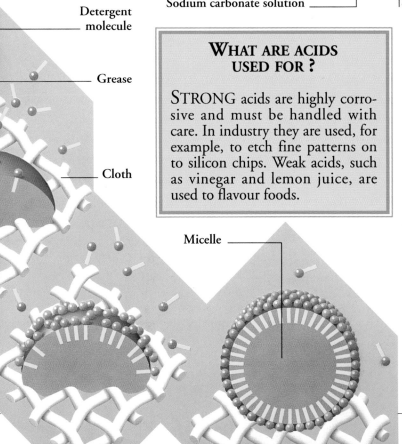

Micelle

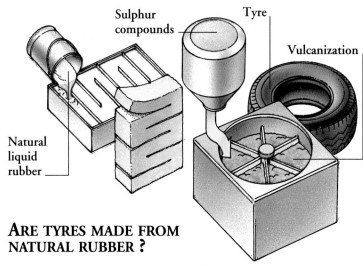

Sulphur compounds

Tyre

Vulcanization

Natural liquid rubber

ARE TYRES MADE FROM NATURAL RUBBER ?

NATURAL rubber is soft and elastic. It quickly wears out if used to make tyres. For the rubber to be strong enough, it has to be vulcanized. Vulcanization is a chemical process in which sulphur compounds are added to change the molecular structure of rubber to make it tougher and harder. Most rubber is now made artificially by the plastics industry. But it still has to be vulcanized to make tyres.

WHAT IS GLASS MADE FROM?

GLASS is made from sand, limestone, soda ash (sodium carbonate) and recycled waste glass. Boric oxide is added to make heat-resistant glass (called Pyrex). The ingredients are heated to a high temperature in a furnace until they melt together. The molten glass from the furnace cools to form sheets, or may be moulded to make objects such as bottles.

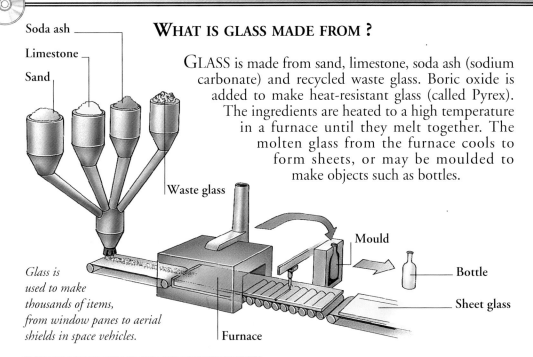

Soda ash
Limestone
Sand
Waste glass
Mould
Bottle
Sheet glass
Furnace

Glass is used to make thousands of items, from window panes to aerial shields in space vehicles.

WHO FIRST MADE GLASS?

PEOPLE probably first realized glass was possible when they saw melted sand in the bottom of a fire. Among the earliest users of glass were the ancient Egyptians. They made glass bottles as early as 2000 BC. These were found in the tombs of the pharaohs. About a thousand years later the Chinese were making coloured glass into imitation gemstones.

CAN PLASTICS BE RECYCLED?

YES, one way of recycling waste plastic is by controlled burning. The plastic is fed into the top of a furnace and heated as jets of hot air are forced up through it. Half of the fuel gases produced are used to power the process. The remaining gases and liquids are used to make new plastics.

WHAT ARE PHOSPHATES USED FOR?

PHOSPHATES are extracted from phosphate rock by adding sulphuric acid. They are used to make fertilizers, because phosphorus is essential for root growth. They are also used in detergents, baking powder and flame-proofing.

In the recycling process, plastics have to be burnt carefully to prevent adding to air pollution.

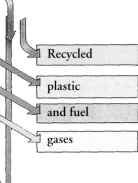

Furnace
Waste plastics
Recycled
plastic
and fuel
gases
Compressed air

CAN METALS BE RECYCLED?

MOST metals can and should be recycled if we are to save energy. Much less energy is needed to re-use scrap metals than to process metals from ores. For example, scrap steel can be added to blast furnaces in which iron is being made from iron ore.

The best timber planks are sawn from the middle of a tree trunk.

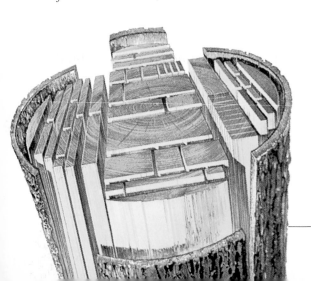

WHICH TREES MAKE THE BEST TIMBER?

THERE are two types of timber trees. Those with broad leaves, such as oak, ash and mahogany, are called hardwood. They take up to 100 years to grow, and the timber is used mainly for furniture. Trees with needle-shaped leaves, such as firs, pines and spruces, are called softwood trees. Those grown in plantations mature in about seven years. The timber is used to provide wood pulp for paper making, and for construction.

WHAT IS AN ALLOY?

AN ALLOY is a metal made by mixing two or more substances. Examples include brass (a mixture of copper and zinc), duralumin (aluminium and copper) and steel (iron and carbon). Most alloys are stronger than the materials from which they are made.

WHAT ARE THE DIFFERENT TYPES OF PLASTICS?

THERE are two main types of plastics. The plastics known as thermosets harden on heating and cannot be re-melted. They include polyurethane and melamine, and are used for making electrical fittings and work surfaces. Plastics known as thermoplastics soften on heating and can be melted and re-melted. They include polystyrene and nylon, and are used for packaging and clothing.

HOW IS ARTIFICIAL SILK MADE?

ARTIFICIAL silk, or rayon, is made from cellulose, obtained from cotton or wood pulp. The cellulose is dissolved in a substance called alkaline carbon disulphide to make a thick liquid. This is squirted through tiny holes into a bath of acid. It reforms as fibres, which can be spun into yarn.

WHAT IS CHIPBOARD?

CHIPBOARD is made from small pieces of timber obtained by shredding waste or recycled wood. The wood chips are mixed with a liquid plastic, which hardens when it is heated under pressure. The resulting sheets may be coated with wood veneer or another plastic.

After the springy cotton bolls have been picked, they are taken to a ginning plant, where the seeds are removed.

WHAT NATURAL FIBRES ARE USED TO MAKE CLOTH?

COTTON is made from the soft mass of fibres that surround the seeds of the cotton plant. Linen is made from the stem fibres of the flax or linseed plant. The main animal fibres are wool from sheep and goats. Silk is made from the cocoons of a moth.

The Statue of Liberty was a gift from France to the people of the United States of America. It was dedicated in 1886.

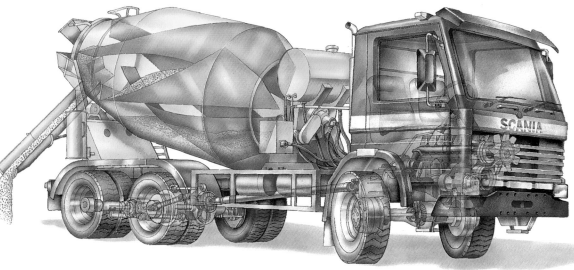

A large, ready-mixed-concrete truck can carry up to 25 tonnes of concrete.

WHAT MATERIAL IS THE STATUE OF LIBERTY MADE FROM?

THE Statue of Liberty is 91.5 m tall (including its base), and stands on an island in New York Harbour. The statue itself, without its pedestal, weighs almost 204 tonnes. Its inner framework consisted originally of a skeleton of iron rods joined to four wrought-iron posts. The iron rods have now been replaced with stainless steel. The outer skin is made from 300 overlapping copper plates.

WHY DOES CONCRETE SET HARD?

CONCRETE is a mixture of sand, gravel and cement. It is the cement that sets in liquid concrete. It binds together the other ingredients, which give concrete its strength and wear resistance. Cement is made by roasting a mixture of powdered limestone rock and clay. Heating removes water from the rock and clay and it becomes a fine grey powder. When water is added to the cement, it turns back into rock and dries to form a hard solid.

WHAT IS ENERGY?

ENERGY is the ability of something to do work. There are two kinds of energy: potential (stored) energy and kinetic energy (energy associated with movement). The different kinds of energy include heat, light, sound, electrical, chemical and nuclear.

WHAT IS A FORCE?

A FORCE is anything that moves a stationary object or alters the direction or speed of a moving object. The English scientist Sir Isaac Newton first studied force in the 17th century.

Solar cells

Solar panels

Wind-powered generator

Heat insulation

Heat exchanger

WHY ARE FORCES IMPORTANT IN SPORTS?

ALL sports involve forces. Athletes could not run without the force of friction to prevent their feet slipping. In every ball game, a force applied to the ball makes it move, whether from the kick of a footballer or the action of a tennis racket. In motor sports, forces make the vehicles move, and other forces are needed to stop them.

About 30 percent of the Sun's energy that reaches the Earth's atmosphere passes through it, and so can be exploited as a source of power.

WHY IS THE SUN'S ENERGY SO IMPORTANT?

AS WELL as providing heat and light, the Sun causes the weather, which provides wind and water power. Solar panels heat water, and solar cells convert sunlight directly into electricity. Electricity can also be obtained from a generator driven by a windmill. In addition, the Sun's energy allows plants to grow, and the plants give energy to humans and animals when eaten. They can also be used as a fuel; coal was formed from plants millions of years ago.

WHAT IS FRICTION?

FRICTION is the force that resists movement between two things that are in contact with each other. Without friction, a ball would go on rolling across the ground at the same speed for ever. The reason it eventually stops is because friction is acting on it.

The loudness of a jet fighter's engines is 170 decibels, which is beyond the pain threshold.

170

All sports players, for example hammer throwers and American footballers, make use of forces.

HOW IS SOUND ENERGY MEASURED?

THE amount of energy in a sound wave depends on its intensity or loudness, measured in decibels. The quietest sound we can hear is given a value of 0 decibels (0 dB). The rustle of leaves has a loudness of 10 dB, and conversation is about 55 dB. Sounds over 100 dB begin to cause us pain.

Galileo proved that a light object and a heavy one fall at the same rate.

WHICH FORCES ACT ON A JET AIRCRAFT ?

AS A jet aircraft moves through the air, the force of gravity pulls it down. But its wings provide an upward force, called lift, which keeps it in the air. The forward force of the engines overcomes the resistance of the air, called drag.

A chain reaction occurs when particles released by one atom splitting go on to split others. This is nuclear fission.

WHAT IS GRAVITY ?

GRAVITY is a force of attraction that exists between any object and the Earth. You can feel this force when you try to lift an object; its weight is due to the force of gravity pulling the object back to Earth. In the 1600s, the Italian scientist Galileo discovered that all objects fall back to Earth at the same rate, whatever their weight.

CAN ONE FORM OF ENERGY BE CHANGED INTO ANOTHER ?

ALL forms of energy can be changed into other forms, but the total amount of energy remains the same. Sound energy turns into electrical energy and back again when we use the telephone.

130

WHAT IS NUCLEAR ENERGY ?

ONE type of nuclear energy is made by fission. In this process a heavy atom, such as uranium, splits into two smaller fragments after being hit by an incoming neutron, releasing large amounts of energy. Particles produced at the same time cause more fission in a chain reaction. The energy of nuclear fusion, which takes place in the Sun, is released when lighter atoms join to form heavier ones.

Incoming neutron

Uranium atom

Atom splits

Fission fragment

HOW ARE FORCE AND ENERGY MEASURED ?

FORCE is measured in newtons. A newton is the force that gives 1 kg an acceleration of 1 m per second per second. Energy is measured in joules. A joule is the work done by a 1-newton force moving 1 m.

WHAT IS THE DIFFERENCE BETWEEN MASS AND WEIGHT ?

MASS is the amount of matter in an object. It is measured in units such as grams and kilograms. Weight is the gravitational force that attracts an object to the Earth. It is measured in newtons, a unit that measures force.

HOW DOES A TURBINE WORK ?

A TURBINE is a machine that uses gas or liquid to make a shaft turn. In a water turbine, water hits or flows through a set of blades on a wheel, attached to a shaft. This makes the shaft turn. Turbines are often used to drive electricity generators.

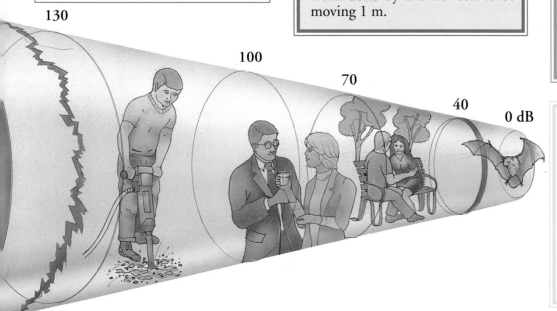

100

70

40

0 dB

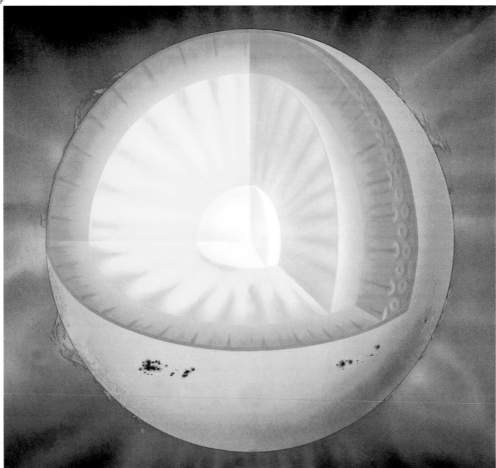

The central core of the Sun, where heat and light are produced, has a temperature of 15 million degrees.

WHAT HAPPENS WHEN COLOURS ARE MIXED?

THE result depends on whether you mix coloured lights or coloured paints. The three primary colours of light — green, red and blue — combine to produce the secondary colours: yellow, magenta and cyan. All three primaries mix to make white light. The primary paint colours are yellow, cyan and magenta. They combine to make black. The corresponding secondary colours are red, green and blue.

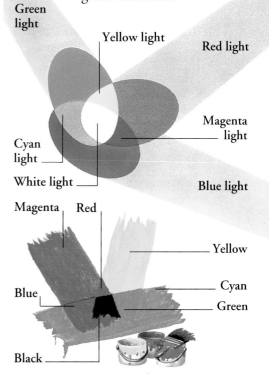

Coloured lights mix differently from coloured paints.

HOW DOES THE SUN PRODUCE LIGHT?

THE Sun produces light by a nuclear reaction called fusion. As atoms of hydrogen combine to form helium, they produce vast amounts of heat and light. Sunlight appears white, but it contains a mixture of all the colours of the rainbow: red, orange, yellow, green, blue, indigo and violet.

WHAT IS LIGHT?

LIGHT is a form of energy called electromagnetic radiation. Its waves fan out in all directions from the light source. Light rays travel in straight lines. When they hit an object, they are either reflected or absorbed.

WHAT IS HEAT?

HEAT is a type of energy that an object has when its atoms or molecules are vibrating rapidly. The faster they vibrate, the hotter the object is. At absolute zero (-273°C), vibrations stop and the object has no heat.

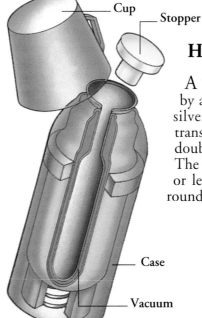

Because heat cannot travel through a vacuum, a vacuum flask keeps hot things hot or cold things cold.

HOW DOES A VACUUM FLASK WORK?

A VACUUM flask does not allow heat transfer by any of the three ways that heat can travel. The silver coating on the inner bottle prevents heat transfer by radiation, and the vacuum between its double wall prevents heat moving by convection. The thinness of the glass walls stops heat entering or leaving the flask by conduction. The case surrounding the flask provides additional insulation.

WHAT IS COLOUR?

COLOUR is a property of light. When white light hits a "red" object, for example, we see it as red because only red light is reflected; the other colours are absorbed.

WHAT IS TEMPERATURE?

TEMPERATURE is the measure of how hot an object is. If two objects at different temperatures are brought together, heat always travels from the hotter object to the cooler one until they are the same. Temperature is measured in degrees Celsius (°C), Kelvin (K) or degrees Fahrenheit (°F).

HOW DO THERMOMETERS WORK?

A LIQUID-IN-GLASS thermometer has a bulb containing a liquid that expands along a graduated tube to show temperature. The pointer on a bimetallic thermometer moves along as two metals expand at different rates causing the coil to tighten. The probe of a digital thermometer generates a small electric current as it gets hot.

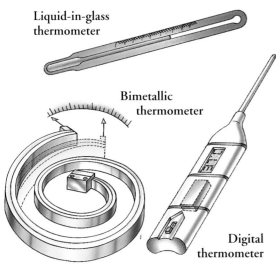

Liquid-in-glass thermometer

Bimetallic thermometer

Digital thermometer

Thermometers measure the degree of hotness of an object, which we call its temperature.

HOW DOES HEAT TRAVEL?

HEAT can travel in three main ways. If one end of a metal bar is heated, its atoms vibrate more vigorously. The "hot" atoms nudge their neighbours, and heat travels along the bar by conduction. In a gas or liquid, heated areas expand and become less dense. As they rise, cool gas or liquid moves in to take their place, with the result that the heat circulates by convection. Objects also radiate, or give off, heat.

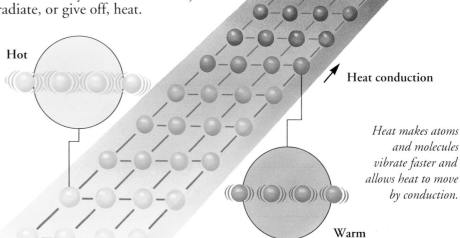

Cold

Hot

Heat conduction

Heat makes atoms and molecules vibrate faster and allows heat to move by conduction.

Warm

WHAT IS THE COLDEST-POSSIBLE TEMPERATURE?

THE coldest temperature is absolute zero. It is zero on the Kelvin scale, which is equal to -273°C or -460°F. Scientists have not yet been able to cool a substance to this temperature.

HOW FAST DOES LIGHT TRAVEL?

LIGHT travels extremely fast. In air or a vacuum, the speed of light is almost 300,000 km/sec. At this speed, it takes just over 8 minutes for light from the Sun to reach the Earth.

HOW DO OUR EYES DETECT LIGHT?

AT THE back of the eyeball is a layer of light-sensitive cells, called the retina. Photons (packets of energy) in lightwaves stimulate the cells of the retina and send messages to the brain, enabling us to see. The retina's rod-shaped cells work best in dim light, and its cone-shaped cells, which detect colour, in bright light.

HOW DO GLASSES WORK?

THE lens in the eye of a person with normal eyesight focuses light rays on to the retina at the back of the eye. A long-sighted person has an eyeball that is too short when measured from front-to-back. Glasses to correct the condition have convex lenses, which focus light rays on to the retina, instead of behind it. A shortsighted person's eyeball is too long from front-to-back. Glasses to correct short-sightedness have concave lenses, which focus light rays correctly on to the retina instead of in front of it.

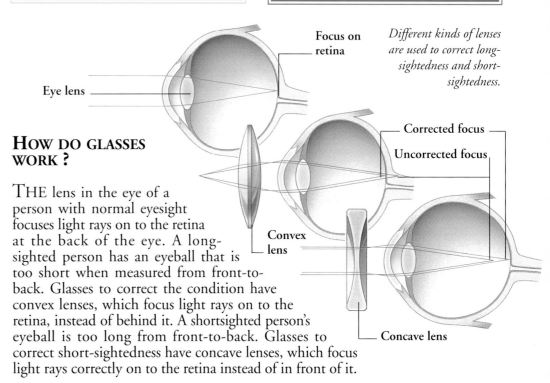

Focus on retina

Different kinds of lenses are used to correct long-sightedness and short-sightedness.

Eye lens

Corrected focus

Uncorrected focus

Convex lens

Concave lens

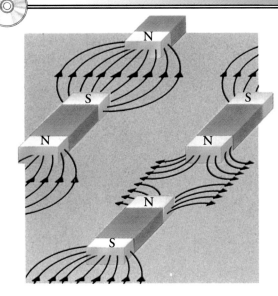

Lines of force between the poles of magnets trace out the magnetic fields.

WHAT IS A MAGNETIC FIELD?

A MAGNETIC field is the space around a magnet in which the magnet's force can be detected. The field can be represented as lines of force. The lines link a magnet's north pole at one end, and its south pole at the other end. North and south poles attract each other. Poles of the same type (two north poles or two south poles) repel each other.

An electric bell's electromagnet is activated by an electric current passing through the coils of wire.

WHY DOES A COMPASS NEEDLE POINT NORTH?

THE Earth behaves as if it had a giant magnet along its axis between the north and south poles. Confusingly, the south pole of this supermagnet is near the Earth's north pole. The pointer in a compass is a small magnet pivoted at its centre. Its north pole is attracted to the supermagnet's south pole. It is thought that the Earth's magnetism is caused by electric currents circulating in the molten iron core of the Earth.

The Earth's magnetic field extends for many kilometres out into space.

Earth's axis

Magnetic north pole | Geographic North Pole

WHAT IS AN ELECTRIC CURRENT?

AN ELECTRIC current is a flow of electrons along a conductor, such as a piece of wire. The electrons come from the metal making up the conductor. They are forced to move by a voltage applied between the ends of the conductor.

HOW DOES AN ELECTROMAGNET WORK?

AN ELECTRIC current flowing along a wire creates a magnetic field around it. If the wire is wound into a coil, the fields combine to give a field like an ordinary magnet's. A piece of iron in the centre of the coil makes the field stronger.

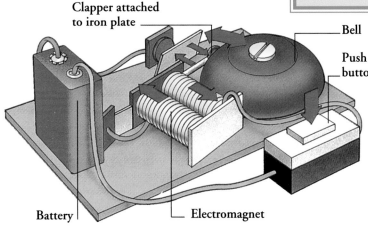

Clapper attached to iron plate

Bell

Push button

Battery

Electromagnet

HOW DOES AN ELECTRIC BELL WORK?

AN ELECTRIC bell contains an electromagnet, consisting of coils of insulated wire wound round iron rods. When an electric current flows through the coils, the rods become magnetic and attract a piece of iron attached to a clapper. The clapper hits the bell and makes it ring.

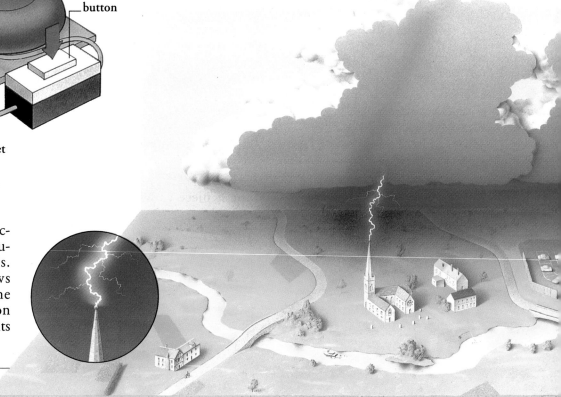

HOW ARE ITEMS ELECTROPLATED ?

WHEN certain chemicals are dissolved in water they split into ions. Copper sulphate, for example, splits into copper ions and sulphate ions. If two electrodes are dipped into the solution and connected to a battery, the ions move towards the electrodes. Copper ions move to the electrode connected to the negative terminal (the cathode). As a result, the cathode is covered, or electroplated, with a layer of copper metal.

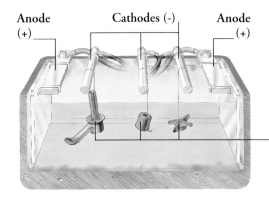

Anode (+)   Cathodes (-)   Anode (+)

Objects being electroplated

WHAT IS LIGHTNING ?

LIGHTNING is a huge electric spark. During a thunderstorm, clouds become electrically charged to a very high voltage. When the voltage reaches a certain strength a giant spark jumps from the cloud to the ground, or between two clouds. A shock wave in the air causes a loud clap of thunder.

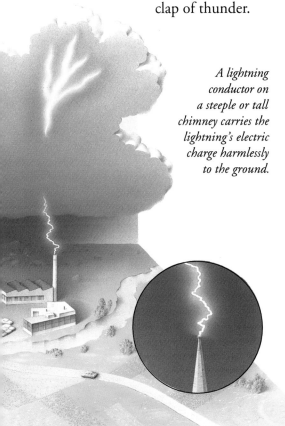

A lightning conductor on a steeple or tall chimney carries the lightning's electric charge harmlessly to the ground.

HOW CAN YOU MAKE AN ELECTRIC CURRENT ?

DIRECT, or one-way, current (DC) is made by a battery or by a dynamo. A dynamo rotates a coil of wire in a magnetic field to produce a current. Alternating current (AC) changes direction, and is produced by an alternator.

Parts of a tap are chromium electroplated by being wired to the cathodes of a plating tank.

WHAT IS STATIC ELECTRICITY ?

STATIC electricity consists of stationary electric charges. It can be produced by rubbing a non-metallic object, such as plastic, with a piece of cloth. You can charge a comb by running it through your hair.

HOW IS SOLAR POWER USED ?

SOLAR power is used to generate electricity in a photo-electric, or solar, cell. The electricity can be used in various ways. The large "wings" of a satellite are panels of solar cells. They provide the electricity to power the craft's instruments. A more down-to-earth use is a solar-powered bike. Solar cells generate enough electricity to work an electric motor, which in turn gives the bike power.

Solar power can be used to generate enough electricity to drive an electric motor in a bicycle.

WHAT HAS BEEN THE MOST IMPORTANT ELECTRICAL DEVICE INVENTED ?

THE most important electrical device invented is the light bulb. Its invention in 1879 by Thomas Edison in the United States and Joseph Swan in Britain changed everyday life across the world. Until then, the only artificial lights were oil and gas lamps.

WHO BUILT THE FIRST ELECTRICAL GENERATOR ?

THE first electrical generator was built by Michael Faraday in 1831. Electric current was produced by a copper disc spinning between the poles of an electromagnet. By the 1860s small electrical generators, powered by steam, were being used in Europe and the United States.

HOW DOES AN ELECTRIC MOTOR WORK ?

WHEN an electric current flows along a piece of wire in a magnetic field, the wire moves. In a simple motor, the wire is in the form of a coil placed between the poles of a magnet. The ends of the coil are attached to a pair of split rings called a commutator. Current is fed to the commutator through a pair of carbon brushes. When the wires move in the magnetic field, the coil rotates.

A simple electric motor is a coil of wire inside a magnet.

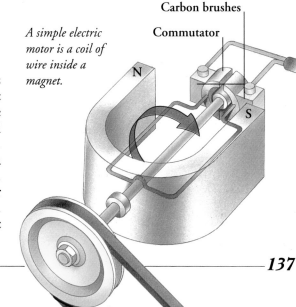

Carbon brushes

Commutator

N   S

HOW ARE OIL AND GAS EXTRACTED FROM UNDER THE SEA BED ?

CRUDE oil and natural gas occur in "pockets" under the ground. Sometimes the deposits are found under the sea bed. Like other deposits, they are extracted by drilling a hole down through the rocks into the oil or gas. For undersea deposits, the drills are mounted on a platform called a drilling rig. The oil or gas is usually pumped ashore through pipelines.

WHAT HAPPENS AT AN OIL REFINERY ?

AT AN oil refinery, crude oil is distilled in a process called fractionation. The oil is heated at the bottom of a tall column. Gas and light fuels like petroleum collect at the top, leaving heavy oils like bitumen to settle at the bottom.

WHAT HAPPENS TO NUCLEAR WASTE ?

WASTE nuclear fuel rods are processed to extract plutonium and uranium that can be used again. Other radioactive waste may be sunk beneath water or buried deep in the ground until its radioactivity decreases.

HOW DO ENGINEERS BORE A LARGE TUNNEL ?

TO MAKE large tunnels through rock, engineers use a TBM (tunnel-boring machine). This has a rotating cutterhead studded with hardened-steel picks that cut through the rock. The cut rock is passed back on a conveyor belt to wagons, which take it to the surface. The TBM shown here helped to bore the two parallel main tunnels of the 50-km long Channel Tunnel between England and France.

The huge cutterhead that bored the Channel Tunnel measured about 7.6 m across.

Hundreds of people work on a large oil rig. They are carried to and from the rig by helicopter.

HOW DEEP IS THE DEEPEST MINE ?

THE deepest mine is a gold mine in South Africa; in 1977 the Western Deep Levels Mine reached a depth of 3,581 m. Generally, though, mines descend to about 1,000 m or so.

HOW DOES A NUCLEAR POWER STATION MAKE ELECTRICITY ?

IMMENSE heat is generated by the nuclear reaction that takes place inside the reactor core. This makes pressurized water extremely hot. The water passes to a steam generator, where the heat is used to boil more water to make steam. The steam spins the blades of a turbine, generating electricity. Steam from the turbine passes to a condenser, where it cools and becomes water, which is then recycled.

The most common type of nuclear reactor is called a pressurized-water reactor.

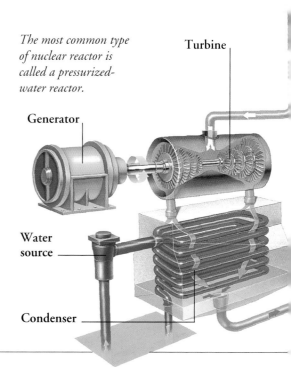

Turbine

Generator

Water source

Condenser

HOW MUCH OIL CAN A SUPERTANKER CARRY?

LARGE supertankers can carry more than 2 million barrels (320 million litres) of crude oil. The biggest supertanker is 458 m long and 68 m wide. Accidents and oil spills have made oil companies design smaller, safer ships.

IS ENGINEERING USED IN THE FOOD INDUSTRY?

THE food industry uses engineering in the preparation and packaging of foods. For example, baked products, such as cakes and biscuits, are cooked on conveyor belts that pass through ovens. Special packaging keeps the food fresh until it is opened.

HOW IS ALUMINIUM MADE?

ALUMINIUM comes from an ore called bauxite. It is extracted by mixing bauxite with other chemicals, melting it, and passing an electric current through it. The process produces a very pure type of aluminium.

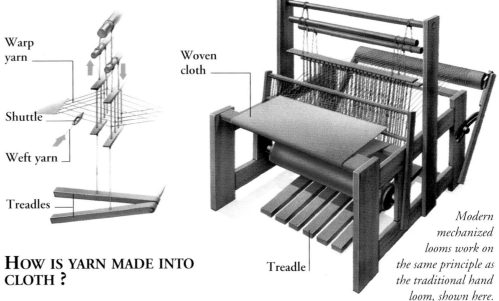

HOW IS YARN MADE INTO CLOTH?

LONG threads called yarn are woven into cloth on a loom. A hand-operated loom has foot-peddles, called treadles, which, when pressed, cause wires to separate the lengthwise threads. These are called warp threads. This enables the weaver to pass a shuttle carrying a thread across the loom. This is the weft thread. By pressing different combinations of treadles, the weaver can build a design into the cloth.

HOW IS PAPER MADE?

MOST paper is made from wood that has been ground into a pulp or treated chemically. Sometimes torn-up rags are added. A creamy pulp, consisting of fibres and water, passes on to a wire-mesh belt. The water drains through the mesh, sometimes aided by suction from below. The matted web of fibres is then squeezed between rollers, some of which are heated. The dried paper is finally wound on to large reels.

Modern mechanized looms work on the same principle as the traditional hand loom, shown here.

WHAT IS A SERVICE INDUSTRY?

A SERVICE industry provides services, rather than producing goods. Such services include banking, insurance, public transport and retailing (such as shops and supermarkets). They make an important contribution to a country's economy.

HOW IS STEEL MADE?

MOST steel is made by forcing oxygen down a long pipe into a vessel containing molten iron from a blast furnace. This burns off impurities in the iron, such as sulphur and phosphorus, to form high-quality steel.

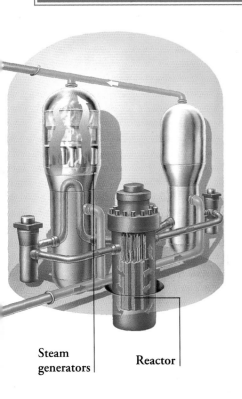

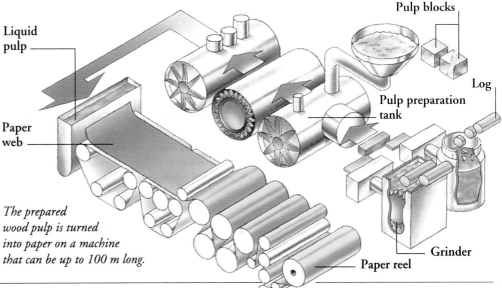

The prepared wood pulp is turned into paper on a machine that can be up to 100 m long.

HOW DID PEOPLE PUMP WATER IN ANCIENT TIMES?

THE Archimedes' screw is a pumping device named after the ancient Greek scientist Archimedes (282–212 BC). It is thought that he invented it to pump water from ships. The pump consists of a screw fitted inside a sloping cylinder. The lower end of the cylinder is placed in a stream and the screw rotated by a handle. This "screws" the water up the cylinder through the screw's thread, until it reaches the top.

An Archimedes' screw is a simple kind of pump used for raising water.

HOW DOES A ROBOT ARM WORK?

ROBOT arms are mechanical devices which have joints that can bend and rotate. They are driven by computer-controlled electric motors. Tools can be fitted to the "hand" end of the arms, and the computer programmed to make them perform different tasks such as cutting, drilling, welding and painting. They are also used for dangerous tasks, such as handling radioactive materials or unexploded bombs.

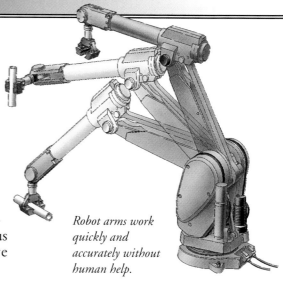

Robot arms work quickly and accurately without human help.

WHAT IS THE SIMPLEST MACHINE?

A MACHINE is any device that provides a mechanical advantage. That is, it allows a small force (the effort) to move a larger force (the load). The simplest machines to do this are levers.

WHAT IS A CRAWLER-TRANSPORTER USED FOR?

AT THE Kennedy Space Center in Florida, a 40 x 34.7 m crawler-transporter carries the Space Shuttle from the assembly building to the launch pad. Its eight caterpillar tracks are over 3 m high.

WHICH WERE THE FIRST MACHINES NOT POWERED BY HUMANS OR ANIMALS?

THE first machines that did not use muscle power were probably windmills. Early mills had sails resembling a boat's sails and were used for grinding corn around AD 600.

HOW DID EARLY GRAMOPHONES WORK?

EARLY gramophones recreated music by revolving a grooved disc, or record, on a turntable. A stylus, or needle, sits in the groove and is vibrated against little bumps. The vibrations picked up are converted back into the original sounds and amplified through a large horn.

HOW DOES A STEAM LOCOMOTIVE WORK?

A STEAM locomotive is a steam engine on wheels. Fuel burning in the firebox heats the water in the boiler until it turns to steam. The steam enters the cylinder and moves the piston. A connecting rod links the piston to a crank on the axle of the main driving wheel, making it turn. A coupling rod connects all the driving wheels together. Exhaust steam and smoke are released from the chimney.

The steam locomotive revolutionized transport in Europe and America in the 19th century.

Cylinder

Boiler

WHO INVENTED THE MOTOR CAR ENGINE?

THE earliest motorized road vehicles, made in the 1800s, had steam engines. By the 1880s, the German engineers Karl Benz and Gottlieb Daimler had fitted petrol engines to cars and motorcycles. In 1892 Rudolf Diesel invented the diesel engine.

WHAT ARE LASERS USED FOR?

LASERS produce a narrow beam of high-energy light that is all exactly the same colour. A laser beam can be used for welding metals and cutting cloth. Three-dimensional pictures, called holograms, are produced using lasers. But perhaps the most important uses are in communications. For example, in a CD or CD-ROM player, a laser beam "reads" the information on the compact disc. Laser beams also carry information along fibre-optic cables.

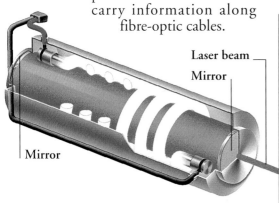

Laser beam

Mirror

Mirror

The beam from a laser is made of intense light of the same wavelengths.

WHEN WAS THE FIRST BICYCLE MADE?

THE first bicycle was made in 1818 by Baron von Drais. Called a hobby horse, it was propelled by pushing it along with the feet! The first pedal cycle was built by Kirkpatrick MacMillan in 1839, and improved by the Michaux brothers in France in 1861.

WHO INVENTED THE JET AEROPLANE?

ENGLISHMAN Frank Whittle patented the jet engine in 1930, but in 1935 Hans von Ohain of Germany took out a similar patent, and the first jet aeroplane to fly was the German Heinkel He-178, in 1939. The British Gloster Whittle E-28 flew in 1941.

IS IT POSSIBLE TO MAKE A PERPETUAL MOTION MACHINE?

NO! A perpetual motion machine would go on forever without needing energy. But machines have moving parts, which cause friction. Without extra energy to overcome friction, all machines eventually come to a halt.

A modern all-terrain bike has an average of 21 gears. This helps the rider to get up steep hills.

HOW DO A BICYCLE'S GEARS WORK?

WORKING the pedals of a bicycle makes a chain turn cogs on the back wheel. When a cyclist changes gear, a lever lifts the chain from one cog-wheel to another. Small cogs allow the back wheel to turn quickly, making it easier to cycle fast or uphill. Large cogs make the back wheel turn more slowly, which is useful when cycling downhill.

HOW DOES A ROLLER-COASTER WORK?

A ROLLERCOASTER works by using gravity. A cable hauls the train to the top of the highest incline. This gives it potential energy (energy of position). As the force of gravity makes the train speed down the first slope, potential energy is converted to kinetic energy (energy of movement). This is sufficient to carry it up the next incline. Each peak must be smaller than the last, because the train loses energy through friction.

The world's tallest rollercoaster, in Blackpool, England, is 72 m high.

Firebox

WHAT IS A PERSONAL COMPUTER ?

A PERSONAL computer (PC) is one which can be used in homes, schools and·offices. It consists of the computer itself, with the central processing unit, RAM (random access memory), disc drives, and a keyboard and mouse for inputting data. There is also a visual display unit (VDU), or monitor.

The heart of a PC is the microprocessor chip in the central processing unit (CPU).

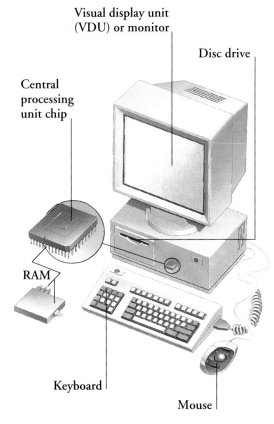

Visual display unit (VDU) or monitor

Disc drive

Central processing unit chip

RAM

Keyboard

Mouse

HOW DO COMPUTERS FLY AIRCRAFT ?

THE control of an aircraft by computer is called fly-by-wire, and is designed for maximum safety. Three computer programmers write the same programme. On the aircraft, the three programmes are run at the same time on two separate computers, so that if one fails there is always a back-up. If one programme contains an error, it is unlikely that the other two will.

WHAT IS THE INTERNET ?

THE Internet is an electronic network that links together office and home-computers throughout the world. It consists of many local networks connected together. Data is sent between networks along telephone lines and between continents using satellite links. It also allows people to share information via the World Wide Web. The Web is an ever-growing library of information supplied by individuals or organizations, which can be easily accessed in the home via a computer.

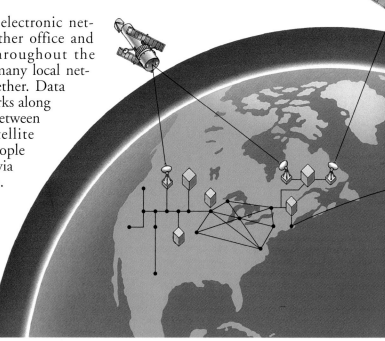

WHEN WAS THE FIRST COMPUTER MADE ?

THE first electronic device able to process data was built in 1937, but the first computer with a stored programme came in 1946. At 30 tonnes, and with 18,000 vacuum tubes, it filled a large room!

WHAT ARE SEMI-CONDUCTORS USED FOR ?

A SEMICONDUCTOR is a material, such as silicon or germanium, which has the property of conducting electricity under certain conditions. Semiconductors are used to make small electronic components such as transistors and diodes.

As a safety check, a fly-by-wire aircraft's two computers run three versions of the same programme.

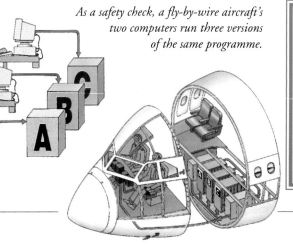

WHAT IS A CD-ROM ?

CD-ROM stands for Compact Disc, Read-Only Memory. It is a computer-storage device that can hold up to 600 million individual pieces of information, including text, sound, still pictures, video and animation.

WHAT IS MULTIMEDIA ?

MULTIMEDIA is a computer system that includes sound and video. The information is usually held on a CD-ROM. Some multimedia applications are interactive, which means that the user can add additional data while the application is running, and can therefore affect the output.

WHAT IS A SILICON CHIP ?

A SILICON chip is a tiny electronic circuit on a piece of silicon crystal. It can contain a million components, all in an area a few millimetres square. Silicon chips are found in the printed circuits of, for example, personal computers, cars and washing machines.

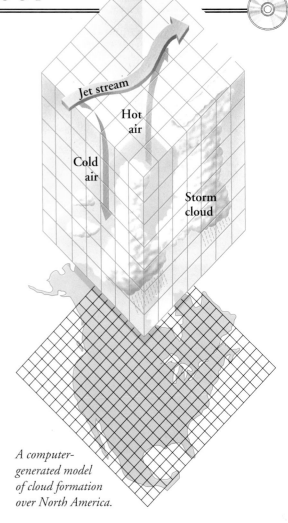

The Internet uses telephone lines and satellite links to interconnect computers all over the world.

HOW DO COMPUTERS FORECAST THE WEATHER?

COMPUTERIZED weather forecasting uses some of the most powerful computers in the world. This is because there is such a vast amount of data, and the calculations have to be made very quickly. Measurements of temperature, pressure, humidity and other weather conditions are taken from around the world. This information is used by the computer to calculate how it will affect the weather model held in its memory.

Jet stream

Hot air

Cold air

Storm cloud

A computer-generated model of cloud formation over North America.

WHAT IS A TRANSISTOR?

A TRANSISTOR is a tiny electronic component used to control a current flowing through it. It was invented in 1948 at the Bell Telephone Laboratories in the USA. Today, billions are made every year, and are used in most electronic equipment, including computers, TVs, radios, videos and satellites.

WHAT IS DESKTOP PUBLISHING?

DESKTOP publishing (DTP) is a method of using a computer to prepare pages of text and pictures ready for printing. The pages may have complicated designs, or page layouts, and may use many different styles of type. DTP systems are used by many newspapers and publishing companies.

WHAT IS A SMART CARD?

A SMART card is used by telephone companies, banks and other organizations involved in money transactions. It consists of a piece of plastic similar in size to a credit card. Embedded in it is a tiny computer microprocessor and a memory. A telephone smart card, for example, records the number of units the user has bought in its memory. Each time the card is used, units are deducted from the memory.

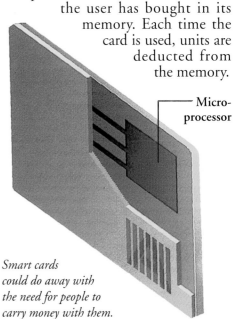

Micro-processor

Smart cards could do away with the need for people to carry money with them.

WHAT IS VIRTUAL REALITY?

VIRTUAL reality is a computer technique that uses sound and vision to simulate a real environment. The user wears a helmet, which projects three-dimensional moving images for each eye. The helmet detects if the user's head moves, and adjusts the images. The person wearing the helmet can look around and even "walk" through the projected image. Earphones provide stereo sound. A wired-up glove enables the user to "feel" the virtual image.

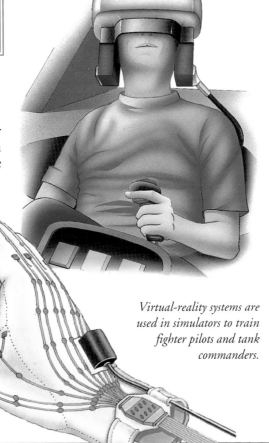

Virtual-reality systems are used in simulators to train fighter pilots and tank commanders.

Benz three-wheeler, 1885

Daimler, 1885

The first cars were modified tricycles and carriages fitted with small petrol engines.

WHAT IS AN ARTICULATED TRUCK?

AN ARTICULATED truck has two main parts. At the front is a tractor unit, carrying the engine and the driver. The tractor pulls a trailer, which usually has wheels only at the rear. The two parts are pivoted together or articulated, to make it easier to steer the long vehicle round corners. Different types of trailers are designed to carry different types of loads.

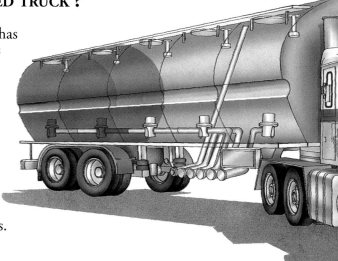

WHEN WAS THE FIRST CAR BUILT?

THE first car was a three-wheeler built by the German engineer Karl Benz in 1885. In the same year another German, Gottlieb Daimler, built the first four-wheeled car. Both cars were made from wood and were steered with a tiller rather than a wheel. The two engineers founded separate companies to build their cars. In 1926 they merged to form the Daimler-Benz Company.

WHICH WAS THE FIRST MASS-PRODUCED CAR?

THE first car to be produced in large quantities was the Ford Model T. First built in 1908, it remained in production until 1927, by which time more than 15 million had been built. The car was relatively cheap, and introduced motoring to families throughout the United States and parts of Europe.

HOW ARE CAR BODIES MADE?

EARLY cars were made by building a body on a separate frame or chassis. This method continued until the 1950s, when one-piece or monocoque construction was introduced. The car body is a complete "shell", made by welding together pressed steel plates. The other parts are then attached to the body shell.

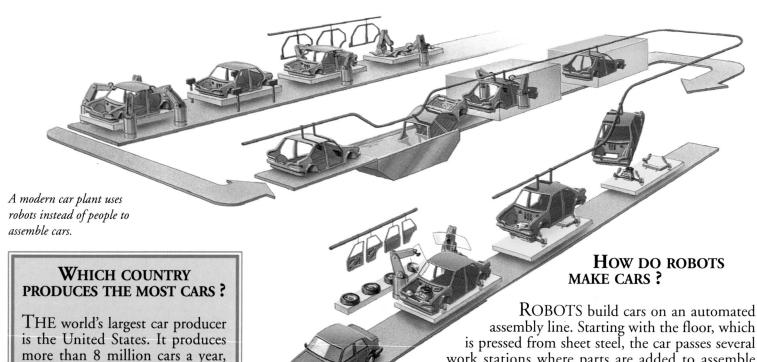

A modern car plant uses robots instead of people to assemble cars.

WHICH COUNTRY PRODUCES THE MOST CARS?

THE world's largest car producer is the United States. It produces more than 8 million cars a year, mostly for the home market. Japan makes a similar number, but mostly for export to other countries.

HOW DO ROBOTS MAKE CARS?

ROBOTS build cars on an automated assembly line. Starting with the floor, which is pressed from sheet steel, the car passes several work stations where parts are added to assemble the body shell and weld it together. The body is then rust-proofed and painted. Finally the engine, transmission, axles, suspension, seats, doors, windows and wheels are added before the completed car rolls off the production line.

A large tanker is divided into sections inside to stop the contents from sloshing about dangerously.

HOW DOES A TIPPER TRUCK WORK ?

TIPPER trucks normally carry bulk materials such as sand, gravel, grain or even potatoes. They are usually loaded from overhead hoppers. At the destination, the back of the truck is tipped to discharge the load. The body of the truck is pivoted at the back. At the front, hydraulic rams extend to raise the front of the body. The rams operate using oil under pressure, pumped by the main engine or by a separate diesel engine.

A bulk-carrying tipper truck has an aluminium body that can hold up to 22 tonnes.

WHAT IS AN ENGINE MANAGEMENT SYSTEM ?

AN ENGINE management system uses a microcomputer to control the performance of a car. It measures temperature, pressure, composition of the exhaust gases and engine speed, and adjusts the engine if necessary.

WHAT DOES A CATALYTIC CONVERTER DO ?

A CATALYTIC converter removes poisonous gases from a car's exhaust system. The main pollutants are carbon monoxide, nitrogen oxides and unburnt fuel. The converter changes these to harmless carbon dioxide, nitrogen and water.

WHAT ARE THE ALTERNATIVES TO PETROL AND DIESEL ENGINES IN CARS ?

AN ALTERNATIVE to petrol and diesel engines is to use electric motors. The motors are easy to make, but a major problem with them is their electricity supply. One solution is to use batteries, but these are heavy and an electric car cannot be used while its batteries are being recharged. An alternative power source is a solar panel, but this only works well when there is plenty of sunshine!

Some electric cars are "composites"; they use batteries in town and a petrol engine out of town.

WHAT IS THE MOST EXPENSIVE ROAD CAR ?

THE world's most expensive car that can be driven on the road is the McLaren F1 6.1. It costs £634,500! McLaren are known for their Formula One Grand Prix racing cars, for which speed and expert engineering are essential. The same skills and technology have been applied to the F1 road car.

The McLaren F1 6.1 develops in excess of 627 bhp (brake horsepower).

Richard Trevithick's 1804 locomotive was the first machine to run on rails.

WHICH WERE THE BIGGEST LOCOMOTIVES EVER BUILT?

THE world's biggest locomotives were 534-tonne steam locomotives, nicknamed "Big Boys". Built for the Union Pacific Railroad in the early 1940s, they hauled 70-car freight trains, weighing 3,000 tonnes, at speeds of up to 129 km/h.

"Big Boy" locomotives were built to haul heavy freight trains over the Rocky Mountains.

WHO BUILT THE FIRST LOCOMOTIVES?

THE first locomotive was built by Englishman Richard Trevithick in 1804. It weighed 5 tonnes and ran at 8 km/h, but was inclined to break the cast-iron rails it ran on. The next advance came in 1813 with George Stephenson's locomotive *Blucher*. In 1829 Stephenson built his famous *Rocket*, which reached a top speed of 46.6 km/h.

The largest and most powerful gun ever carried on a railway was the German gun, Schwere Gustav.

WHAT WERE THE FIRST RAILWAYS USED FOR?

THE first railways were used in mines for carrying rock and coal. They used horse-drawn wagons running on wooden rails. When steam locomotives replaced horses, they were still employed on mine railways. Within a few years, however, passenger-carrying railways were built.

WHAT IS THE RECORD SPEED FOR A TRAIN?

THE world speed record for a steam train is 202.7 km/h. It was set by the *Mallard* in 1938 and the record still stands. The overall world rail speed record was set in 1990 by a French high-speed *TGV* electric train. It reached a top speed of 515.3 km/h.

WHAT WAS THE BIGGEST GUN-TRAIN EVER BUILT?

DURING the First World War, several armies put machine guns and artillery on railway trucks. But the largest-ever rail-mounted gun was built in the Second World War by the Germans. They called it *Schwere Gustav*. Weighing 1,329 tonnes, it could fire 4-m long shells at targets nearly 48 km away, at a rate of one every 15 minutes.

WHEN WAS THE FIRST UNDERGROUND RAILWAY BUILT?

THE first underground railway was built in London in 1863. Other early underground systems included Glasgow, Boston and Paris. The steam locomotives had a device on them to absorb the smoke they created. Electric loco-motives were first used in 1890.

WHICH IS THE WORLD'S LARGEST UNDERGROUND STATION?

THE largest underground station is London's Piccadilly Circus. It was built in the 1920s and was designed to carry more than 5 million people a year. Its 11 reversible escalators move at 30.5 m per minute.

Piccadilly Circus, in the heart of London, is a deep-level interchange, built to connect the Piccadilly and Bakerloo lines.

WHAT DOES "GAUGE" MEAN ON RAILWAYS ?

GAUGE is the distance between the rails. The gauge used for the first public railway, the Stockton and Darlington, in England, was 1.43 m. Adopted nearly everywhere, it is called standard gauge.

HOW DOES STREAMLINING SPEED UP TRAINS ?

WHENEVER an object moves through the air, it meets wind resistance. This creates a force, called drag, which slows it down. A pointed or rounded object creates less drag than an angular one. For this reason, fast cars and trains are designed with a rounded front, called streamlining. One of the world's most famous streamlined trains was the *Twentieth Century Limited*, which ran between New York and Chicago in the 1930s.

Ten streamlined locomotives were built to pull the Twentieth Century Limited. *They could haul the 1,000-tonne train at over 160 km/h.*

WHAT IS A MONORAIL ?

A MONORAIL is a railway that has only one rail. This reduces friction and allows the trains to move faster and use less energy. On most monorails the train rides on top of a concrete beam. Magnetic levitation (maglev) trains of the future will use a magnetic field to "float" over the track, eliminating friction altogether.

ARE STEAM TRAINS STILL BEING BUILT ?

OLD-FASHIONED steam trains are still being built for the state-owned railway in China, where transportation has suffered from lack of investment. They carry freight and passengers huge distances across the country.

WHICH ARE THE LONGEST RAIL AND METRO TUNNELS ?

THE longest rail tunnel is the Seikan rail tunnel, which runs under the Tsugaro Strait between Honshu and Hokkaido, Japan. Opened in 1988, it is 53.85 km long. The longest continuous metro tunnel is the Moscow metro, at 37.9 km long.

WHAT SORT OF MOTORS POWER TODAY'S FAST TRAINS ?

THE original British high-speed trains used 200-horsepower diesel engines, and in 1973 set a record for diesels of 230 km/h. These were superseded by today's gas turbine (jet) engines. The fastest modern trains, such as the French TGV, use electric motors.

WHAT IS THE FASTEST TRAIN IN USE TODAY?

THE fastest train running a regular daily service is the Eurostar, which runs from London to Paris and Brussels through the Channel Tunnel. It regularly reaches 299 km/h on the new high-speed lines in France. Each trainset is made up of 18 coaches, with an electric power car at each end; in total it measures 394 m in length. The power supply is drawn from overhead wires in France and Belgium, and in Britain current is supplied via a third rail.

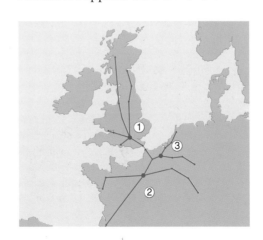

The map shows how the Eurostar network is planned to give high-speed access between major cities in Britain (1), France (2) and Belgium (3).

HOW FAR DID ANCIENT SHIPS TRAVEL?

ANCIENT ships travelled some remarkable distances. About 1500 BC, trading ships were sent from Egypt to the land of "Punt" (modern Somalia), a distance of some 4,000 km. From 1000 BC, the Phoenicians sailed from the Mediterranean to Britain to trade for tin. In the 9th century AD, Vikings from Scandinavia sailed across the Atlantic, via Iceland, to Greenland and North America in their longships. They also travelled northeastwards to Russia.

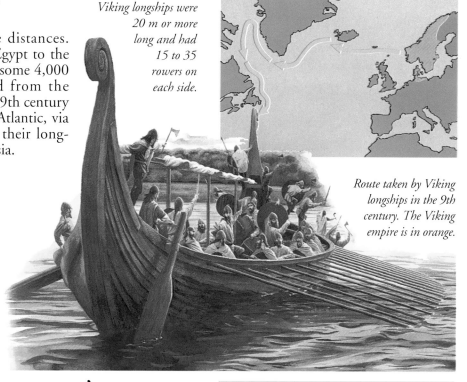

Viking longships were 20 m or more long and had 15 to 35 rowers on each side.

Route taken by Viking longships in the 9th century. The Viking empire is in orange.

WHO BUILT THE EARLIEST SEA-GOING SHIPS?

THE Egyptians built single-masted sailing ships over 5,000 years ago. The hulls were made from tightly lashed bundles of papyrus reeds, which grew along the banks of the River Nile.

HOW DO SHIPS' NAVIGATORS FIND THEIR WAY?

EARLY navigators used the astrolabe (1) to measure the altitude of the stars, and the sextant (2) to measure the angle of the Sun above the horizon. From these, they could work out the ship's latitude. The direction of the ship relative to north was found using a compass (3). Radar (4) and satellite (5) are used today to help reduce the risk of collision at sea.

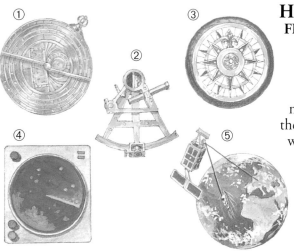

Early navigational instruments paved the way for the sophisticated satellite systems used today.

WHAT WAS A TRIREME?

A TRIREME was a wooden warship used in battle by the Greeks. The vessel had three levels of oars, a single sail, and was equipped with a ram.

IN WHAT TYPE OF SHIP DID COLUMBUS SAIL TO AMERICA?

THE three ships used by Columbus in 1492 were three-masted caravels. In this new ship design the hull planks met edge on, rather than overlapping, making it more streamlined. Caravels were the forerunners of the galleon.

WHAT WAS A GALLEON?

A GALLEON was a three- or four-masted sailing ship adapted for use as a warship in the 16th and 17th centuries. The largest carried more than 800 men. Galleons were armed on two or three decks with cannon, fired through portholes at enemy vessels. Galleons were used by several sea-faring European nations. They remained in service until the late 18th century.

A 17th-century galleon's rich carvings and gold leaf showed off its country's wealth.

The ship's crew included the captain (1) and the ship's master (2), who commanded the seamen (3). A ship's boy (4) kept the ship clean.

WHICH WAS THE LARGEST PASSENGER LINER?

THE largest passenger liner ever built was the *Queen Elizabeth*, with an overall length of 314 m and a displacement of almost 84,000 tonnes. It was launched in 1940 and had a cruising speed of 28.5 knots (52.5 km/h).

HOW DOES A SHIP MADE OF STEEL STAY AFLOAT?

A STEEL ship floats because its hull displaces (pushes away) a weight of water equal to its own weight. Displaced water causes an upthrust — a force that pushes the hull upwards and keeps the ship afloat.

WHAT IS A MODERN CRUISE LINER LIKE?

A CRUISE liner is a floating hotel. It has all the facilities people need to enjoy a complete holiday without having to leave the ship. Passengers have luxury cabins and play areas are provided for children. There are several bars, restaurants and swimming pools, and entertainment is laid on in cinemas and theatres.

A luxury cruise liner is a huge, floating hotel. The largest can accommodate almost 2,000 passengers.

WHAT IS THE LARGEST WARSHIP AFLOAT TODAY?

THE largest warship is the nuclear-powered aircraft carrier *USS Enterprise*, which was launched in 1960. It measures 335.5 m long, and the flight deck is almost 77 m wide. The flight deck has an area in excess of 18,000 sq m. Its maximum speed is 35 knots (64 km/h).

HOW DOES A SHIP'S PROPELLER WORK?

A SHIP'S propeller has three or more angled blades. When the propeller turns on its shaft, the blades act like a screw that moves the ship through the water.

WHAT KIND OF ENGINES DO MODERN SHIPS HAVE?

MOST modern ships have slow-running diesel engines, with one engine per propeller. Large vessels have steam turbine engines, often with oil-burning boilers to produce the steam. Nuclear-powered ships also have steam turbines, but use a nuclear reactor to provide the heat for making steam.

HOW POWERFUL IS A MODERN AIRCRAFT CARRIER?

A MODERN aircraft carrier is equipped with jet fighters and vertical take-off aircraft, and may have a steam catapult and a "skijump" to assist planes into the air. Two or more helicopters are carried for reconnaissance, submarine detection and rescue work. The ship is defended by missiles that are launched against other missiles, aircraft and submarines. Radar-directed guns are used at close range.

A modern aircraft carrier is a self-contained fighting unit that can both attack the enemy and defend itself.

HOW DOES THE JET ENGINE WORK ?

THE jet engine is the most efficient type of aircraft engine. Using jets, aircraft can fly higher, faster and further than with airscrews or turboprops. The jet works by sucking air in at the front and mixing it with inflammable liquids. As the mixture burns it produces gases that expand rapidly and are forced out of the rear of the engine. As the gases rush out, they push the engine, and the aircraft it powers, forwards. As the gases leave the engine they turn turbines that power a fan, which sucks in air at the front.

The enormous power of the turbofan engine makes it ideal for large passenger aircraft.

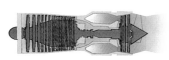

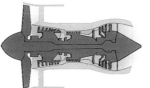

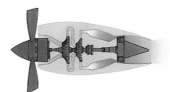

A turbojet engine is used on supersonic flights.

Most jets have turbofan engines.

Small craft at low altitude use turboprop engines.

WHEN DID HUMANS FIRST FLY ?

MANY ancient legends tell of people flying like birds, but the earliest properly recorded outdoors flight took place in 1793. Two French brothers, Joseph and Jacques Montgolfier, made a hot air balloon that carried two people.

WHEN DID THE FIRST POWERED AEROPLANE FLY ?

THE Wright brothers' *Flyer 1* biplane first flew in 1903. It was airborne for only 12 seconds and travelled for about 30 m at roughly the speed of a galloping horse. Today, planes can fly at several times the speed of sound.

WHEN DID AIRCRAFT FIRST GO INTO BATTLE ?

FIGHTER planes were first used in the First World War (1914–1918). Initially, they were used to spy on the enemy, but later guns were fitted and bombs carried.

WHAT IS THE WORLD'S LARGEST PASSENGER AIRCRAFT ?

THE Boeing 747 can carry over 550 people; more passengers than any other aircraft. It is so large that it has been nicknamed the Jumbo Jet by air crew. A Boeing 747 measures 70 m long, 20 m high and has a wingspan of 65 m. Its fuel tanks are so large that it can carry enough fuel for flights of over 13,000 km without landing.

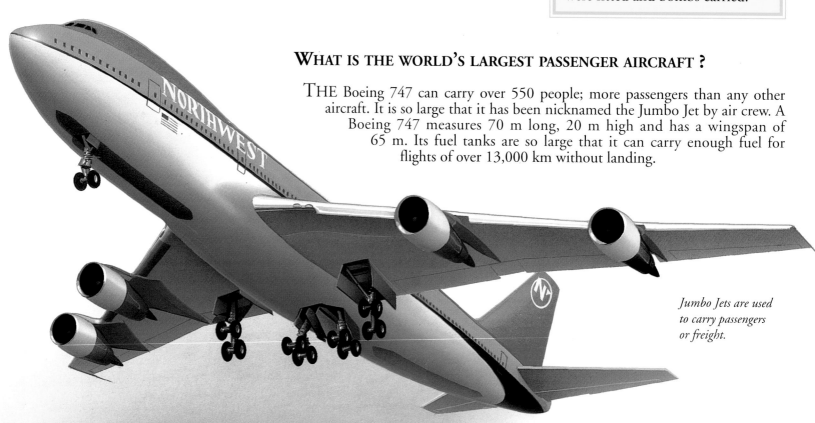

Jumbo Jets are used to carry passengers or freight.

A fully equipped Harrier taking off vertically on a mission.

HOW DO HELICOPTERS WORK ?

A HELICOPTER'S spinning rotor blades act as powerful wings. As they whirl around, air flowing over them produces an upwards force, called lift. By altering the speed and angle of the rotor blades the pilot can make the helicopter rise, fall or hover. Helicopters are also able to fly forwards or backwards.

WHAT IS VTOL ?

THE letters VTOL stand for Vertical Take-Off and Landing. Few aircraft are capable of VTOL as it requires very powerful engines and lots of fuel. The most successful VTOL aircraft is the Harrier. This military jet is used for bombing targets on the ground and for attacking other aircraft. VTOL allows the Harrier to take off from ships or from small areas of flat ground.

This McDonnell Douglas helicopter has a T-shaped tail that acts as a stabilizer and long skids for landing.

WHICH AEROPLANES ARE INVISIBLE ?

SOME fighter planes are sprayed with a material that absorbs radar waves, rather than bouncing them back to their source. This enables them to avoid detection on enemy radar screens. Known as "stealth" aircraft, they are also specially shaped to deflect radar signals.

WHAT IS THE SHORTEST AIRLINE FLIGHT ?

THE islands of Westray and Papa Westray in the Orkney Islands, Scotland, are linked by an air route across the stormy channel that separates them. The flight usually takes two minutes, but has been completed in just 58 seconds in good weather.

WHAT FUELS DO AIRCRAFT USE ?

AIRCRAFT with different engines use different fuels, although they are all based on oil. The piston engine, which powers propeller-driven aircraft, uses a fuel similar to petrol. Jet engines normally burn kerosene, a fuel similar to paraffin.

HOW DOES A GLIDER WORK ?

GLIDERS are aircraft that fly without any engines. Instead they rely on air currents to remain in the air. Gliders are built of light materials and usually have very large wings in proportion to their body size. This enables them to gain the maximum effect from the currents. If a glider pilot finds patches of rising air, often under clouds, the aircraft can stay aloft for hours on end.

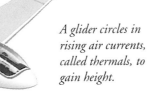

A glider circles in rising air currents, called thermals, to gain height.

HOW FAST CAN CONCORDE FLY ?

CONCORDE is the fastest passenger airliner in the world. Its top speed has been recorded at 2,179 km/h, over twice the speed of sound. When carrying passengers, it usually averages about 1,900 km/h, crossing the Atlantic in less than three hours.

During flight, Concorde's nose is raised to reduce air resistance, but when landing the nose drops so that the pilot can see the ground.

HOW IS MILK PRODUCED ?

ON THE farm, the milk yield is measured and the milk kept cool in a bulk storage tank. Road or rail tankers take the milk to the dairy, where it is pasteurized to kill off any bacteria. Pasteurization involves heating the milk and then rapidly cooling it. Pasteurized milk is separated into cream, low-fat milk and skimmed milk. Some is made into butter, yoghurt and cheese. Long-life milk is made by the UHT (ultra-high temperature) process, which allows it to be kept for months.

From milk, a range of dairy products are made, including cream, butter, yoghurt and cheese.

Farm
Milk pump
Graduated recording jar
Bulk storage tank
Milk tanker
Separator
Pasteurization
Insulated tank
Cooling to 10°C
Heating to 72°C

Packaging and distribution | Cream and butter | Low-fat milk | Skimmed milk | Cheese | Homogenized | Sterilized | (UHT) Ultra-high temperature treatment
Yoghurt

In addition to the familiar banana and pineapple, a wide variety of tasty tropical fruits can be found in the shops.

WHAT ARE THE MOST POPULAR TROPICAL FRUITS ?

TROPICAL fruits, rich in vitamins, are imported by developed countries with cooler climates, and are often sold as luxury items. Shown above are (1) pineapple, (2) durian, (3) carambola, (4) mango, (5) papaya, (6) soursop, (7) persimmon, (8) mangosteen, (9) pomegranate, (10) litchi, (11) akee, (12) cherimoya, (13) banana, (14) guava, (15) sapodilla, (16) passion fruit, (17) loquat, (18) Cape gooseberry and (19) rambutan.

WHAT ARE THE MOST IMPORTANT CEREAL CROPS ?

THE most important cereal crop worldwide is wheat, although in Asia rice is the staple crop. Barley, oats and rye are grown in cooler regions, and maize is a major crop in Africa and America.

WHICH REGIONS PRODUCE THE MOST WHEAT ?

THE major wheat-producing regions are the Ukraine, the prairies of the United States and Canada, and the Punjab region of India. Wheat is milled to produce flour, semolina and bran.

WHERE DID POTATOES ORIGINALLY COME FROM ?

POTATOES originally came from the Andes mountains of South America. They were introduced into Europe by Spanish explorers in the 16th century and into Britain by Sir Walter Raleigh.

WHAT VEGETABLES ARE GROWN IN TEMPERATE REGIONS ?

THE chief temperate vegetables are root crops such as potatoes, turnips, parsnips and carrots. Cabbages are also commonly grown. Other popular vegetables include (1) chives, (2) shallots, (3) onion, (4) garlic, (5) leeks, (6) tomato (technically a fruit), (7) artichoke, (8) spinach, (9) lettuce, (10) rhubarb, (11) asparagus, (12) fennel, (13) chicory and (14) celery.

Vegetables are important in our diet because they contain carbohydrates, fibre and minerals.

WHAT CROPS ARE GROWN TO PRODUCE SUGAR?

SUGAR comes from two main crops. Sugar beet is a root crop grown in temperate regions. Sugar cane, a type of grass, is grown mostly in tropical countries. In sugar refining, the beet or cane is chopped up and boiled in hot water, from which sugar is crystallized. By-products include treacle and molasses.

WHAT IS FISH FARMING?

FISH farming is the raising of fish for food. Parts of a lake or river are closed off with nets, and young fish are introduced into the water. They are fed daily and quickly grow. Many salmon and trout are produced in this way in temperate regions. In Asia, fish are sometimes raised in flooded paddy fields.

HOW DOES A COMBINE HARVESTER WORK?

A COMBINE harvester is used for harvesting cereal crops. At the front, a rotating pick-up reel forces the crop against the cutter bar. A rotating screw feeder carries the cut grain on to an elevator, which carries it to the fast-spinning threshing cylinder. This separates the grain from the straw. The grain is off-loaded into a truck and the straw is ejected from the back of the harvester on to the ground.

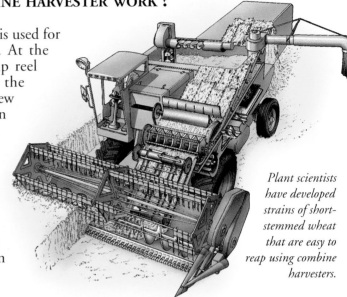

Plant scientists have developed strains of short-stemmed wheat that are easy to reap using combine harvesters.

WHICH FISH ARE CAUGHT FOR THE FOOD INDUSTRY?

IN SHALLOW temperate waters the main fish caught are pilchard, herring, whiting and mackerel. Anchovies are caught off the Pacific coast of South America. Ocean fish include cod and tuna.

WHAT CROPS ARE GROWN TO FEED ANIMALS?

CROPS grown specifically to feed animals are called fodder crops. They include lucerne (alfalfa), clover, kale and beans. Grass is grown to make hay and silage. Cereal crops such as barley, oats and rye are also fed to animals.

WHY ARE FISH SO IMPORTANT AS FOOD FOR PEOPLE?

FISH are important because they are an extremely nourishing source of food. They are rich in protein, which is necessary for body growth and repair. They also contain many essential vitamins, such as niacin. The oil from fish livers is a particularly good source of vitamins A and D. Similar food sources include shellfish (mussels and oysters) and crustaceans (crabs, lobsters and prawns).

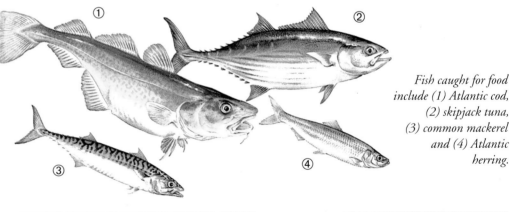

Fish caught for food include (1) Atlantic cod, (2) skipjack tuna, (3) common mackerel and (4) Atlantic herring.

WHERE ARE THE WORLD'S MAJOR FISHING GROUNDS?

THE major fishing grounds are in shallow waters off the shores of the continents. These areas correspond to the warmer parts of the oceans, which are rich in phytoplankton. These tiny plants provide food for fish. Over-fishing has reduced fish stocks to dangerously low levels in some areas.

This map shows the major fishing grounds off North America and Europe.

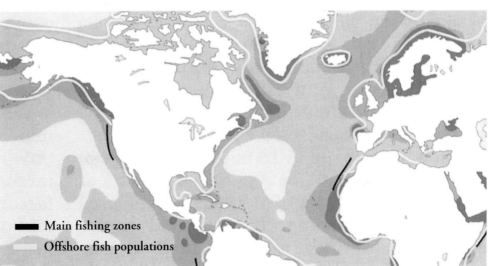

■ **Main fishing zones**
▨ **Offshore fish populations**

The ocean depths have been called inner space because we probably know less about them than we do about outer space.

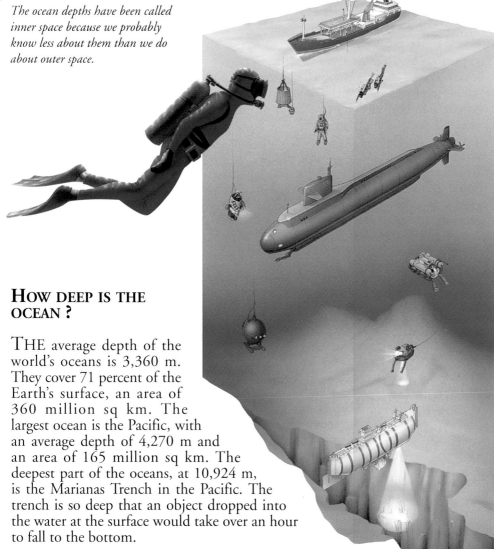

WHAT CREATURES LIVE AT THE BOTTOM OF THE OCEAN ?

GIANT worms measuring 27 m long live on the ocean bed. There are also fish whose only food consists of other fish or the dead remains of sea creatures. In the pitch-black water, some fish, such as angler fish, lure their prey with their luminous tentacles.

HOW DEEP IS THE OCEAN ?

THE average depth of the world's oceans is 3,360 m. They cover 71 percent of the Earth's surface, an area of 360 million sq km. The largest ocean is the Pacific, with an average depth of 4,270 m and an area of 165 million sq km. The deepest part of the oceans, at 10,924 m, is the Marianas Trench in the Pacific. The trench is so deep that an object dropped into the water at the surface would take over an hour to fall to the bottom.

WHO INVENTED THE SUBMARINE ?

THE submarine took many years to perfect, with each new stage being an improvement on the last. The first attempt was made in the 1620s by a Dutchman, Cornelius Van Drebel, who built a wooden shell covered with greased leather and propelled by oars. The next successful craft, called the *Turtle*, was constructed in 1776 by an American, David Bushnell. It was built so that explosives could be planted under enemy ships. In about 1800, Robert Fulton built a functional all-iron submarine.

WHAT IS A SUBMERSIBLE ?

A SUBMERSIBLE is a small submarine. A large, manned submersible is usually called a bathyscaphe. In the type shown here, the two crew members sit in a thick metal sphere beneath the craft. The sphere's air is at normal atmospheric pressure. To make the craft float, a tank in the upper part is partly filled with petrol, which is less dense than seawater. To make the vessel sink, water is let into the tank. Metal weights are released to make the bathyscaphe rise again.

Submersibles regularly go down to depths of 6,000 m to explore the ocean bed.

HOW DEEP HAVE HUMANS DIVED ?

THE deepest dive made by humans took place on 23 January, 1960. The two crew members of the bathyscaphe *Trieste* descended 10,916 m into the Pacific Ocean's Marianas Trench. No deeper part of the world's oceans than the trench has yet been discovered.

HOW ARE SUBMERSIBLES CONTROLLED?

MANNED submersibles are controlled by their crew. Unmanned craft, controlled from a surface vessel, are used to investigate wrecks and pipelines. They are lowered on cables, and are equipped with sound-detection equipment, lights and television cameras for photographing the sea bed. Some are fitted with mechanical robot arms that can pick up objects. The control ship receives pictures from the boat.

Submersibles are used to examine shipwrecks and faulty underwater pipelines and cables.

ARE THERE ANY USEFUL MINERALS ON THE OCEAN BED?

AT THE ridges in the bottom of the major oceans, new rocks well up from volcanic fissures as the sea bed expands. Hot gases and liquids also escape from vents, carrying many useful minerals, such as gold and titanium. There are also rocky nodules containing metallic elements like manganese.

WHO OWNS TREASURE FOUND ON THE SEA BED?

LAWS about treasure vary from place to place. When found in international waters, treasure belongs to the finder. If something valuable is found in national waters, it also belongs to the finder unless it was hidden deliberately, in which case it belongs to the state. Many of the objects found in shipwrecks are not valuable, but may be of great interest to historians.

Among the items raised from the wreck of Henry VIII's warship Mary Rose, *sunk in 1545, were gold coins and a surgeon's chest containing flasks and implements.*

WHAT DOES SCUBA STAND FOR?

SCUBA is short for Self-Contained Underwater Breathing Apparatus. Also called an aqualung, it is the breathing apparatus favoured by divers who want to descend lower than is possible using a snorkel, which can only take them 1 m below the surface.

WHAT ARE THE "BENDS"?

WHEN a diver breathes compressed air, some nitrogen in the air dissolves in the diver's blood via the lungs. When the diver surfaces, the nitrogen escapes from the blood around the joints, causing an intense pain known as the bends.

HOW IS THE DEPTH OF THE SEA MEASURED?

THE chief method is echo-sounding. The sounder directs an ultrasonic signal at the sea bed, and measures the time it takes for an echo to return. From this measurement, and a knowledge of the speed of sound in water, the depth can be calculated.

HOW DID EARLY DIVING SUITS WORK?

THE first diving suits date from the 1600s. An enlarged metal helmet covered the diver's body down to the hips, with holes for the arms. Air pumped through a hose into the "suit" enabled the diver to breathe. The pressure of the air also kept the water out. A diver could only dive the length of the hose.

Divers in old-fashioned suits had to breathe air under pressure, which meant they risked getting the "bends".

A modern atmospheric diving suit.

HOW DOES A MODERN DIVING SUIT WORK?

A MODERN diving suit encloses the whole of the diver's body. Called an atmospheric suit, it contains air at atmospheric pressure (the same pressure as at the surface). Although the pressure inside the suit is normal air pressure, the water pressure outside may be very high, depending on the depth. For this reason, the suit is made of thick metal so that it cannot be crushed. Atmospheric suits can withstand pressure down to a depth of 300 m.